THE PHILOSOPHICAL CANON
IN THE 17TH AND 18TH CENTURIES

THE PHILOSOPHICAL CANON IN THE 17TH AND 18TH CENTURIES

Essays in Honour of JOHN W. YOLTON

edited by

G. A. J. Rogers and Sylvana Tomaselli

University of Rochester Press

First published 1996

University of Rochester Press
34–36 Administration Building, University of Rochester
Rochester, New York, 14627, USA
and at PO Box 9, Woodbridge, Suffolk IP12 3DF, UK

ISBN 1–878822–64–0 (Hardback)

Library of Congress Cataloging-in-Publication Data
The philosophical canon in the 17th and 18th centuries : essays in
honor of John W. Yolton / edited by G.A.J. Rogers and Sylvana
Tomaselli.
    p.   cm.
Includes bibliographical references
ISBN 1–878822–64–0 (alk. paper)
1. Locke, John, 1632–1704. 2. Philosophy, Modern—17th century.
3. Philosophy, Modern—18th century. I. Rogers, G.A.J. (Graham
Alan John), 1938–   . II. Tomaselli, Sylvana. III. Yolton, John W.
B1297.P45 1996
190′.9′032—dc20   96–16388
                                                       CIP

British Library Cataloguing-in-Publication Data

A catalogue record for this book
is available from the British Library

This publication is printed on acid-free paper
Printed in the United States of America
Typeset by Cornerstone Composition Services

CONTENTS

INTRODUCTION

Sylvana Tomaselli

John W. Yolton's contribution to the history of philosophy is outstanding. He has enhanced our knowledge of some of the most eminent figures within the canon and of a great many outside of it. His work has especially enriched our understanding of the central texts of the seventeenth and eighteenth centuries and of what they were taken to mean by readers in subsequent periods and in different countries. He has established the intentions behind the writings and rhetoric of influential thinkers in those two hundred years and analyzed the history of the ideas and hypotheses put forward by them. Above all else he has taught pupils and colleagues alike to read. He has urged us to develop, as he put it, "a sensitivity to an author's use of words,"[1] and never to stray beyond the evidence afforded by the texts. His distinction as a scholar and a teacher resides partly in the fact that he has unfailingly practiced what he has preached.

Yolton was first drawn to philosophy in his second year at the University of Cincinnati by an introductory course taught by a dynamic teacher. He went on to major in philosophy and English literature. The person who then gave a more distinctive shape to his philosophical interests and broadened his historical knowledge was Julius R. Weinberg. Supervised by Weinberg, Yolton's M.A. thesis on perception theory set the tone for much of his subsequent research.

Early in his undergraduate career Yolton came across the writings of George Santayana. He found the philosopher's style attractive, his vocabulary challenging, and his world view exciting. The philosophical novel, *The Last Puritan*, and Santayana's poetry appealed to Yolton's combined interests in philosophy and literature. He began what was to become a comprehensive collection of Santayana's books and went on to publish several articles on the author as well as review some of his works for *The Philosophical Review* and *Mind*. This led to a correspondence between the two men, and Santayana remains a key figure in Yolton's intellectual landscape

---

[1]   *A Locke Dictionary* (Oxford: Blackwell, 1993), 1.

to this day. Thus in 1991, Thoemmes Antiquarian Books published a reprint of Santayana's *Character and Opinion in the United States* (1921) with an Introduction by Yolton.

After completing his M.A. at Cincinnati, Yolton spent four years at the University of California, Berkeley, as a teaching assistant and University Fellow. His historical work was encouraged by several members of the philosophy department, especially Edward Strong. It was Strong who suggested that Yolton should consider examining the reception by Locke's contemporaries of his *Essay Concerning Human Understanding* for his doctoral thesis. Little was known about that subject at the time. Since a large collection of Locke's papers, the Lovelace Collection, had recently been purchased by the Bodleian Library at Oxford, it seemed imperative for Yolton to cross the Atlantic. A Fulbright Fellowship made this possible in the autumn of 1950. Thanks to its renewal, the thesis was completed and our understanding of Locke and his period was much enlarged as a result.

John Locke is of course the intellectual figure one most readily associates with Professor Yolton. Among the many reasons for this is the simple fact that he has greatly added to the accessibility of Locke's works and thoughts, through for instance, *The Locke Reader: Selections from the Works of John Locke with a General Introduction and Commentary* (Cambridge: Cambridge University Press, 1977), and *A Locke Dictionary* (Oxford: Blackwell, 1993). Indeed, his Everyman edition of *An Essay Concerning Human Understanding* (1961) is the most comprehensively annotated paperback edition available and is widely used by students on both sides of the Atlantic, including those at the Open University, where it is a set text. Like all of Yolton's writings, its introduction shows him to be the eminent Locke scholar he is internationally known to be, as well as uniquely able to explain, even to the most uninitiated, Locke's epistemology in all of its philosophical subtlety. Among his concerns is the need to dispel the enduring misconception of Locke as a mere sensationalist. Locke, as Yolton stresses, did not counter innatism by arguing that the mind is utterly passive in the acquisition of knowledge. On the contrary, knowledge is the product of both experience *and* reason, and, while it does not consist of innate principles, it emphatically does depend "upon the right use of those powers nature hath bestowed on us."[2] It has been one of the main strands of Yolton's scholarship to examine what Locke took to be "the right use" of our mental powers and how he thought these should be developed.

This has led him to give particular attention to Locke's advice on the rearing of children and especially to *Some Thoughts Concerning Education*

---

[2]   Ibid., xxix.

and its relation to the *Essay*. Apart from being the subject matter of his *John Locke and Education* (New York and Toronto: Random House, 1971), it is probably one of the more helpful qualities of Yolton's writings that they demonstrate the importance of a careful reading of *Some Thoughts* to a proper comprehension of Locke's theory of the mind. Conversely, the Yolton edition of *Some Thoughts* for the Clarendon Edition of *The Works of John Locke* (Edited with an Introduction, Notes and Critical Apparatus by John W. and Jean S. Yolton, Oxford, 1989) benefits hugely from the editorship of someone bringing to it a profound understanding of the *Essay* and indeed of the Lockean corpus in its entirety. For Yolton highlights not only the interconnection between the pedagogical and philosophical works, but also between these and Locke's *Two Treatises*:

> The themes of the origin and growth of knowledge, the development of awareness, the formation of character, virtue, and social responsibility: these themes span much of his writing. The links between *Some Thoughts* and *Two Treatises* are especially important; the former provides a training and educational programme for the development of a moral person, the latter places that person in the political arena. The rationale of Locke's civil society is the protection of property: the possessions, the life, the individuality of the person. The list of virtues praised by Locke in *Some Thoughts* includes some individual-oriented properties (e.g., industrious-ness, prudence), but also contains social virtues (e.g., kindness, generosity, civility). The individualism of his philosophy is nicely balanced by his twin concepts of the community of mankind and the civil polity. The person as a moral being belongs to both communities; both communities set the standards for and preserve the values of Locke's morality. Locke's person is, in short, a socialized and Christianized individual.[3]

This said, Yolton stresses that for all the links which exist between Locke's works "we must be careful not to saddle him with more systematic theory than is found in his writing."[4] *Some Thoughts* must not be seen merely as an attempt to draw out the educational implications of the *Essay*. Each of Locke's works have, first and foremost, to be considered on their own terms. What Yolton shows can be, and indeed, has to be underlined, is Locke's own insistence on the need to attend to character-building in children, as he clearly saw it to be fundamental to the process of rearing responsible

---

[3] *John Locke, Some Thoughts Concerning Education*, Edited with an Introduction, Notes and Criticial Apparatus by John W. and Jean S. Yolton (Oxford: Clarendon Press, 1989) 1–2.

[4] Ibid., 2.

members of civil society. Yolton also argues that Locke was far from being a simple-minded believer in the unlimited potential of nurture. Locke urged parents and tutors to take account of the natural dispositions of children and modify their approach accordingly. He took it as a given that we are endowed with certain traits and dispositions, just as we are with mental faculties. The Lockean self is not a blank. Its development is a complex process which must be informed by a recognition of the distinctiveness of each individual. Only this makes it possible to establish how best to prepare the latter for an adulthood shaped by the desire to fulfil God's revealed purpose for mankind. Parents and guardians have a duty, in other words, to ensure that their children and charges are capable of obeying God's laws, and this, Yolton emphasizes, crucially depends for Locke on reason's control over the passions and the appetites. Enhancing that control in those they educate should therefore be the primary object of all educators.

That Locke's empiricism did not in the least entail the belittling of reason in his account of human understanding, that his contest with innatism did not mean that he conceived of the mind as passive in any general sense, and that his educational writings in no way ignored the reality of natural temperament are all part and parcel of Yolton's depiction of the seventeenth-century thinker as the author of a subtle theory of the mind and nuanced account of its comprehension of the natural and the moral world, in contrast to the enduring caricatures of Locke as the proponent, the "discoverer" even, of the *tabula rasa* view of the mind. Such was one of the aims of *John Locke and the Way of Ideas* (Oxford: Clarendon Press, 1968; reprint Bristol: Thoemmes Press, 1993), Yolton's first book, and each and every entry in *A Locke Dictionary*, one of his latest major publications, counters any lingering tendency to think of Locke as anything short of one of the very greatest philosophers in history. This, of course, could only be truly effected by someone with a thorough command of Locke's thought, from its scientific to its moral and religious aspects—a point further illustrated by *Locke: An Introduction* (Oxford: Blackwell, 1985).

To be able to explain what makes a philosophy a great one, to show what made and continues to make the *Essay* an interesting work is a rare gift, and it is for this reason that Yolton's *Locke and the Compass of Human Understanding* (Cambridge: Cambridge University Press, 1970) will remain essential reading for anyone interested in philosophy and its history. Both this and *John Locke and the Way of Ideas* reveal how Locke's epistemology was a response to the theological disputes of his age; both works, as indeed all of Yolton's scholarship, are attentive to Locke and his contemporaries' use of language and examine their conception of the nature of language, its descriptive potential and its relation to ideas. Moreover, in keeping with

Yolton's method, both books seek out how the texts they study were received and understood in their own time and beyond. Much of the success of Yolton's writing and teaching resides in the fact that the philosophy he explicates is presented by him within the context of the debates it was contributing to, the problems it was devised to answer, as well as the controversies, misunderstandings, and elucidations it generated in its turn.

A most notable account of the extent to which Locke's suggestions, let alone his pronouncements, were taken up is afforded by both *Thinking Matter: Materialism in Eighteenth-Century Britain* (Minneapolis: University of Minnesota Press, and Oxford: Blackwell, 1984) and *Locke and French Materialism* (Oxford: Clarendon Press, 1991). In tracing the "adventure" of Locke's hypothesis that God could have endowed matter with thought, Yolton evinces the nature of Locke's impact on the Enlightenment as he appears to have influenced radical and more orthodox thinkers alike. At every turn, the Locke which emerges from Yolton's pen is a more absorbing and complex philosophical figure than most writings about him would ever have led one to suspect.

Great as Yolton's improvement on our understanding of Locke is, his scholarship has not been confined to the latter, as will be made evident by the chapters of this volume. His publications cover the entire history of philosophy from Plato onwards. He has touched on nearly every philosophical topic, including the philosophy of science, and partaken in numerous debates, especially on the nature of the history of philosophy and the validity of the various approaches to it.

Gathered in this collection are contributions by fellow scholars and former pupils. They illustrate some, but not all, of Yolton's intellectual interests. Discussing one of his main topics of research in recent years and doing so in strict accordance with his methodology, the first chapter by François Duchesneau is a closely argued piece about the theme of *Thinking Matter*, and one which reconsiders Locke's position on this subject. Duchesneau does not directly challenge what he calls Yolton's "metaphysical" account of Locke's argument that while the materialists are wrong, the existence of an immaterial substance cannot be taken to follow necessarily from the existence of the power of thought and that God could have endowed matter with thought. In a manner which will no doubt meet with Yolton's approval, Duchesneau begins by presenting what he takes to be the seventeenth-century philosophical backdrop to Locke's views on the soul. He argues that the vast array of positions on the subject on both sides of the Channel shows the issue to have been not only metaphysical, but also epistemological, and that it therefore must be treated as such.

Continuing on this epistemological theme, Richard Popkin's "Scepticism with Regard to Reason in the Seventeenth and Eighteenth Centuries," juxtaposes Locke's views about the extent and limits of human certainty to those of his near-contemporaries and followers, and explores varieties of epistemological scepticism which, he argues, seem to be enduring features of the Western philosophical condition. Whilst Popkin presents Locke as rather dismissive of the Cartesian hypothesis that our perception of the external world might be nothing but a dream, he also insists that the philosopher conceived of his theory of knowledge as one which showed how limited human knowledge actually was: sufficient to self-preservation, it did not extend beyond our needs because our rational and sensory faculties were suited to them.

As its title indicates, "Locke and the Sceptical Challenge," G.A.J. Rogers's chapter also takes up the subject of Locke's response to the challenge of scepticism and demonstrates its merits, whilst agreeing with Popkin about the tenacity of scepticism. Both Popkin and Rogers's contributions thus discuss aspects of the subject matter of one of Yolton's most influential works, *Perceptual Acquaintance from Descartes to Reid* (Minneapolis: University of Minnesota Press, and Oxford: Blackwell, 1984). Closely related to *Thinking Matter: Materialism in Eighteenth-Century Britain, Perceptual Acquaintance* shows the extent to which in the seventeenth and eighteenth centuries a principle, that "no thing can be or act where it is not," and a phrase, "presence to or with the mind," shaped epistemological debates in France and Britain. Although Yolton presents a detailed analysis of the ways in which this spatial language was modified in an attempt to resist the widespread tendency to take it literally, he also shows not only its pervasiveness, but how it was used in support of the view that God might have endowed matter with the property of thinking. Covering the history of the epistemological debate from Descartes to Hume, *Perceptual Acquaintance* has convincingly undermined what had been conventional views about the central tenets of the period's philosophical arguments.

An interview Peter Laslett gave to Rogers makes the third chapter. Laslett's account of the recovery of John Locke's library is a lively and interesting one, which also brings to mind Yolton's own extensive collection of editions of Locke's works and other seventeenth- and eighteenth-century publications. This collection will eventually be housed in York University, Toronto, of which Yolton was a member in various capacities, including that of Acting President (1974–75).

Michael Ayers continues the discussion of scepticism with his chapter on "Natures and Laws in Early Modern Philosophy." At issue here are competing claims about the extent of God's interference in the world beyond the point of Creation. In particular, Ayers contrasts the different forms which voluntarism took in the period. His investigation echoes Yolton's own efforts in *Locke: An Introduction* to clarify what Locke meant by the Law of Nature and what he thought it comprised; for while references to Locke's conception of God's Law abound in scholarship about him, few interpreters have provided their readers with an account of the rules which derive from it.

Ayers's chapter includes a close study of Berkeley, whose view of the nature of common sense is the object of scrutiny in Geneviève Brykman's "Common Sensibles and Common Sense in Locke and Berkeley." Again, Brykman's careful inquiry into the two philosophers' explications of the source of our common sense ideas is both thematically and methodologically in keeping with the spirit of Yolton's written work and teaching. The same is true of M.A. Stewart's examination of what was meant by "abstract idea" in the seventeenth and eighteenth centuries, a chapter in which Locke and Berkeley also feature prominently. Both these chapters partake in the deliberations which *Thinking Matter* and more especially *Perceptual Acquaintance* scrutinize. Stewart reconsiders Berkeley's misconstruction of Locke's epistemological stance and in so doing helps us come to grips with Berkeley's complex views about the relationship between notion and idea. Furthermore, he elucidates the nature of Hume's debt to Berkeley and in so doing extends the present collection's sustained discussion of the connection between Locke's epistemology and epistemological considerations inspired by him, materialism and scepticism.

Arthur W. Wainwright's "Reason, Revelation, and Experience in the Hymns of Addison and Watts" reminds us of the importance of Locke's discussion of the relation between reason and revelation as it pursues this theme in the writings of the two eighteenth-century thinkers, while John Stephens gives us an insight into the teaching of philosophy in the early part of the eighteenth century in "Edmund Law and His Circle at Cambridge." John P. Wright's "Hume, Descartes, and the Materiality of the Soul" pursues a long-standing argument with Yolton and challenges the latter's interpretation of Hume's theory of perception as put forward in both *Thinking Matter* and *Perceptual Acquaintance*. It does so within the context of a study of Hume's rejection of the Cartesian principle of metaphysical reasoning except in relation to the soul. Wright usefully compares aspects of Descartes's *Meditations* to Hume's *Treatise of Human Nature* and brings into his discussion Bayle and Locke as well as Spinoza. This lively contribution attests to the fact that Yolton encouraged his students to question all received interpretations, not excepting his own, by always checking them against the word and letter of the texts.

"Foucault's Critique of the Enlightenment" by Shadia B. Drury provides an apt conclusion to this volume. It emphasizes the necessity of a proper understanding of the concept of reason as used by early modern philosophers, not only for the sake of scholarship, but also because of the ideological force which the twentieth century's many facile critiques of the Enlightenment have all too often had. Drury's chapter is a counter-attack on Postmodernism's vilification of the period. It exposes the crassness of the preconceptions about eighteenth-century philosophy which still underlie much of contemporary critical debates, and demonstrates the crucial importance to our future as rational beings of nuanced and discerning readings of the works of the past. Like all of his writings, Yolton's latest book, *Ideas, Representation and Realism: An Historical Perspective* (Cornell University Press, 1996), which traces the development of direct realism from Descartes to Kant, will not only enhance our confidence in the feasibility of this vital project, but also confirm his standing as one of the great historians of philosophy of the twentieth century.

LOCKE AND THE PHYSICAL
CONSIDERATION OF THE MIND

François Duchesneau

In *Thinking Matter*,[1] John Yolton has attempted to survey and analyze the numerous controversies which arose among Enlightenment philosophers from Locke's stated paradox about the mind in *An Essay concerning Human Understanding* 4.3.6. To summarize, Locke's argument aims at establishing that we have no means of deciding whether God has made us capable of thinking by associating an incorporeal substance to the material substance we experience we are, or whether he has given the material substance an additional power of thinking. There are other aspects to Locke's argument in this instance, but the core of it is the analytic unfolding of an absence of necessary connection between our idea of thought and that of the essence of body, while we have to acknowledge at the same time that our idea of what a finite substance is leaves room for various powers whose derivation from essence remains unaccountable for our understanding. Yolton's account of the argument is in a way "metaphysical." He relates *Essay* 4.3.6 to the rejection of the materialist hypotheses in the chapter Locke devoted to our demonstrative knowledge of God's existence. The other interpretative elements for his analysis derive mainly from the *Second Reply to Stillingfleet* (1699), which reflects Locke's concern for justifying his theory of knowledge in the light of more traditional metaphysics. The aim of my contribution is not to challenge directly Yolton's interpretation, but rather to focus on the "methodological" significance of Locke's skeptical position on the nature of mind in the context of his inquiry into the empirical derivation of knowledge contents. I wish to clarify what Locke meant in *Essay* 1.1.2 when declaring: "I shall not at present meddle with the physical consideration of the mind."[2]

---

[1] J.W. Yolton, *Thinking Matter: Materialism in Eighteenth-Century Britain* (Minneapolis: University of Minnesota Press, 1983), especially chapter 1, "Locke's Suggestion," 14–28.

[2] References will be to J. Locke, *An Essay concerning Human Understanding*, ed. P. H. Nidditch (Oxford: Clarendon Press, 1975).

I

According to Yolton, Locke in 4.3.6 is basically rejecting the ontology of materialists, while acknowledging that we have no means of necessarily relating the power of thought with the required existence of an immaterial substance. It is appropriate to follow first this line of analysis before turning to the methodological approach which I feel is more congenial to Locke's purposes in the *Essay*.

One must recall that the nature of the soul forms one of the major philosophical issues in seventeenth-century philosophy. The question was the more important since the mechanistic methodology extended its rule over a large part, and ideally, the whole of physics. Since animal and man belong to the physical universe, how and to what extent ought we to apply to their specific properties those models of analysis which prevail in geometrico-mechanical science? What is at stake is not only scientific progress, for the problem entails metaphysical and ethical implications. For most seventeenth-century philosophers, the scholastic doctrine of the three souls corresponding to various modalities of the substantial form seemed to contradict the methodological principles of the new science of physical realities. Alternatively, any theoretical attempt to account for biological and mental functions in accordance with mechanistic principles would be deemed acceptable, at least on a provisional basis. This is especially true for the period after 1650. It then became more and more evident that specific geometrico-mechanical models were to be proposed in order to account for various vital or animal functions of the organism. Indeed, in the posterity of J. B. Van Helmont for instance, vitalistic or animistic theories were still being developed.[3] But, whatever hypothesis one professed on the principle(s) of animation, the prevailing scientific methodology would require that organic and psychological operations be made dependent upon microstructures that one could in principle investigate through analysis. If needed in order to sustain that system of explanation, one could suppose specific "seeds" (*semina*) from which such structures would derive as well as the corresponding functional properties. Such "seeds" would act as micro-systems or organic devices instituted by God within compass of the natural order.[4]

---

[3]   On Van Helmont, cf. W. Pagel, *Joan Baptista Van Helmont. Reformer of Science and Medicine* (Cambridge: Cambridge University Press, 1982).

[4]   Cf. for an illustration, J.-B. Du Hamel, *De corporum affectionibus cum manifestis, tum occultis, libri duo, seu promotæ per experimenta philosophiæ specimen* (Paris: A. Le Petit & S. Michallet, 1670). After having asserted that all can be explained mechanically in the

The main metaphysical attempts to provide a theory of the soul and account for the vital and/or mental dispositions in nature can be ascribed to Descartes and Gassendi, provided we admit that there is a vast array of variant interpretations in other philosophers. But even if we focused on the issue from a metaphysical perspective, we should not forget that the issue was jointly an important methodological one for the more scientifically-inclined minds, who had to deal with the explanation of vital and psychological phenomena. Under this provision, theories like those of Willis, Steno or Malpighi exerted an overwhelming influence on contemporary philosophers.[5] As a philosopher, Locke was not so prone to draw a clear borderline between metaphysical problems and those methodological and epistemological issues which were found relevant to the establishment of scientific knowledge under the form of natural philosophy. Indeed, one of the major areas of concern for him was the continuity of experimental with demonstrative knowledge when dealing with our potential understanding of phenomenal realities.[6]

The thesis of *Essay* 4.3.6 reads as follows. We possess ideas of matter and thinking. But we cannot actually perceive a necessary connection between the one and the other such that we are able to determine whether it is in the power of a material being to think. Conversely, though this is less explicit, we cannot determine whether it is impossible for a material being with an appropriate organization of parts, whatever that be, to have cognitive activities. Because of our status as thinking agents with corporeal

---

physical order, Du Hamel adds 56: "Sed neque id fieri posse putem, ut mirabilis illa plantarum, & animalium structura, quam vix animo assequi possumus, ex ea vorticum rotatione, aut inquieta materiæ agitatione prodierit. Quodcirca id mihi sapienter ridetur D. Boyle, ut rem verisimillimam supponere, quasdam materiae portiones in prima rerum semina ab authore naturæ inclusas, quæ quidem prima velut rudimenta certis locis tanquam matricibus recondita, vel certe plantarum, & animalium sint corporibus indita."

[5]   On the paradigmatic case of Malpighi, cf. F. Duchesneau, "Malpighi, Descartes, and the Epistemological Problem of Iatromechanism," in: M.L. Righini-Bonelli & W.R. Shea, eds., *Reason, Experiment, and Mysticism in the Scientific Revolution* (New York: Science History Publications, 1975), 111–30. For a more general treatment of theories of the organism at the turn of the eighteenth-century, cf. F. Duchesneau, *La Physiologie des Lumières. Empirisme, modèles et théories* (The Hague: Martinus Nijhoff, 1982).

[6]   Cf. J. W. Yolton, *Locke and the Compass of Human Understanding* (Cambridge: Cambridge University Press, 1970), especially chap. 2, "The Science of Nature", and chap. 3, "The Method to Science," 44–103; F. Duchesneau, *L'empirisme de Locke* (The Hague: Martinus Nijhoff, 1973), especially chap. 1, "Locke et la doctrine sydenhamienne," and chap. 2, "L'empirisme médical de Locke," 1–91.

characteristics, there must at least be some linkage in us between the power
to think and the specific features of our corporeal existence. Both our power
of perception and the cluster of material properties we identify as our own
body require substantive grounding. The main ontological issue involved
in such a reference to substance is that of determining whether we should
hypothesize a single material substance with an unknown intrinsic foundation for its cognitive operations, or a combination of two substances with
distinct but separately coherent systems of properties and with indetermi-
nate linkage between these.

The reference to divine creation in this instance is to be interpreted in
an analogical fashion. Locke introduces this part of the argument with a
significantly comparative phrase: "It being, in respect of our notions, not
much more remote from our comprehension to conceive . . ." (Essay, 4.3.6).
The concept of thinking entails no determinate knowledge of the causal
requirements for supporting this type of activity in existence. As with the
various other powers, we get no access in the case of the power of thinking
to the inner "mechanism" behind or beneath its being enacted. Interestingly
enough, Locke takes as instances of acts of thinking, the perceptions of
pleasure and pain. How can we ascertain that they do not happen in the
body itself, which interpretation by the way seems to match the facts of our
immediate sensitive experience? Why would it be more rational to suppose
that pleasure and pain take place as mental events in an immaterial
substance, concomitant with some motions in the system of material parts
forming our body proper? It is important to note that the case of such feelings
does not differ significantly from that of secondary qualities. As such,
secondary qualities may not be more than subjective appearances to the
mind, though in fact we postulate their inherence in certain corporeal
substances affecting our sense perception; we also presuppose that those
secondary qualities are grounded in primary qualities of clusters of corpuscles
which afford the causal requirement for their empirical manifestation. But
as such, they are but appearances to the mind, and the corresponding ideas
cannot be directly analyzed so that we may determine the specific connecting link they possess with the primary qualities of elementary bodily structures.[7] Locke insists on the disparity of secondary qualities with the motions

---

[7]   On the arbitrariness of our ideas of secondary qualities as mere appearances to the
mind without discoverable connection with primary qualities of corresponding bodies,
cf. Essay, 2.8.13 and 4.3.12–14. In the Nouveaux essais sur l'entendement humain, Leibniz
counteracted significantly on that issue, cf. N.E., 2.8.13, G.W. Leibniz, Sämtliche
Schriften und Briefe (Berlin: Akademie-Verlag, 1923–____), 6.6: 131: "Il ne faut point
s'imaginer, que ces idées comme de la couleur ou de la douleur soyent arbitraires, et sans

of bodily parts which are supposed to produce them as appearances to the perceiving mind. In the same way, could we not pursue the analogy and presume that cognitive activities take place as the unaccountable result of bodily structures and operations?

In my opinion, the most important argument Locke brings forward in 4.3.6 is a negative one, resulting in the rejection of a rational dilemma which is central to traditional metaphysics and regulates any attempt at "demonstrating" the immateriality, and thus the immortality, of the soul. Locke's position is that such a question eludes our rational capacity and that we cannot reach the level of true demonstration in our attempts at solving the dilemma about the nature of mind. In this respect, I shall quote the passage which embodies an evident statement of antinomy:

> And therefore it is not of such mighty necessity to determine one way or the other, as some over zealous for or against the Immateriality of the Soul, have been forward to make the World believe. Who, either on the one side, indulging too much to their Thoughts immersed altogether in Matter, can allow no existence to what is not material: Or, who on the other side, finding not *Cogitation* within the natural Powers of Matter, examined over and over again, by the utmost Intention of Mind, have the confidence to conclude, that Omnipotency itself cannot give Perception and Thought to a Substance, which has the Modification of Solidity. He that considers how hardly Sensation is, in our Thoughts, reconcilable to extended Matter; or Existence to anything that has no Extension at all, will confess that he is very far from certainly knowing what his Soul is. It is a Point which seems to me to be put out of the reach of our Knowledge: and he who will give himself leave to consider freely and look into the dark and intricate part of each Hypothesis, will scarce find his Reason able to determine him fixedly for or against the Soul's Materiality (4.3.6).

In a way, this passage may be taken to refer to some elements of Cartesian metaphysics. The use of the term *cogitatio* would suggest it, as well as the strategy invoked, which consists in trying to reconcile concepts in

---

rapport ou connexion naturelle avec leurs causes: ce n'est pas l'usage de Dieu d'agir avec si peu d'ordre et de raison. Je dirois plustost qu'il y a une maniere de ressemblance non pas entiere et pour ainsi dire *in terminis*, mais expressive ou de rapport d'ordre; comme une Ellipse, et même une Parabole ou Hyperbole ressemblent en quelque façon au cercle dont elles sont la projection sur le plan: puisqu'il y a un certain rapport exact et naturel entre ce qui est projetté et la projection qui s'en fait, chaque point de l'une répondant suivant une certaine relation à chaque point de l'autre. C'est ce que les Cartesiens ne considerent pas assez, et pour cette fois vous leur avés plus deferé, Monsieur, que vous n'avés coustume, et que vous n'aviés sujet de faire."

our thoughts, such as those of matter and cogitation, through an analysis of the intrinsic *implicata* of these concepts as they express the nature of their respective objects. But, on the other hand, the concept of existence refers to the bodily existence of the agent of cogitation; it is intimated that any disincarnated, immaterial existence would elude our capacity of representation. Also, the idea of a material being is presented as if it should be analyzed as the concept of a cluster of given modifications which one may try and relate to the basic concepts of corporeal nature (= ideas of primary qualities), for instance extension and solidity. These features of the argument point in a direction that differs considerably from the Cartesian line of analysis. Indeed, one could take one of the horns of the dilemma to translate a Cartesian approach, the other being perceived as expressing a materialist position. But one should not forget that both the thesis and antithesis are phrased in the context of the Lockean notion of idea. For someone familiar with Locke's combined semantic and referential doctrine of ideas, based on acquaintance of the meaning of the object in its actual instantiation through our experience of sensation and reflection,[8] this is especially evident in a sentence like: "He that considers how hardly Sensation is, in our Thoughts, reconcilable to extended Matter; or Existence to anything that has no Extension at all, will confess that he is very far from certainly knowing what his Soul is"(4.3.6). In this instance, simple ideas of reflection appear underivable from those other simple ideas which signify material properties. At the same time, a question is raised concerning the simple idea of existence, which in 2.7.4 is indeed presented as "suggested to the Understanding by every Object without and every *Idea* within." The justification afforded for this statement reads as follows: "When *Ideas* are in our Minds, we consider them as being actually there, as well as we consider things to be actually without us"(2.7.4). What it means for one who tries to account for our immediate sensitive apprehension of knowledge contents, is that existence is not bestowed on the mind and on external realities in the same way. In the latter case, the idea of existence immediately signifies a reality outside the mind which possesses the features of bodily presence. In the former case, the existence apperceived is that of ideas *qua* mental states, modifications of the knowing agent; they do not refer to a *res cogitans* whose nature would be experienced to differ categorically from the reality of objects external to the perceiver.

---

[8] Cf. F. Duchesneau, "L'analyse d'idées selon Locke," *Les études philosophiques*, 1977, 67–94, and J. Yolton's endorsement of a similar position in *Perceptual Acquaintance from Descartes to Reid* (Minneapolis: Minnesota University Press, 1984), 216–21.

The concluding section about the antinomy of the mind as a distinct substance or a power superadded to a material substance supports this interpretation. As for Descartes, the certainty of the *cogito* escapes any doubt, because true judgement is implied in the very awareness of our doubting about the nature of our own mind.[9] But behind the stage of our mental operations which evidently refer to an existing entity, we get no access to the essence of such an entity, nor *a fortiori* do we perceive the necessary implication of cogitation in this essence. The situation is not presented as strictly parallel in the case of bodies, the existence of which sense perception reveals. We can ascertain their substantive nature up to a given point because of their possessing qualities which can be taken to represent their essence, such representations being determinate, if not fully sufficient, expressions of it. As a matter of fact, our intellective access to material substances, though far more determinate than our access to the substantive underpinning of cognitive operations, still lacks in analytic comprehensiveness: and this is especially the case with the various powers which we experience to pertain to bodies. "For I would fain know, Locke confesses, what Substance exists that has not something in it, which manifestly baffles our Understandings" (4.2.6). So one can speak of a partial asymmetry in the case of the mind, whose substantive nature is fully unknowable, when compared with so-called material substances, whose nature is imperfectly known, since the full connection and grounding of the ideas signifying it escapes our grasp. However, though partial, such an asymmetry cannot but entail significant implications for the "metaphysical" analysis of mind as a potentially material or immaterial entity. Having thus set the epistemological context, it is time to turn to and retrace the ontological treatment of the Lockean paradox which Yolton sketched.

Following on a rather incidental argument in 4.3.6,[10] Yolton connects the analysis of the antinomy with the concept of the eternal first thinking being, whose existence Locke takes to be demonstrable against the

---

[9]   Cf. *Essay*, 4.9.3: "As for *our own Existence*, we perceive it so plainly, and so certainly, that it neither needs, nor is capable of any proof. For nothing can be more evident to us than our own Existence. *I think, I reason, I feel Pleasure and Pain*; Can any of these be more evident to me than my own Existence . . . ?"

[10]   *Essay*, 4.3.6: "For I see no contradiction in it, that the first eternal thinking Being should, if he pleased, give to certain Systems of created sensless matter, put together as he thinks fit, some degrees of sense, perception, and thought: Though, as I think, I have proved (4.10), it is no less than a contradiction to suppose matter (which is evidently in its own nature void of sense and thought) should be that Eternal first thinking Being."

speculations of the materialists. There is an apparently sound reason to draw the link here since the inadequacy of our concepts of matter and thinking, which we cannot succeed in spelling out, and analyzing down to some necessary connection, forces us to admit that an omnipotent God could have indifferently endowed matter with a power to think or associated two different substances, one material the other not, for the purpose of mind-body interaction.

The demonstration of God's existence in a Lockean perspective is based on the notion of an eternal self-sufficient cause for actual existents. This rational requirement applies first to the phenomenal *cogito*. The eternal being required to account for the existence of the thinking agent must possess a power adequate to the nature of this property. Locke insists on the fact that the idea of matter as an extended solid being, if transposed to apply to an eternal being, would not meet the requirement of accounting for the emergence of thinking in any finite and contingent reality. The same is presumed about the connection between the eternal precondition and the advent of motion among the realities of the physical universe. The structure of the argument is that of a hierarchy of ontological conditions applying to the primary sufficient reason: "So that if we suppose nothing first, or eternal; *Matter* can never begin to be: If we suppose bare Matter, without Motion, eternal; *Motion* can never begin to be: If we suppose only Matter and Motion first, or eternal; *Thought* can never begin to be." (4.10.10) We are thus drawn to conclude that there exists an eternal cogitative being.

The interesting feature of the demonstration is that such a being could after all qualify also as a material being, if it were not for certain significant deficiencies such an hypothesis would reveal in a notion which is presumed to be adequately determined. For Locke, the emergent sequence of properties in the phenomenal world, from bare entity to matter, from matter to motion, and from motion to thought, entails an inverted ordering of power in the eternal being who is required for the basic causal explanation of those phenomenal characteristics. The analysis is built in such a way as to show that, for instance, from the notion of matter as an extended solid entity no causal understanding is provided for the advent of motion among bodies. Evidently, this line of analytical reasoning is systematically developed in the transition from physical characteristics to mental features expressing cognitive operations. As a result, the Lockean God is presumed to possess the compensatory causal structure that will make for the absence of perceivable connection between the notions signifying the various stages of ontological determination. Yolton is right in stressing that God so defined is meant to account for the unknown correlation of natural sets of properties in finite beings, whenever such sets of properties do not seem to be analytically derivable from each other. The main key to Locke's ontological position consists in the emptiness of our concept of substance, whose essence, in a way void of any power to act, may precede in God's creation the giving of causal dispositions for generating phenomenal properties. Indeed, one is left to hypothesize the nature of this superadded causal disposition, but we tend to conceive of the global intelligibility of nature on the assumption, empirically-based but teleologically-oriented, that our concepts representing natural sets of properties indicate stages of ontological perfection.[11]

On the other hand however, Yolton takes Locke to reject the possibility that matter as such might be able to enact thinking. The arguments in 4.10.14–17 are recounted for the purpose of this interpretation. And Yolton concludes: "Locke is thus firmly of the opinion that thought cannot be a property of matter if all there is is matter and motion, but he insists that it would be possible for God—that omnipotent, eternal, cogitative being—to add to a system of matter the power of thought" (*Thinking Matter, 17*).

Those anti-materialist arguments are particularly important. Locke considers three successive hypotheses. (1) *Every particle of matter thinks*. If this were the case, one would be faced with the absence of causal unity for the system of nature, and the problem would resume of reconstituting the thought process out of an infinite plurality of extended parts. (2) *A single atom thinks*. If this were the case, one ought to establish the special reason why this particle should possess an infinite power of thought, and that reason could not be found in any "material" characteristic of such an atom. (3) *Some determined corporeal system thinks*. This hypothesis is more in line with the notions we have of ourselves and other thinking beings. And we tend to ascribe by analogy this type of ontological status to God. The difficulties with it are the following: one makes the thinking process in its unity dependent on contingent contextures of corporeal parts, subject to an infinite variety of separate motions; there is no regulative process among such discrete and fleeting elements that could emulate the orderliness of cognitive operations. Locke's inference is crucial: " . . . let this thinking System be all, or a part of the Matter of the Universe, it is impossible that any one Particle should either know its own or the motion of any other Particle, or the Whole know the motion of every Particular, and so regulate its own Thoughts or Motions, or indeed have any Thought resulting from such Motion." (4.10.17)

---

[11]   For an analysis of this aspect of Locke's ontology, cf. M.R. Ayers, "Mechanism, Superaddition, and the Proof of God's Existence in Locke's Essay," *Philosophical Review* 90 (1981), 210–51.

Does this mean that such properties as perception and thought could not emerge, or at least be conceived to emerge, from a complex correlation of moving material parts?[12] This interpretation is not at all excluded by Locke's way of arguing. The fact is that from the notion of moving material parts one cannot analytically derive a sufficient reason for the cognitive operations of the mind. And this is reflected in the cogitative power one must primordially assign to God's nature if he is to account for the orderliness and cognitive features of phenomenal reality. There is however a clear empirical connection between the phenomenal characteristics of thought and the interplay of moving organic parts, and no one would deny that there is an identity of the organism and that this identity seems to form a prerequisite for the empirical analysis of voluntary motion and sense perception.[13] In this instance, a rereading of 4.10.19 appears to be in order.

There, Locke challenges the *ignoramus* position on the basic causal requirement concerning the universe of finite realities. One must admit a power of the eternal being that may match the nature of the effects to be accounted for. Conversely indeed, when faced with contingent connections of powers at the phenomenal level, we cannot but admit that there must exist a sufficient cause for such connections, even though it proves inaccessible to our understanding. Voluntary motion is the appropriate instance. Undoubtedly, we lack an analytical apprehension of the way the will in us determines motions in our body. Even a solution like Descartes's proves unsatisfactory, according to which the mind does not determine such motions causally but only redirects the course of the hypothetical (material) "animal spirits." The causal mechanisms presupposed in any mind-body operation should be admitted even though they escape our understanding and cannot be dealt with under the schematism of ontological hypotheses. If the antinomic statements of 4.3.6 can be evoked in this instance, it should be conceded that they seem to express a straightforward skepticism on the possibility of untying conceptual knots about the emergence of mental features in an organic body. These knots result from the rational attempts at unifying the various clusters of phenomenal properties and powers under

---

[12]   One of the most interesting attempts in that direction was Spinoza's, cf. *Ethica*, II, Prop. 13, and the attending series of corollaries, scholia, axioms, lemmatas, and postulates. Cf. F. Duchesneau, "Modèle cartésien et modèle spinoziste de l'être vivant," *Cahiers Spinoza 2* (Paris: Éditions Réplique, 1978), 241–85.

[13]   It would be appropriate in this instance to take into consideration the empirical criteria of identity put forward in *Essay*, 2.27.4–8 for living organisms up to the level of human being.

notions of substantive essences that the understanding on its own could unfold through analysis.

The major element in the ontological presentation is afforded by Locke's *Second Reply to Stillingfleet*. There, Locke considers the possibility of superadding to a substance consisting of matter, that is an extended, solid substance, various sets of properties, like the Newtonian power of gravity in the case of physical bodies, the power to organize, grow and reproduce in plants, the same in animals plus the power of sensation and of generating motion, to end up with the hypothesis of an additional power of thinking in the special animals we are. The argument against this hypothesis is inspired by Cartesian metaphysics: superadding thought to a material sub-stance would negate the specific essence of matter; insofar as it proves analyzable, the concept of material substance entails conditions that would be inconsistent with the conceptual essence "thinking". The material substance would thus need to be destroyed in its materiality, so to speak, in order to ground the possibility for the essence signified by the notion of thinking to inhere in the "same" substance. Following M.R. Ayers, Yolton has focused on the main argument invoked by Locke. This is an hypothesis about God creating two substances, the one material, the other immaterial, but without adding any principle of activity in either. In the notion of any finite (= created) substance as such, there does not seem to subsist any essential ground for action:

> God has created a substance: let it be, for example, a solid extended substance: is God bound to give it, besides being, a power of action? that, I think, nobody will say. He therefore may leave it in a state of inactivity, and it will be nevertheless a substance; for action is not necessary to the being of any substance, that God does create. God has likewise created and made to exist, *de novo*, an immaterial substance, which will not lose its being of a substance, though God should bestow on it nothing more but this bare being, without giving it any activity at all. Here are now two distinct substances, the one material, the other immaterial, both in a state of perfect inactivity. Now, I ask, what power God can give to one of these substances (supposing them to retain the same distinct natures, that they had as substances in their state of inactivity) which he cannot give to the other?[14]

Yolton is keen to point out that the condition of the two inactive substances is not similar: the material substance is endowed with an essence consisting of two minimal properties, namely extension and solidity; the immaterial

---

[14]   *The Works of John Locke*, 10th ed. (London, 1801), 4: 464.

one has a very abstract kind of essence since it seems to be merely conceiv-able in terms of plain being and to be slightly more that a bare *ens rationis*. Ayers connects this argument with the Aristotelian and scholastic distinc-tion between inseparable and separable properties when speaking of the essence of some natural kind ("Mechanism," 226–31). This would mean that for Locke, thought might be considered a separable property in a context of essential identification of finite substances. Using a more Cartesian terminology, I suggest it means that thought, and more precisely acts or states of thought, would appear as modes of a substance whose essence or nature could not be specified through the notion of a principal constant attribute. As a matter of fact, Yolton connects the interpretation suggested by Ayers with a passage in the correspondence with Limborch where Locke states that the attribute of thought could not serve to define God as a substance, since we need to exclude any mode that might be connected with corporeity in thinking of Him, and thought would not meet this restrictive conceptual requirement.[15] Yolton takes the notion of an inactive immateri-al substance (= with no actual state of thought) as congruent with the conception of an omnipotent Creator. But since no analysis can be offered for the inseparable properties of such a substance that would draw a parallel with extension and solidity in the inert material substance, have we not a reason to disqualify this ontological construct, which can only serve as a polemical device? Within the abstract frame built around the "artificial" antithesis of material and immaterial substance, the need to add active powers comes into play when one has to account for phenomenal entities and their observable properties. Those active powers cannot be taken to derive from mere extension and solidity, but they cannot either be supposed to imply the negation of extension and solidity. As a result, the ontologizing of essential attributes such as extension and solidity, or the negation of the same, offers no real inlet to the explanation of the human mind in a context of natural philosophy. In short, setting up antinomies about thinking matter can be considered a strategy to shift the emphasis of inquiry to a different, more epistemological, type of approach.

---

[15]   Cf. Locke to Limborch, 4 April 1698, Letter 2413, *The Correspondence of John Locke* (Oxford: Clarendon Press, 1976–88), 6: 365: "[. . .] the term 'incorporeal' or 'immaterial' would not on that account [= the Cartesian reliance on the term 'thought' to express the essence of a spiritual substance] have to be omitted from the definition of God since whoever wants to think rightly about God ought to remove all matter or corporeity from Him. 'Thought' certainly does not do this, whatever the men devoted to Descartes's opinions suppose to the contrary."

II

It is definitely my suggestion that Locke had decided to take a skeptical stand on the problem of the mind's substantive nature. This attitude results mainly from his adhering to a conception of knowledge akin to Gassendi's. But precisely because of this affinity, Locke is keen to elude the presumed ontological implications of such an empiricist epistemology. In which instance, he is ready to borrow from the Cartesians an apparent reduction of the knowledge process to the phenomenal aspect of thought processes within compass of the perceiving agent's sensitive and reflective experience. So Locke is transforming the way of ideas into a descriptive analysis of our way of achieving a system of objective and rational representations in conjunction with the data of sense experience and mental self-awareness.

What kind of theory of the mind one could expect to find in Locke? It is evident that for most seventeenth-century philosophers the question could not be treated in abstraction from a reflection on the animal's structural and functional specificity: indeed, the notion of soul itself involved a basic reference to the agent of physiological functions. And so the main problem was to conceive how mental operations expressive of a rational activity might be connected with this physiological entity, which itself belonged to the physical order. However obliquely treated, the nature and characteristics of mental operations formed an object of inquiry in natural philosophy, and therefore were in need of a "scientific" treatment. Two main options might prevail in this instance. The Gassendi type of approach would consist in trying to derive from a phenomenal consideration of complex organized bodies the conditions for the supervenience of mental operations. The Descartes type of approach, on the contrary, would distinguish two different types of essences representative of the substantive natures comprised in the created universe; and it would attempt to derive from the distinct conceptual characteristics of these essences, *extensio* and *cogitatio*, a system of representations for the mental operations: such operations may be considered in isolation from the corporeal phenomena, when dependent upon the sole intellect, as well as in conjunction with those phenomena, when the intellect operates in an unknown kind of correlation with the physical conditions of sense perception and imagination.

As stated in the epistle to the reader, Locke's endeavour in the *Essay* is at once different from the usual goals of inquiry in natural philosophy. His philosophical analysis presents itself as subordinate to the constructions of a science of phenomena. Its function is to be mainly critical: it should allow scientific knowledge to develop freely by avoiding aporias which result from an inadequate use of terms (*Essay*, 9–10). With Locke, philosophy gives up the building of science as its own task. This is a significant demarcation from the Cartesian project. The demarcation from Gassendi's may be viewed as less radical; nevertheless, Locke dissociates himself from the idea of drawing up an integral system of natural philosophy, and in this instance, he parts with Gassendi and his followers.[16] When the solving of scientifical questions rests finally in the employment of a descriptive and classificatory method-ology, like that which the *virtuosi* of the Royal Society would advertise and Locke himself accepted as the sole basis for experimental philosophy,[17] philosophers cannot find their way to a "physics" of the soul and mind in good standing anymore. Locke will submit these theoretical entities to a "skeptical" treatment, which was not to be found as such in either Descartes or Gassendi. Concerning the "discerning faculties of a man," this is well translated in the analytical objectives set forth in *Essay* 1.1.2, which refer to the sole use of the "historical, plain method."[18] This strategy aims at placing in parentheses a good part of what used to form a theory of the soul and mind among previous philosophers. To sum up, if there is such a theory in Locke, it is due to manifest a lack of direct ontological reference.

It can be easily shown that Locke is relatively eclectic on the subject of soul and mind. There are in the *Essay* a variety of sketched analyses which remind of Descartes's at times, of Gassendi's in some other instances. But I would insist that none of the sketches provides a real "physics" of the mind; and even the synthesis drawn from those various sketches would not suffice

---

[16]   On Gassendi's natural philosophy and the tensions which arise in his system, cf. O.R. Bloch, *La philosophie de Gassendi* (The Hague: Martinus Nijhoff, 1971), chap. 6. "De rebus naturæ universe: I. L'espace et le temps," 172–201; chap. 7. "De rebus naturæ universe: II. La matière et le mouvement," 202–32. The more recent study by L.S. Joy, *Gassendi the Atomist* (Cambridge: Cambridge University Press, 1987), is less instructive for our purpose since it focuses mainly on the role Gassendi played in the historical recasting of atomism. A more useful reappraisal of Gassendi's philosophy is provided by B. Brundell, *Pierre Gassendi. From Aristotelianism to a New Natural Philosophy* (Dordrecht: Reidel, 1987).

[17]   Cf. Yolton's analyses in *Locke and the Compass of Human Understanding*, mentioned in note 6 above.

[18]   Cf. *Essay*, 1.1.2: "It shall suffice to my present Purpose, to consider the discerning Faculties of a Man, as they are employ'd about the Objects, which they have to do with: and I shall imagine I have not wholly misimploy'd my self in the Thoughts I shall have on this Occasion, if, in this Historical, plain Method, I can give any Account of the Ways, whereby our Understandings come to attain those Notions of Things we have, and can set down any Measures of the Certainty of our Knowledge, or the Grounds of those Perswasions ... "

to this end. In searching the *Essay* for what it may not give, we can at best recast a bundling together of theses somehow truncated from their onto-logical implications. Does analyzing the nature of this algebraic *x* which *mens* means, differ from inventorying the several registers of phenomena which seem to link to it, without having any guarantee that we can get to a necessary connection between these and their substantive ground? The critique of the notion of substance (2.23 and passim), the distinction of real and nominal essences (3.3.15–20), the empirical derivation of our ideas of power (2.7.8; 2.8.23–25; 2.21.1–4; 2.26.1–2): these are some among the epistemological theses that contributed in relativizing and phenomenaliz-ing, so to speak, the investigation on the nature of *mens*.

How does Locke appropriate the Cartesian schemes? The following points summarize the operation in its essentials. Reflective experience is one source of simple ideas, a source which cannot be reduced to external sense experience. The understanding gets its ideas of the various mental operations through this channel. These operations are apprehended as the properties of the cognitive agent. And this cognitive agent forms a subject of inherence, a *substratum* or substance, on which those properties depend and from which they are taken to flow. It is impossible to determine what essential attribute such a substance owns beyond its operations. One cannot therefore deduce the various mental properties from a specific nature rationally circumscribed. From the Cartesian *cogito*, Locke thus retains the intuitive certainty of the existence of the knowing subject, the linking with the same *substratum* of all acts of thought apprehended in the reflective experience of a conscious self, the reduction of the perception of ideas to what the understanding is presently aware of. But, at the same time, the *mens* gets reduced to what appears of it in inner experience: it has no ontological dimension anymore. Nothing, for instance, allows us to suppose that the *substratum* of thought processes ceases to exist when the continu-ousness of our conscious experience is suspended. And the apparent antin-omy developed in *Essay* 4.3.6 witnesses to this, setting the real nature of the substantial principle in parentheses: it is no more inconceivable that God may have linked the operations of the thinking subject with the *sui generis* organization of a material substance than it is inconceivable that he may have united a spiritual substance with a material one so that conscious experience be concomitant with the modifications of our own body. In a way, Locke is content with dismissing together the champions of the material soul in Epicurean style and the partisans of the Cartesian *mens*. In both cases, are we not faced with purely speculative hypotheses which nothing can warrant, not even an analogy with the data of experience? In contrast with hypotheses received in science, such speculative hypotheses do not serve at all in assembling data into a coherent system. The limitation of the Cartesian scheme for Locke shows up clearly in his analysis of personal identity in *Essay* 2.27. The reality of a person is abated to fit the "phenomena" of his or her activity as a *cogito* and thus, the person is said to subsist within the limits of experienced self-awareness: personal identity rests in continuity of consciousness. The substantial inherence of this *conscientia sui* is in fact considered as suspended, at least insofar as our conceptual analysis can get access to it. The various paradoxes Locke builds concerning the unattainable substantial reference for personal identity bear witness to this philosophical agnosticism (2.27.23–25). In the same manner, Locke had built paradoxes about the presumed substantial status of the Cartesian *cogito* (2.1.10–19).

Let us turn now to Gassendi's potential influence on Locke's treatment of the mind. Within purview of the present analysis, we can but cover scantily the texts of the *Syntagma philosophicum* concerning this issue. Following O.R. Bloch, the dominant aspect of Gassendi's work previous to 1644–1645 was a systematic materialism, according to which every known phenomenon should be accounted for in terms of atoms endowed with such characteristics as extension, figure, solidity and motion; indeed, this state of affairs would apply in the case of the vital and cognitive operations of animals and human beings. This is the position for instance one finds expressed in Gassendi's objections and instances against Descartes's *Meditationes de prima philosophia*, which were reproduced in the *Disquisitio metaphysica* (1642).[19] But the *Syntagma philosophicum*, the main elements of which were assembled in 1644–1645, aims at achieving some kind of conciliation between an atomist ontology and empiricist epistemology on the one hand, and the main tenets of traditional theology on the other. In this new context, the notion of an immortal soul had to be confirmed without entailing major disruptions for natural philosophy: the natural philosophy involved was such as the mechanistic analysis of phenomena seemed to require and for which an empiricist epistemology would provide necessary support. The result is known as a doctrine of the two souls: one soul is akin to the Epicurean corporeal soul and consists in a specific organization of atoms, endowed with the most active properties of material parts, those which express certain higher level modalities of the material substance:[20] it is taken to operate the vital and cognitive functions exem-

---

[19]   P. Gassendi, *Disquisitio metaphysica seu dubitationes et instantiæ adversus Renati Descartes metaphysicam et responsa*, ed. and trans. B. Rochot (Paris: Vrin, 1962).

[20]   Gassendi, *Opera omnia* (Lugduni, Sumptibus L. Anisson & J.B. Devenet, 1658), 2: 250b: ". . . videri ergo potius esse Animam substantiam quandam tenuissimam, ac veluti

plified in animal life; the other soul is the *mens* and as such, it is a specific immaterial substance from which the cognitive operations associated with human intellect flow. The outstanding feature of Gassendi's analysis about the respective activities of the two souls consists in a straightforward parallelism which makes it possible to acknowledge their ontological continuity notwithstanding the "analogical" reasons supporting the immateriality of *mens*. The arguments boil down to an admission of the fact that the operations of the intellect might after all be conceived as an extension of those of the "phantasy" (*phantasia*), which forms the core of the material soul's actions. But some arguments of a verisimilar nature may be adduced that would tend to tip the scale on the side of an immaterial soul.

According to the program of analysis in the *Syntagma*, the complex corpuscular structure of the animal and the dynamical interactions of the atoms involved in the most active part of it, the brain, pursuant to the influx of material parts from the external objects on the periphery of the body and the sense organs, may account for the emergence of sophisticated physiological functions. This scheme seems the more acceptable and real the more we admit of a general teleological plan for the intervention of efficient causes. Thus a specific, densely-organized cluster of active material parts ought to afford a sufficient reason for the complex biological functions, including those of sense perception, imagination and animal reasoning (*ratiocinatio*), which seem to depend more directly on brain structure and operation. In this context, Bloch links what he calls the "mechanism of an atomistic pneumatology" with the teleology of a seminal plan for the created world.[21]

---

florem materiæ, cum speciali dispositione, habitudineve, & symmetria partium intra ipsam massam crassiorem corporis degentium."

[21] Cf. O.R. Bloch, *La philosophie de Gassendi*, 363–64: " . . . si la vie n'est rien d'autre que la possession de l'âme et de son pouvoir d'agir, si l'âme est cette 'force interne présente en nous et dans nos membres, par laquelle nous vivons, sentons, imaginons, nous mouvons; et dont le départ fait que nous nous dissolvons, et ne manifestons plus rien de tel', si enfin la vie . . . est essentiellement *mouvement*, ce mouvement vital, cause efficiente de tous les processus biologiques, ne peut être rapporté à une Forme immatérielle, dont ne sauraient procéder des mouvements réels, ni à une qualité ou à un arrangement des parties de la matière qui, n'étant que relation, ne sauraient constituer un principe actif, mais seulement à une âme qui soit à la fois matérielle et mobile. . . . Mais si cette âme matérielle et active rend compte du mécanisme des processus vitaux . . . il reste que, d'une part, son mouvement et son activité mêmes renvoient à la création simultanée par Dieu des atomes et de leurs mouvements, que, d'autre part, ces explications restent dans l'ordre des causes efficientes, difficiles à pénétrer, alors que la finalité biologique saute aux yeux, et manifeste immédiatement, par-delà ou en-deçà du mécanisme d'une pneumatologie atomistique, l'intention providentielle du Créateur."

If we take for granted this type of analysis in the case of vital functions and of sense organ operations, psychological activity proper seems to depend on the phantasy or imagination. This phantasy is considered as exerting a plurality of cognitive functions: it is the sole cognitive faculty in animals; it qualifies as *æstimatrix, cogitatrix, memoria* (*Opera omnia* 2:402b), and the description of its various functions is by no means limited, provided we do not distinguish them as so many scholastic real qualities, or forms. Part of the arguments in the *Disquisitio* aimed at showing that there is no distinction of nature between the intellect and that imagination which is taken to exert a plurality of cognitive functions: for instance, one can actually perceive the sun, or recall its perceivable aspect through memory, or build a geometrical representation of its size and figure according to astronomical measurements: in all those instances, one relies on the same cognitive process which could be equally disturbed by pathological brain states.[22] Along the same line, both ideas of the sun, the perceptual and the conceptual, are referred to the same operation of thought because there is need to admit an homogenous power of representation for both, if one idea is to be compared with, and eventually substituted for the other.[23] The same in the case of our apprehension of the general notion of substance: it entails abstractive and argumentative operations which tend to be assigned to the intellect proper, but no thinking goes on in the process without the support of some imaginative representation; and in fact the discrimination of intellectual and imaginative contents in the notion *qua* representation is impossible to achieve.[24]

If we turn to the later *Syntagma* and omit from our reading the conciliatory part entitled *De Intellectu seu Mente*, the phantasy doctrine seems to develop as an integral account of cognitive operations. Essentially, the imagination perceives representations, which are termed phantasms; these

---

[22]   *Œuvres de Descartes*, ed. C. Adam and P. Tannery (Paris: Vrin, 1964–74), 7: 266–67; Gassendi, *Opera omnia*, 3: 300b.

[23]   Cf. O.R. Bloch, *La philosophie de Gassendi*, 370: "L'intellect n'est qu'une imagination plus avertie, qui compare les images au lieu de les appréhender simplement."

[24]   *Opera omnia*, 3: 325b: "Dicis *substantiam non imaginatione, sed intellectu solo percipi.* Ego Intellectu percipi non nego; neque enim potest ut quidpiam distinctum ab accidentibus concipi sine abstractione, et consequentis deductione, quæ Intellectus propria est; at contendo imaginatione quoque simul percipi, seu imaginatrix sit facultas distincta, quæ cum intellectu concurrat; seu potius sit una, eademque facultas, sensu mox ante exposito." It should be noted that in a speculative way, Gassendi is stating the equivalence of the two hypotheses: that the intellect may be acting in conjunction with the imagination or that they boil down to the same faculty. From the psychological viewpoint, the difference between the two hypotheses seems irrelevant.

present twofold characteristics: they are "impressed species" insofar as they are occasioned or caused by some bodily impression or its remaining trace (*vestigium*) in the *sensus communis*; they are "expressed species" insofar as they form what we can be said to see or apprehend, whenever we imagine *stricto sensu* or conceive.[25] What characterizes the operation of phantasy is precisely the perceiving of phantasms, and therefore "expressing" them. And so it is not bound to actual sensation: it may consider objects which are absent as well as present. It can also comprehend in a single act several species by assembling them: hence the possibility of judging or inferring that something is not something else. Extending the doctrine of expression according to the various ways the phantasy perceives allows Gassendi to distinguish three sets of cognitive operations. The first relates to "the simple apprehension, meaning by that the bare [*nuda*] imagination of a certain thing, without affirmation or negation" (*Opera omnia*, 2:409a). "The [second] operation of the phantasy is composition and division, or assent and dissent, which is also termed affirmation and negation, proposition, enunciation, and [enunciative] judgment" (2:410a). In fact, our imagination cannot turn to a plurality of distinct objects at once: witness the fact that in binocular vision, a single image is perceived, the impression of the eye the axis of which is stretched, being stronger, more lively and distinct than that of the other eye, and therefore attracting more attention from the phantasy. In the second operation, the cognitive power considers several objects in the fashion of a single one, which can be united or disjoined. In this manner of knowing, there is an agreement or disagreement between the elements represented, which depends on the imagination being able to maintain the representation of one element within the apprehension of the other so as to join or separate them. "The third operation is reasoning, which is also named argumentation, discourse and judgment of consecution" (2:411b). Attributing this operation to the phantasy might let believe that animals are granted reason, while it seems to be the exclusive property of man. To avoid this objection, Gassendi phrases a terminological distinction between *ratio sensitiva* and *ratio intellectiva*, the former only being common to men and beasts. But, with sensitive reason, which is a simple function of the imagination, one can draw inferences; and syllogistic reasoning can be accounted for by such inferences. The core of the operation is the power of

---

[25]   *Opera omnia*, 2:405b: "Expressa vero nihil est aliud quam illud ipsum quod quasi intuemur, apprehendimusve, cum reipsa imaginamur aut cogitamus; iuxta illud apud Ciceronum *nulla species cogitari potest nisi appulsu imaginum*. . . . Impressa autem non tam species, aut imago est, quam causa, et occasio, ut huius modi speciem, seu imaginem effingamus."

discovering inclusion relations between more or less general representations. At the beginning of the *Syntagma* in the part entitled *Institutio
logica*, Gassendi develops his empiricist account of the formation of general
and abstract ideas, and he proceeds analogically therefrom to account for
the judicative and ratiocinative functions of the phantasy without any
significant discrimination between the achievements of *ratio intellectiva* and
those of *ratio sensitiva*.

So much being said in favour of a reductive position concerning
cognitive operations, let us consider the conciliatory strategy which such
sections as *De Intellectu seu Mente* illustrate. The following passage summa-
rizes this strategy well:

> [The demonstration of the soul's immortality] has been given when,
> discoursing about the intellect or mind, or the rational soul, we showed
> with diligence, with all the force we could, that it is immaterial; and this
> mainly by taking into consideration the functions of the intellect, among
> which we have revealed and clearly established that many are not imagi-
> nations, that is to say they are produced without images presenting
> themselves to the soul. This is why they can absolutely not be produced
> by the phantasy, a material faculty bound to species or images in perceiv-
> ing any object. Indeed we abundantly inferred these conclusions when we
> dealt with the substance of the soul itself after having rejected the dogmas
> of Plato and Aristotle — this is where we also appealed to arguments
> drawn from reflective actions, from the notion of the universals and of
> universality itself, from the status of the object of the intellect, in which
> as every being, so particularly the immaterial one is comprised; but we also
> did so later, when after having declared the origin, the "information", the
> seat of the soul, we discussed about its mode of action and, distinguishing
> the actions of the intellect or mind, according to common opinion, as
> simple apprehension, enunciation and argumentation, we retained many
> such actions in the three categories, which require an immaterial faculty,
> considerably surpassing the highest (*suprema*) phantasy of material reali-
> ties.[26]

According to François Bernier in his summary of Gassendi's analysis,[27]
arguments in favour of the rational soul hypothesis flow from the fact that
the understanding can reach demonstratively objects which surpass the
capacity of actual sense perception: it is, for instance, the case when we
substitute an astronomical notion of the sun's size and distance to the basic

---

[26] *Opera omnia*, 2:629a–b, quoted by O.R. Bloch, *La philosophie de Gassendi*, 399.

[27] Cf. F. Bernier, *Abrégé de la philosophie de M. Gassendi*, (Lyon: Anisson & Posuel,
1678).

observational one. Indeed, the understanding makes use of phantasms at the starting point of, and throughout its discursive processes, but it ends up with an intentional object which does not admit of immediate material exemplification. All this boils down to recognizing the specificity of logical constructs and inferences as means for extending your knowledge of phenomenal objects beyond the reach of sense experience. A second stream of argument relates to the *cogito*: its reflective knowledge lacks any material equivalent in terms of self-intending motion, since the motion of a part is always directed to an other part.[28] In short, it is impossible to perceive or imagine a mechanism of parts that would operate intellectual reflection as we experience it internally. As a third category of reasons in support of the immaterial soul, Gassendi brings forth the fact that we can think of objects, which may be incorporeal as well as corporeal: in this instance, he has in mind the notions we use to represent the most general metaphysical categories, such as the abstract notion of substance. A more epistemological argument has to do with the fact that we conceive and reason about universals and acknowledge their universality in the case of a certain number of our mental representations. In all instances, clearly the argumentation for an immaterial soul is hypothetical and obtains at best a higher degree of probability than the alternative view, which seemed to underlay Gassendi's anti-Cartesian critique in the *Disquisitio*. When summing up the arguments in favour of the immaterial soul, Gassendi establishes that the end result is a negative and abstract conception which presumes that the ontological basis for our cognitive operations may surpass the limits of a material phantasy.[29]

28　*Opera omnia*, 2: 441a: "Quamobrem et exinde fit, ut neque visus aut videre seipsum possit, aut suam visionem cognoscere, aut animadvertere se videre; neque ulla alia facultas, quæ corporea sit, præstare quidpiam simile valeat; atque idcirco, ne Phantasia quidem corporea cum sit, seipsam, suamque imaginationem percipiat, aut animadvertat se imaginari."

29　Summarizing a set of arguments in *De intellectu seu Mente* (*Opera omnia*, 2:442–43), F. Bernier clearly states this relativistic feature of the immaterial soul hypothesis, *Abrégé de la philosophie de M. Gassendi*, 6: 350–51: "À la vérité, l'Entendement ne connaît pas positivement, comme on parle, cette sorte de substance (l'immatérielle) en sorte qu'il la voie, pour ainsi dire, selon qu'elle est en soi, parce que la liaison étroite qu'il a avec le corps tant qu'il fait sa demeure dedans, l'en empêche; mais c'est assez pour nous faire remarquer son immatérialité qu'il la connaisse négativement, et abstractivement, c'est-à-dire qu'il s'élève par sa propre force, et par son raisonnement à connaître ou inférer, et conclure qu'outre ce qui lui est représenté par son imagination, il y a quelque nature plus noble et plus parfaite qui ne peut être représentée par une espèce corporelle, et que cette nature est ou existe effectivement et réellement."

But by building this additional system of immaterialist conceptions concerning the mind, Gassendi is perfectly aware that he is unable to surmount the antinomy about the soul by means of an effective demonstration: there is no final test, whether rational or empirical, to discard one of the alternatives: a strictly material soul able to operate rational functions through a material phantasy, or a system of two souls, one material, the other immaterial, conjoined in the cognitive operations characteristic of human beings.

In *L'empirisme de Locke* (105–6), I had suggested that Locke was directly influenced by the paradoxical nature of Gassendi's arguments about the two souls in stating his skeptical position in *Essay* 4.3.6 and thus avoiding the entanglement of metaphysical issues about the mind's substantive nature. The complex and finally inconclusive analyses in the *Syntagma philosophicum* may have played a significant rôle in persuading Locke "at present [not to] meddle with the physical consideration of the mind" (1.1.2) while pursuing his analysis of human knowledge.

Notwithstanding this skeptical stand for the present, there might be in the *Essay* some indications that such an inquiry about the physical consideration of the mind could be sketched for the future: then it would more likely belong to the domain of experimental philosophy. In which case the influence of Gassendi, filtered through the sieve of the historical, plain method as applied to an analysis of powers of acceding to and/or building knowledge contents, would have had a persistent residual effect. One finds in Locke a genesis of our complex ideas from the initial level of representations (= phantasms); the abstractive functions of our understanding depend on, and emerge from, a *ratiocinatio* combining signs, that is ideas or words expressing ideas, which ultimately refer to data of sense experience, whether reflective or sensitive: these features are quite akin to certain principal elements of the Gassendist epistemology.

The importance Locke attaches to the determination of the identity of a man in 2.27.8 has been rightly underlined in the literature. This determination consists in an empirical connection between the idea of a thinking or rational being, which is drawn from the reflective experience of the *cogito* on its operations, and the idea of an organized body fit to maintain the vital functions according to the descriptive characterization of an animal.[30] Attempting to derive the rational operations physiologically is not an

---

[30] *Essay*, 2.27.8: "For I presume 'tis not the *Idea* of a thinking or rational Being alone, that makes the *Idea* of a *Man* in most Peoples Sense; but of a Body so and so shaped joined to it; and if that be the *Idea* of a *Man*, the same successive Body notshifted all at once, must as well as the same immaterial Spirit go to the making of the same *Man*."

aberration in this context. After all, Locke admits of certain instruments to generate probable inferences: these will generalize and unify the various contingent coexistence relations that form the major part of our knowledge of phenomenal realities. One of these instruments of experimental philosophy is the corpuscular hypothesis (*Essay* 2.8 and passim). But another is the principle of an *analogical* gradation of life forms from less to more complex, that principle being signified by the metaphor of the *great chain of beings* (3.6.12, 4.6.12). We could add that the model for the empirical derivation of ideas in Book II of the *Essay* presupposes the progressive emerging of intellectual processes from an initial stage which Locke does not hesitate in assimilating with the operations of a sort of animal psychism. Such is by the way the type of arguments that serve to repudiate Descartes's radical mechanistic model about the soul of animals.

The descriptive model for the genesis of ideas framed in accordance with the "historical, plain method" seems in fact to legitimize a rather emergentist conception of the rational functions along with the representation of a progressively increasing complexity in the "manipulations" of ideas. Might not this complexity depend on an underlying physiological organization which complexifies gradually? Locke would probably reply that hypotheses of that kind, though they may signify unknown connections from which to draw some explanation for our notions of the mental operations, cannot result in any demonstrative body of knowledge that would form a *physics of the mind*. At best, such an hypothetical representation might prove useful in connecting various sets of phenomena without ever reaching true rational ground of the type metaphysicians would be seeking. In these circumstances, there is no surprise that historically, Locke disappointed both materialists and spiritualists. But should he be blamed for refusing to overdetermine the knowledge processes and grant them unwarranted a priori ontological significance? At the same time, however, Locke may be seen as opening up new avenues for the empirical investigation of the intellect, within compass of scientific enquiries bearing on natural phenomena.

*   *   *

As shown by John Yolton, Locke drew up a remarkable critique of ontological paradoxes about the mind-body substantive connection; his critique was at least partly grounded in the analytical incompatibility of our determinate notions about mind and body respectively, when we try to connect the distinct sets of mental and corporeal properties with our scanty knowledge of the essences involved. But, for Yolton, Locke's solution to the paradoxes hinged on a metaphysical consideration of God's causal power in light of our relative notions about separable and inseparable properties of finite substances. I have attempted to show that this metaphysical way is only part of the story: Locke intended not to "meddle with the physical consideration of the mind" for reasons that had essentially to do with the employment of an empiricist methodology in analyzing knowledge processes. In this context, the ontological paradoxes grew out of an unresolved epistemological antinomy between a single material soul and a conjunction of immaterial and material soul. Such an antinomy was part of the Gassendist heritage: in the *Syntagma philosophicum*, Gassendi had fostered a dual analysis of the intellectual functions with no final epistemological criterion to decide between the alternative versions. Recasting an analogous analysis, Locke is prone to get rid of the undecided issue since the enquiry is supposed to bear solely on the materials and processes of knowledge within scope of our mental experience. This epistemological strategy may leave room for further investigation of the mind-body relationship, but in the non-metaphysical context of experimental philosophy. As proposed by Locke, such a methodological shift redefines the issue radically but it could not but lend itself to fierce polemics during the Enlightenment and afterwards. It is my belief that Locke's fine epistemological arguments deserve to be revisited for their own meaning and within their original context, apart from the antagonistic interpretations that have been superimposed on them in subsequent history.

SCEPTICISM WITH REGARD TO REASON IN THE 17TH AND 18TH CENTURIES

Richard H. Popkin

In the history of scepticism from Sextus Empiricus onward much attention is given to undermining confidence in human sensory faculties. Most of the famous tropes in Sextus deal with the unreliability of our senses, and with why we should suspend judgment about all assertions of sensory knowledge. On the other hand, much less attention is given to undermining confidence in our reasoning faculty. Sextus and later Montaigne pointed out that people have made mistakes in reasoning, that reasoning is influenced by non-rational factors like the effects of drinking alcohol or lack of sleep. They pointed out that reasoning can lead to paradoxical results, as Zeno had shown. Further they sought to show that even in the most rational activity of doing mathematics, that strange, incredible conclusions can result. And Sextus, Montaigne and Gassendi had all said that our reasoning faculty might be fine, but that human beings in any particular case could use it erroneously and end up with dubious results.

These doubts concerning reason were hardly the strongest part of the sceptical arsenal. However, with the presentation of Descartes's method of doubt in the early 17th century, a much more forceful scepticism with regard to reason was set forth. It was not just that one might misapply one's rational faculty. The faculty itself, even when used most carefully, might be demonically infected, so that we are forced to reach false or dubious conclusions even when doing what we call "reasoning correctly." There may be an evil demon who deliberately leads us astray whenever we reason, and prevents us from realizing this.

Descartes made this sceptical possibility more cosmic when he raised the possibility that maybe the all-powerful God is the deceiver, and there is no way we can overcome His or Her forced deceptions. Having raised this ultimate scepticism with regard to reason, Descartes then calmly sought to remove the horrendous doubts by "proving" that God cannot be a deceiver, and hence we can really trust our faculties.

It was seen that the problem posed by Descartes: namely, can our rational faculty be deceptive?, is not so easily solved, if it can be solved at all. What I wish to explore here is the way the problem of justifying the reliability of reason developed after Descartes in English thought up to Hume, and then reached a still higher point of doubt in Condorcet. Hume said,

> There is a species of scepticism, antecedent to all study and philosophy, which is much inculcated by Descartes and others, as a sovereign preservative against error and precipitate judgment. It recommends an universal doubt, not only of all our former opinions and principles, but also of our very faculties, of whose veracity, say they, we must assure ourselves, by a chain of reasoning, deduced from some original principle, which cannot possibly be fallacious or deceitful. But neither is there any such original principle, which has a prerogative above others, that are self-evident and convincing, or if there were, could we advance a step beyond it, but by the use of those very faculties, of which we are supposed to be already diffident. The Cartesian doubt, therefore, were it ever possible to be attained by any human creature (as it plainly is not) would be entirely incurable; and no reasoning could ever bring us to a state of assurance and conviction upon any subject.[1]

Though Descartes himself seemed convinced that he had overcome this Cartesian doubt of the reliability of our reasoning faculty, the problem Hume saw became a basic problem in 17th century discussions. Pascal had said that it was only by faith and revelation that we could overcome the doubt involved there.[2] In England one of Descartes's first converts who soon became a major opponent, Henry More, saw the centrality of the issue of the reliability of our faculties in justifying any knowledge claims, and also saw the inadequacy of Descartes's way of solving the issue. In his *An Antidote against Atheism. Or An Appeal to the Natural Faculties of the Minde of Man whether there be or not a God*, of 1655, More felt that in order to refute atheism he had to base his case on the free use of the natural faculties of the human mind, which would overcome the sceptical doubts of the atheist.

He declared that if the atheists "wil with us but admit one *Postulate* or *Hypothesis* , that Our faculties are true," then he will profess there is a God.[3] But More asked, what is the evidence for this "postulate" or "hypothesis"? He quickly admitted that his arguments are not such "that a mans understanding shall be forced to confesse that it is impossible to be otherwise than

---

[1]   D. Hume, *An Enquiry Concerning Human Understanding*, ed. Selby-Bigge (Oxford: 1951), 12. 2:157.

[2]   Pascal, *Penseés*, #131–434 (Lafuma and Brunschvicg numbers).

[3]   H. More, *An Antidote against Atheism, Or, An Appeal to the Natural Faculties of the Minde of Man whether there be not a God*, 2d ed. (London: 1655), B3v–B4r.

I have concluded" (1.2.3). More went on to say that nothing can be so demonstrated, "For it is possible that *Mathematicall* evidence itself, may be but a constant undiscoverable delusion, which our nature is necessarily and perpetually obnoxious unto, and that either fatally or fortuitously there has been in the world time out of minde such a Being as we call *Man*, whose essential property it is to be then most of all mistaken, when he conceives a thing most evidently true" (1.2.3). This possibility of a perpetually deluded human being, close to that offered by Pascal in the *Pensées*, might be the case if there is no God.

At this point More did not say he would, like Descartes, prove God exists and is no deceiver. He would not even produce such arguments "that the Reader shall acknowledge so strong, as he shall be forced to confesse that it is utterly unpossible that it should be otherwise." Nonetheless his arguments, he insisted would be such as shall deserve full assent, and will win full assent from any unprejudiced mind (1.2.4).

More had introduced what Hume called an "incurable scepticism" as a way of eliminating the possibility of necessarily true demonstrations as the basis of any knowledge claims. The value of any argument, he contended, depends on the value or functioning of our faculties. As long as our faculties can be delusive or can be deluded, any result of reasoning "may possibly be otherwise."

At this point, More instead of advocating abandoning rational discourse, then solemnly proceeded to offer his antidote to atheism. For the rest of his intellectual life More worked on presenting what he considered "the true Grounds of the Certainty of Faith in Points of Religion" which would constitute the antidote to atheism.[4] This antidote consists in pointing out that a person who does not assent to certain evidences is "next door to madness or dotage" and does enormous violence to the free use of his faculties.[5] Even if this is the case, this state of affairs does not answer or remove or overcome the incurable scepticism that had been introduced by doubting the reliability of our faculties. The atheist can say over and over again that in spite of all of More's points "it may possibly be otherwise." The clearest mathematical evidence may be false, unless our faculties are true. If we can accept mathematical truths "supposing no distemper nor violence offered to her Faculties," then we can accept a proof of the existence of an absolutely perfect being (ibid., 11).

---

4   This appears in a book dedicated to Jesus of Nazareth, the Crucified Son of God which has on its title page a motto from Sextus Empiricus on why nothing can be proved, *The True Grounds* appears in More's *Theological Works* (London: 1708).

5   More, *Antidote against Atheism*, p. 7.

A few years later in his *The Immortality of the Soul, so Farreforth as it is Demonstrable from the Knowledge of Nature and the Light of Reason,* of 1659, More seems to realize that his scepticism with regard to our faculties could be carried too far by miscreants and perverse types who would try to make any knowledge impossible. So, he announces that "to stop all Creep-holes and leave no place for the subterfuges and evasions of confused and cavilling spirits," he will offer some axioms that are so plain and evident "that no man in his wits but will be ashamed to deny them, if he will admit any thing at all to be true."[6] This begs the question and does not establish the truth of the axioms since they can be doubted. But to do this constitutes "perfect Scepticisme, it is a disease incurable, and a thing rather to be pitied or laughed at, than seriously opposed. For when a man is so fugitive and unsettled that he will not stand to the verdict of his own Faculties, one can no more fasten any thing upon him, than he can write in the water, or tye knots of the wind"(5). More was willing to concede that doubt about the reliability of our faculties may not be answerable but insisted that it only leads to intellectual catastrophe. So, presumably all of those who are reasonable and not demented will accept More's rules, which involve accepting our faculties as reliable.[7]

In the Restoration period two Latitudinarian philosopher-theologians, Bishop John Wilkins and the Reverend Joseph Glanvill further explored that problem of justifying the reliability of our rational faculty.[8] Wilkins, in his *Of the Principles and Duties of Natural Religion,* first published in 1675, stated that the highest kind of certainty, absolute infallibility, which cannot possibly be false, is beyond human beings. Instead they have to base their knowledge and assent on a conditional infallibility, "that which supposes our faculties to be true, and that we do not neglect the exerting of them." If we accept this supposition, then "there is a necessity that some things must be so as we apprehend them, and that they cannot possibly be

---

[6]   H. More, *The Immortality of the Soul, so Farre Forth as it is Demonstrable from the Knowledge of Nature and the Light of Reason* (London: 1659), 4–5.

[7]   Ibid., 9. On More's scepticism and anti-scepticism see R. H. Popkin, "The Incurable Scepticism of Henry More, Blaise Pascal and Soren Kierkegaard", in *The Third Force in Seventeenth Century Thought,* (Leiden: Brill, 1992), 203–221, and Alan Gabbey's somewhat different appraisal of More's discussions of scepticism in his article in Popkin and A. Vanderjagt, *Scepticism for and against Religion in the 17th and 18th Centuries,* (Leiden: Brill, 1993), 71–91.

[8]   On these two thinkers, see H. Van Leeuwen, *The Problem of Certainty in English Thought, 1630–1680,* (The Hague: Nijhoff, 1963), and M. Griffin, *Latitudinarianism in the Seventeenth-Century Church of England* (Leiden: Brill, 1992).

otherwise"[9] Therefore, some kind of genuine knowledge is possible. So, for Wilkins, the acceptance of the reliability of our faculties is a basic assumption. From this he went on to develop his whole probabilistic justification of religious knowledge which is based on the supposition that our faculties are true and reliable. Wilkins did not actually entertain or examine the possibility of what would happen intellectually if we actually did doubt our faculties.

However Joseph Glanvill, who was closely involved with Henry More, saw the central epistemological importance of the acceptance of the reliability of our faculties as well as our inability to establish this reliability. In his *Essays on Several Important Subjects in Philosophy and Religion*, partly written because of things that Wilkins had said, Glanvill saw that ultimate scepticism about all knowledge can only be rejected if one can ignore the possibility of doubting our faculties. He insisted that there is a kind of certainty, which he, like Wilkins before him, called "infallible," which we would have if we were assured that " 'tis impossible things should be otherwise than we conceive or affirm of them."[10] However, this kind of certainty is beyond what humans can attain, "for it may not be absolutely impossible, but that our Faculties may be so contrived, as always to deceive us in the things we judge most certain and assured"(ibid., 50). (This could be just a demonic or accidental constant deception.) Nonetheless, since we have no reason to suspect that this sort of constant deception is going on, we find that we are conditionally certain, "but we may not say 'tis utterly impossible" that we are not deceived in this. Only God can have infallible certainty. We however possess a human certainty which is sufficient for science and religion (ibid., 50). In another essay in the same volume, "The Agreement of Reason and Religion," Glanvill asserted that "*The belief of our Reason is an Exercise of Faith; and Faith is an Act of Reason.*"[11] He contended that we believe that our reasoning comes from God. This is basically an act of faith. Then employing what we believe to be our God-given reason, we can "justify" our faith. By this means we can comfortably put aside the possibility that reason can be deceptive, and leave it as just a purely sceptical possibility that should not disturb reasonable religious people.

---

[9] J. Wilkins, *Of the Principles and Duties of Natural Religion*, (London: 1675), 9.

[10] J. Glanvill, "Of Scepticism and Certainty," second essay in *Essays on Several Important Subjects in Philosophy and Religion* (London: 1676), 49.

[11] This is the fifth of the *Essays*, with its own pagination. The quotation is on p. 21. See also Van Leeuwen, *The Problem of Certainty in English Thought, 1630–1690*, 71–89; and R. H. Popkin, "Introduction" to the photoreproduction edition of Glanvill's *Essays* (London: 1970), esp. xxii–xxvi.

This resolution of the problem of the reliability of our faculties involves a kind of fideism, but not a kind that requires tremendous intellectual struggle about what to believe.

Glanvill, unlike More or Wilkins, saw the sceptical problem about the reliability of our faculties as one that could not be so easily set aside. He agreed that it was unreasonable to doubt our faculties, but it was not impossible. It was unreasonable basically because we had no evidence that they were delusory. But there was always a possibility that they were so. This remained a genuine possibility because of Descartes's demon hypothesis. It could be pointed out that belief in the reliability of our faculties was a prerequisite for the acceptance of the results of any rational activity, like logic or mathematics, the results of any scientific inquiry, and the results of any historical research. We know our faculties can be misused and can mislead us, as the senses sometimes do. But this state of affairs is corrigible *if* we accept the ultimate reliability and indubitable certainty of our faculties. We have no reason at all to believe that they are in general deceptive. Glanvill carried on this sort of reasoning to base acceptance of historical data (and especially that of Scripture) on the alleged indubitable principle that "*Mankind cannot be supposed to combine to deceive, in things wherein they can have no design or interest to do it.*"[12] Of course, there is a remote possibility that just such a conspiracy is going on, "yet no Man in his Wits can believe it ever was, or will be so" (ibid., 49).

On this basis, scepticism can be set aside in mathematics, science, history and theology, because we have no actual reason to doubt the results obtained in these areas. We have to believe various findings and act on them with confidence. Having said all of this, Glanvill immediately made clear that he had not offered or provided any way of eliminating ultimate epistemological scepticism. In spite of what has been said, it still remains possible that all that we believe to be certain, is not actually so. "There still remains the possibility of oure being mistaken in all matters of humane Belief and Inquiry" (ibid., 50), even though we are convinced we have useful knowledge, such as was being developed at the time by the Royal Society. And this knowledge reinforces our evidence of God's governance of the world.

Glanvill's discussion of the relation of reason and religion is perhaps his most original intellectual contribution—that of offering a rational-sceptical fideism as a way of living with irremedial scepticism about the reliability of our faculties. Henry More had advanced his radical scepticism about the reliability of our faculties as a way of pushing aside his opponents's

---

[12]   Glanvill, "Of Scepticism and Certainty", 49. See on this, R. H. Popkin, "The Scepticism of Joseph Glanvill," in *The Third Force*, 246–253.

dogmatism. Then he ridiculed any one who took scepticism seriously, and suggested they were mad or senile. He insisted that one had to accept our faculties as reliable in order to prove God's existence and soul's immortality. Bishop Wilkins after him just insisted that one had to accept the reliability of our faculties as the pre-condition of all indubitable knowledge. Glanvill however made the acceptance of the reliability of our faculties a genuine act of faith. As cited above, he contended that, "*The belief of our Reason is an Exercise of Faith, and Faith is an Act of Reason.*" He had preceded this announcement by stating that "Reason is certain and infallible," which turns out in his view to be based on our knowledge "that first Principles are certain, and that our Senses do not deceive us, because God that bestowed them upon us, is True and Good" ("Agreement," 20–21).

Glanvill in saying this was not emulating Descartes in making true knowledge depend upon the proof that God is not a deceiver. Rather Glanvill was offering what I call "rational fideism." Faith, and faith alone, is the basis for our belief in our reason. We believe in the reliability of our reason because we believe in God's veracity. However, we do not try to prove that God is truthful. This is what we believe. Thus, faith in God gives us faith in the reliability of our reason, which in turn "justifies" our belief that God is no deceiver.

Glanvill did not offer what critics saw as Descartes's circular reasoning in his efforts to establish that God is no deceiver and that our rational faculties used to prove this are therefore reliable. Glanvill saw that the ultimate guarantee of our certitude depends not on what we can prove, but rather on what we can believe. We are able to believe that God is truthful, and hence we can believe in the reliability of our faculties. The first of these beliefs is reasonable, since we have no reason to doubt it. This, then, for Glanvill, enables us to avoid ultimate scepticism by avoiding the fundamental sceptical problem of having to prove our first principles.[13]

Much of Glanvill's thought was developed from More's philosophy. However, Glanvill's rational fideism does not appear in More. It grows out of seeing what conditions are requisite for certain, reliable and unquestionable reasoning. The crucial condition is that God is in fact reliable and hence is not a deceiver.

Glanvill's rational fideism is in sharp contrast to the irrational fideism being offered in the late seventeenth century by both Pierre Bayle and his Calvinist enemy, Pierre Jurieu. Both of them had said that faith was built upon the ruins of reason, and they took the view that faith is above reason

---

[13]   Glanvill, "The Agreement of Reason and Religion," 20–22, and Popkin, "Introduction" to Glanvill's *essays*, xxiii.

to mean that it was contrary (in any meaningful rational sense) to reason.[14] Glanvill posed the possibility that rationality, the reliability of our rational faculty, could be based on faith. Then in terms of what human beings consider reasonable, accepting such faith constitutes an exercise of reason. Using this rational fideism, Glanvill then tried to show the reasonableness of religious belief, and in particular of the liberal Christianity espoused by the Anglican Latitudinarian theologians of the Restoration period.

John Locke no doubt knew or knew of both Bishop Wilkins and Joseph Glanvill in view of their involvement in the 1650s at Oxford with Robert Boyle and the early scientific work there, and then later with the Royal Society. However, Locke does not make the question of the reliability of our faculties central or even relevant. He took for granted that our God-given faculties are what provide us access to knowledge. The question is what can we actually know?, and how certain can such knowledge be? The most certain knowledge, according to Locke, is intuitive knowledge. This type of knowledge "is the clearest and most certain, that humane Fraility is capable of." It is irresistible, and "leaves no room for Hesitation, Doubt, or Examination." All human certainty and evidence of any knowledge de-pends upon this kind of intuition, and one cannot ask for any greater certainty. "He that demands a greater Certainty than this, demands he knows not what, and shews only that he has a Mind to be a Sceptick, without being able to be so."[15] This intuitive knowledge is about our ideas, compar-ing one or more for their agreements and differences. We immediately see and know intuitively and with complete certainty that white is white, and that white is not black.

For Locke there is no possibility of asking whether this intuitive certainty can be deceptive, or can be the result of some deceptive distortion of our faculties. It is the greatest assurance we have or can ask for. What can be inquired into is when and under what conditions we do in fact have the sort of unquestionable assurance. Locke is perfectly willing to admit that in particular cases where we think we possess intuitive knowledge, we can be mistaken. We may confuse names or words with ideas. Or we may think an idea to be clear when it is not so. In such cases our intuitive perception may be faulty. But this does not mean that our knowing faculty can be deceived.

Locke apparently did not take the Cartesian possibility seriously, but only considered that we might misuse or misapply our rational faculty. There-fore, we had to be careful, and make sure that we were not committing the

---

[14]   Cf. R. H. Popkin, "Pierre Bayle's Place in 17th Century Scepticism," in *Pierre Bayle: le Philosophe de Rotterdam*, ed. Paul Dibon, (Amsteram: Elzivier, 1959), 13–14.

[15]   J. Locke, *Essay* 4. 2. 1: 530.

mistakes, and had our mental attention fixed upon clear ideas. Locke did not consider the possibility we shall soon discuss in Hume's writings, that we might be mistaken in thinking we had avoided the possibility of mistakes.

The closest Locke seemed to get to considering radical Cartesian scepticism was when he briefly discussed Descartes's dream hypothesis. If "any one will be so sceptical, as to distrust his Senses, and to affirm, that all we see and hear, feel and taste, think and do, during our whole Being, is but the series and deluding appearances of a long Dream, whereof there is no reality," and is thus led to question the existence of all things, "or our Knowledge of any thing," Locke then deflected this sceptical possibility by pointing out that the raising of it could be part of a dream too. Although this does not directly deal with the sceptical problem, it was sufficient for Locke to make it look like the Cartesian hypothesis was silly and not worthy of an answer. "[I]f all be a Dream, then he doth but dream, that he makes the Question; and so it is not much matter, that a waking Man should answer him."[16]

Immediately after dismissing the sceptic, Locke indicated that his own theory of knowledge only led to a most limited account of what we could know, and how reliable such knowledge is. Our knowledge "is not only *as great* as our frame can attain to, but *as our Conditions needs*. For our Faculties being suited not to the full extent of Being, nor to a perfect, clear, comprehensive Knowledge of things free from all doubt and scruple; but to the preservation of us" (4.11.8).

In sum, for Locke we can have as complete a certainty as possible about our ideas and the comparisons between them. Knowledge beyond this is extremely limited because our faculties, rational and sensory, are not adequate to provide us much access to knowledge of real existing beings (other than ourselves and God), but are adequate to provide us enough quasi-knowledge suited for our preservation and ability to function.[17] The radical scepticism about the very nature of our faculties and about whether they can be deceptive does not come up. Only the application of the faculties can be deceptive.[18]

---

[16]   Ibid., 4. 11. 8.

[17]   On this, see Van Leeuwen, *Problem of Certainty* chap. 5.

[18]   An even more radical scepticism with regard to reason was raised by Locke's contemporary, Pierre Bayle, who claimed that from two true premises strictly logical consequences could be drawn that are demonstrably false. Hence, reason has to be abandoned as a guide. Bayle's possibility was regarded as destroying all rationality, and answers to him were offered by Locke's friend, Jean LeClerc, Isaac Jacquelot and Leibniz. The examination of Bayle's case will not be dealt with here. I have discussed it in my article, "Pierre Bayle's Place in 17th Century Scepticism," *Pierre Bayle* (See n. 14.) 1–19.

This theme is the first version of the question that Hume raised in his chapter in the treatise entitled "Scepticism with Regard to reason." Hume starts off asserting the usual sceptical view on the subject, namely, that the rules of reasoning or the laws of logic are unquestioned or unquestionable, but he then raises problems about whether one can determine in a given instance whether the rules have been properly applied. Hume begins his discussion by asserting that, "In all demonstrative sciences the rules are certain and infallible; but when we apply them, our fallible and uncertain faculties are very apt to depart from them, and fall into error."[19]

He having said this, then the sceptical problem with regard to reason becomes "Can we tell in a given instance that we have employed the rules correctly?" (1.4.1.180). Hume contended that to answer this we have to make a judgment, not about the rules of reasoning, but about our ability to apply them. Whether this judgment is correct will depend upon our ability to judge correctly our ability to apply the rules. Other sceptical writers, such as Pierre Gassendi, had indicated that the problem of the correct application of our reasoning processes could not be overcome, but that it could however be "reasonably" dealt with.[20]

Hume did not accept this, and showed instead that the attempt to check our reasonings generates an endless series of judgments about our previous judgments, each of whose truth value is less than perfect or 1. The product of these truth values will then get smaller and smaller until, supposedly, our belief in the truth of any rational judgment will approach zero. "When I reflect on the natural fallibility of my judgment, I have less confidence in my opinions, than when I only consider the objects concerning which I reason; and when I proceed still farther, to turn the scrutiny against every successive estimation I make of my faculties, all the rules of logic require a continual diminution, and at last a total extinction of belief and evidence."[21]

This should lead to a complete scepticism with regard to reason without questioning the reliability of our reasoning faculty. This should lead to the view "that all is uncertain, and that our judgment is not in *any* thing possest of *any* measures of truth and falsehood" (ibid.). But Hume realized this did not in fact happen. He explained this by insisting that nature would not let us go on doubting and questioning in this manner. In a famous passage, he

[19]   D. Hume, *A Treatise of Human Nature*, ed. Selby-Bigge (Oxford: 1951), 1. 4. 1: 180.

[20]   P. Gassendi, *Disquisitio metaphysica seu, dubtitationes et instantiae adversus Renati Cartesii, et responsa*, ed. B. Rochot (Paris: 1962); and H. Jones, ed., *Institutio Logica* (Assen: 1981).

[21]   Ibid., 183.

declared that, "Nature, by an absolute and uncontroulable necessity has determin'd us to judge as well as to be breathe and feel" (ibid.).

Hume did not claim that doubts about the application of mathematical or logical rules could be overcome. However, such doubts become untenable psychologically. This kind of scepticism with regard to reason is not refuted by the psychological limitations of carrying on the doubting process that Hume has described. In fact, less virulent forms of just this kind of doubt do recur in some 20th century thinkers such as Moritz Schlick, in his comments on this very chapter in Hume, and in Quine and Hilary Putnam. Schlick, in his *General Theory of Knowledge*, first published in 1925, at the very beginning of the logical positivist movement, questions whether any sceptical doubts can be raised about analytical judgments, tautologies. The particular cases he takes up concerning reasons for doubting analytic judgments involve the claim that conceptual relationships are only accessible to us insofar as they are represented by conscious processes. A deduction is not itself open to question, he contends, but the mental process by which deductions are represented in thought can be doubted. At this point Schlick refers to the section in Hume's *Treatise* , which we have just discussed, on scepticism with regard to reason. Schlick comments on Hume's doubts here saying, "When we stand with such thoughts on the highest peak of skepticism, a shudder of intellectual anxiety comes over us."[22]

To overcome this anxiety, Schlick sought to show that the conditions by which we determine the truth of an analytic proposition are dependent on psychological (empirical) considerations. He insisted, much like Locke, that by most careful examination of the data of consciousness, we could relate concepts and assess analytic judgments without fear of sceptical problems. There might be, as Locke too had admitted, cases in which the correspondence between concepts and judgments and their intuitive representations might be faulty, but this kind of mistake could be detected by just repeating the mental process of examining the concepts or judgments one more time. Hume, of course, would insist that if error or mistake could occur once, it could occur twice too. Schlick replied to this possibility by declaring that "it is improbable that this will occur a second time in the same manner, especially if the reexamination is conducted by another person" (ibid., 167).

Schlick kept insisting that no scepticism with regard to reason concerning the application of the reasoning processes was justified because care and

---

[22] M. Schlick, *General Theory of Knowledge*, trans. A. E. Blumberg (Vienna and New York: Springer, 1974), 118. The German original states, "Wenn wir mit solchen Gedanken auf dem höchsten unÜbersteigbaren Gipfel des Skepsis stephen, so Überkommt uns wohl ein Schauder, eine intellektuelle Angst."

careful introspection guarantee the truth of analytic judgments, and the
certitude which we have of these judgments provides the bulwark against
scepticism. But Hume could have easily asked how does one tell if one has
been careful enough, has carefully introspected? This would require further
examination and so forth. And, once again one would be at "the highest
peak of scepticism."

In Schlick one finds a consciously strenuous effort to keep empirical
psychological facts out of truth-determination precisely because of the
problem raised by Hume. But, can this really be done? The knower recognizes certain data, draws certain conclusions. Are these facts in somebody's
life, or independent happenings outside of time and space? A tautology may
be certain, but the recognition that a particular collection of symbols is a
tautology seems, at least to this sceptic, to be an historical event, subject to
questions and doubts. Similarly, the attempt to obviate any such discussion
by using the logical assertion sign, seems to this sceptic to leave the question,
Is the assertion that x is the case an historical occurrence in somebody's life,
or is it outside human consciousness? If the latter, how do we know about
it? If the former, then we are open to Hume's scepticism with regard to
reason all over again. Finally, Is knowing about a mathematical theorem an
historical happening? If it is not, then how and when is it known? If it is,
Can we be sure that we know it? If we have to check, then we are back with
Hume once more. Schlick saw the problem and valiantly tried to avoid it.
Questions about the status of the central claims of logical positivism raised
by Quine, by Putnam and others, indicate that empirical issues open to
question and possible doubt are still involved.[23]

Hume not only saw the possibility of a scepticism with regard to reason
dealing just with the correct application of reasoning procedures, he also
saw, and stated most forcibly, the stronger scepticism with regard to reason
posed by Descartes, More, Wilkins and Glanvill. But, as indicated at the
outset of this paper, Hume insisted that if one entertained at all the
possibility of a deceptive reasoning faculty, one could never resolve the
matter, since any reasoning would be open to question. Hence, in the
Enquiry, after posing what he called "incurable scepticism," he then went
on to offer his "mitigated scepticism," limiting what areas we will explore
and think about so as to avoid eroding all belief and assurance, and allowing
us to have probable knowledge about many things, while escaping from
areas of doubt and uncertainty (12.3).

---

[23] See, for example, W.V.O. Quine, "Two Dogmas of Empiricism", in *From a Logical
Point of View* (New York: Harper & Row, 1961), 41.

The last version of the problem of scepticism with regard to reason that I want to consider is that offered by the *philosophe*, Condorcet. He was one of the greatest mathematicians of his age, and was perhaps the greatest advocate of the theory of the unending progress of human intellectual achievements. Nonetheless, there is a very radical scepticism at the heart of Condorcet's thought that, in fact, emerges from his study of Hume's *Treatise*.[24]

Keith Baker has shown that Condorcet, perhaps the best mathematician amongst the *philosophes*, got his plan for applied mathematics from one of the more baffling sections of Hume's *Treatise*, that on the probability of chances[25] somehow, from all of the confusion in Hume's chapter between psychological and mathematical considerations, Condorcet developed his way of applying mathematical techniques to social problems.

All of his optimism about the value and virtue of applied mathematics notwithstanding, Condorcet was a sceptic of sorts with regard to epistemology. However his sceptical doubt was only part of the story. He declares in his notes to his edition of Pascal's *Pensées* that "all those who have attacked the certainty of human knowledge have committed the same mistake. They have established (nor was it difficult to establish) that neither in the physical sciences nor in the moral sciences can we obtain the rigorous certainty of mathematical propositions. But in wishing to conclude from this that man has no sure rule upon which to found his opinions in these matters, they have been mistaken. For there are sure means of arriving at a very great probability in some cases and of evaluating the degree of this probability in a great number."[26] (Condorcet was the theoretician of the mathematics of probability at that time.)

Condorcet developed his scepticism from a point in Locke's *Essay*, where Locke explains why we cannot arrive at a necessary science of nature due to the limitations of our faculties. We are able to observe empirically what happens all of the time, but not why it happens. Even Newton's laws do not provide a guarantee that nature must behave in certain ways and cannot be otherwise. In the study of nature, Condorcet pointed out, we are not able to achieve the logical demonstrative certainty that we find in mathematics. But should this lead one to adopt the kind of complete scepticism that Pascal and Hume offered?

---

[24] On possible relations between Hume and Condorcet, see R. H. Popkin, "Condorcet and Hume and Turgot," in *The Third Force*, 76–89.

[25] K. Baker, *Condorcet, From Natural Philosophy to Social Mathematics* (Chicago: University of Chicago Press, 1975), 135–55.

[26] Quoted in Baker, *Condorcet*, 129.

The world, for all we know, may be completely determined. However we can only deal with what we know, namely, the empirical observations and intuitively recognized relations of ideas. We can induce laws from the empirical facts. But these laws are only probable, since we do not know whether or not nature will be uniform, and hence we do not know if the future will resemble the past. So, this shows the limits of our empirical knowledge (ibid., chap. 3).

But, Condorcet pointed out, the development of the mathematics of probability allowed people to formulate a mathematics of reasonable expectation, provided that one presumed that nature would remain uniform. This mathematics does not tell us what will happen, but rather tells us what human beings can expect might happen.[27]

In his notes for his inaugural address to the French Academy, Condorcet indicates that scepticism applies even to mathematics. A proposition like 2+2=4 is intuited by us to be certain. The sceptical problem arises when we ask, Can we be sure that our minds will continue to function in the same manner so that the same proposition will seem certain in the future? The kind of doubt that Condorcet was raising has some resemblance to Hume's cause for scepticism with regard to reason in the *Treatise*.[28] But it introduced a new basis for doubt. Mathematics itself became slightly open to question and somewhat empirical in that it depended on the human psyche operating continuously in the same manner. Mathematics like physics and the moral sciences, then, is only probable.

This sceptical conclusion is then turned positive by pointing out that at least the moral sciences can then have the same sort of precision and exactitude as the natural sciences, and *the same kind of certainty*. Hence, notwithstanding all of the sceptical questions, we can know with certainty about the empirical study of nature and of man and society, providing we accept that nature and man will act uniformly. The physical and human sciences can then be developed in terms of probabilities. Our knowledge in these areas can grow endlessly, and can be used to improve the human scene.

---

[27]   Baker, *Condorcet*; and R. H. Popkin, "Condorcet's Epistemology and His Politics," in M. Dascal and O. Gruengard, *Knowledge and Politics, Case Studies in the Relationship between Epistemology and Political Philosophy*, (Boulder, Colorado: Westview Press, 1989), 113–15.

[28]   On Condorcet's knowledge of Hume's *Treatise* see Baker, *Condorcet*, chap. 3, 139–55 and 181ff, and Popkin, "Condorcet and Hume and Turgot," 47–48. Condorcet seems to have been the only of the *philosophers* who read the *Treatise* and knew about Hume's scepticism with regard to mathematics.

So, we have every reason to expect the indefinite progress of human knowledge, and the perfectibility of mankind.[29]

Although Condorcet is mainly remembered for his upbeat optimism, maintained even in the face of the Reign of Terror, he did offer a powerful argument for a scepticism with regard to reason. Even if we could resolve Hume's point by some techniques applicable to the present state of our consciousness, how do we know if this will be relevant in the future? Our mental apparatus may change, and, hence, what seems true today may not be in tomorrow's mental world. Condorcet may have offered this as a caution to his dogmatic contemporaries, but it is a point that is emerging in some present discussions. Astrophysicists talk about the laws of nature having evolved from the moment of the big bang into the present world. They talk about a different set of laws, even a different set of entities, existing that cannot be understood in terms of today's science. If there can be evolution in the laws of nature, why not in the laws of the mental world? Artificial intelligence theorists talk of designing computer programs that have developed emergent further programs with different properties. Insofar as the mind is like a computer, why can't this happen to any of us? Further, the study of brain chemistry and chemopsychotherapy indicates that mental outlooks can be altered, and even altered drastically, so that what seems reasonable, even mathematically certain, can seem false or dubious under different brain states and different chemical conditions. The experiments in so-called brain washing through sensory deprivation, sleep deprivation, and biochemically induced states shows that Orwell's nightmare can be a psychological reality. People can be led to believe $2+2=5$.

In view of all of the now known states of affairs in which our mental life would be radically different, can we be sure that we will not be in a different mental universe at some future time in which today's certainties become tomorrow's doubts? Condorcet may just have raised a possibility. Now we know too many ways in which mental states could be changed through even small additions to the chemicals in our drinking water, through bioengineered food, maybe even through changes in the ozone layer. We know that we are being induced to believe all sorts of things through propaganda, advertizing, authority pressures. Can we really claim

---

[29]   Baker, *Condorcet*, 44, 74, and 181–82, and Popkin, "Condorcet's Epistemology and his Politics," 114.

One always has to remember that Condorcet's most powerful statement of the progress theory and of the perfectibility of mankind was written while the agents of the Reign of Terror were looking for him, and that he died either by his own hand or by execution just after finishing the *Equisse*.

to have some free, independent moment of truth in which we discover a truth that will persevere no matter what else happens in the external and internal world? If we cannot, then Condorcet's scepticism with regard to reason should make us always open to doubt even if we do not entertain the possibility that our very own rational faculties might be deceptive.

Thus, two levels of scepticism with regard to reason, that raised by Descartes, Wilkins and Glanvill: that our faculties could be unreliable or deceptive, and that raised by Locke, Hume and Condorcet: that the results of using our faculties may be unreliable even if the faculties are reliable, generate a fundamental doubt that appears and reappears in modern intellectual history. We may have made tremendous intellectual strides in the last three and half centuries, especially in the sciences, but there seems to be a haunting doubt, sometimes more pronounced, sometimes muted, that never goes away. The attempt to exorcise it by claiming it is a misuse of language, a misunderstanding, a self-referential problem, etc., just leads to doubts and questions about the exorcism, and whether it is in fact an exorcism, or just more of the problem.

The careful study into seventeenth and eighteenth century theories of knowledge carried on by John Yolton during his lifetime and those like him helps us greatly in understanding the problem, even if it does not resolve it.

LOCKE AND THE
SCEPTICAL CHALLENGE

G.A.J. Rogers

Introduction

As John Yolton has demonstrated in many of his publications, Locke's *Essay Concerning Human Understanding* was written as a response to many things just as it embodied premise and argument from a wide variety of sources.[1] It is, therefore, appropriate to ask questions about its relationship to sceptical issues in the seventeenth century, and in recent years several historians of philosophy have addressed this topic, either in general, or by focusing on some particular aspect of the problem.[2]

The scope of this paper is both wide and narrow. It is wide in two rather different senses. First, it offers argument about the general nature of Locke's response to sceptical challenge, and second, looks at Locke's response on moral and theological fronts as well as with the epistemic concerns central to much contemporary philosophy. It is narrow in that it focuses on some particular issues. It will argue that in at least one special sense Locke's

---

[1] See, for example, his *Locke and the Way of Ideas*, *Locke and the Compass of Human Understanding*, passim.

[2] See, for example, H. G. Van Leeuwan, *The Problem of Certainty in English Thought 1630–1690*, 2d ed. (the Hague: 1970), esp. chap. 5; M. B. Bolton, "Locke and Pyrrhonism: The Doctrine of Primary and Secondary Qualities," in *The Skeptical Tradition*, ed. M. Burnyeat (Berkeley: Los Angeles: and London: 1983): 353–75; G.A.J. Rogers's "The Basis of Belief. Philosophy, Science and Religion in Seventeenth-century England," *History of European Ideas*, 6, 1985: 19–39, and M. Ayers, *Locke* (London: Routledge, 1991), 2 vols., *passim*. For the context see R. H. Popkin, *The History of Scepticism from Erasmus to Spinoza* (Berkeley: Los Angeles: and London: 1979); for the context specifically relating to England see B. J. Shapiro, *Probability and Certainty in Seventeenth-century England* (Princeton: Princeton University Press, 1983). For an interesting earlier view of the drafts of the *Essay* in relation to the printed work on the issue of scepticism see S. P. Lamprecht, "The Early Draft of Locke's Essay," *The Journal of Philosophy*, 29, 1932: 701–13. For a recent assessment of Locke's response to scepticism, see M. J. Ferreira, "Locke's 'Constructive Skepticism'—A Reappraisal," *Journal of the History of Philosophy* 24 (1986): 211–22.

response to scepticism is a traditional one, and I shall attempt to outline
how he fits into that tradition. I shall suggest that what I call this traditional
response is not as easily set aside as some modern philosophers have thought.
I shall then suggest that there are also innovative elements in Locke's
position, aspects which point towards later attempts to meet the sceptic.

The Traditional Response to the Sceptic

I begin with a quotation which signals many of the elements of the traditional
response to the sceptical challenge, without at the outset revealing its source:

> Human nature is different from all other animal nature. It is endowed with
> divine wisdom, endowed with divine arts. Therefore we are justly called
> gods and the children of the Supreme Being. For the light of nature is in
> us, and this light is God. Our mortal bodies are vehicles of the divine
> wisdom. . . . For this reason there is no justification for the skeptical
> question: 'Is man able to see the future and is he able to know it?' Such
> doubts imply that not man, but only God, is capable of this knowledge.
> But . . . God . . . is not alone to have the knowledge [which] he has
> entrusted to man.[3]

This statement of a position—it is hardly an argument—captures three
aspects of what I call the traditional response to the sceptical challenge.
The first is the invocation of a deity. The second is to claim for man a special
relationship to the deity, a shared privileged position; and the third is to
extend the price that has to be paid by the sceptic. But I should first reveal
the author of the quoted passage. It was written in the 1520s by Philippus
Aureolus Theophrastus Bombastus von Hohenheim, called Paracelsus.
Paracelsus was not in any sense an important figure in the anti-sceptical
movement. He flourished, after all, before the new scepticism had begun to
make a serious mark. But his position is representative of an important
atttitude towards scepticism which may be detected at many places in the
sixteenth and seventeenth centuries.

Let me now make some comments about the three aspects already
identified. First, the appeal to a deity. It is the existence of a deity which is
seen as the first premise in the case against the sceptic. The implication
would then appear to be that without a deity skepticism may well win the
day. For Paracelsus the form of scepticism that would triumph was one with

---

[3] Paracelsus. *Paracelsus. Selected Writings*, ed. J. Jacobi (Princeton: Princeton University Press, 1979): 127.

regard to the possibility of practical knowledge of nature, and medicine in particular. That in itself might remind us of Locke the physician. But for the moment let us just acknowledge the theological premise and remind ourselves how closely linked the ideas of scepticism and atheism were to become in the seventeenth and eighteenth centuries. We all remember, for example, that Berkeley's *Principles of Human Knowledge* and his *Three Dialogues between Hylas and Philonous* were written "in opposition to sceptics and atheists."[4] And we are all familiar, too, with the fact that Descartes, in the *Meditations*, vanquished sceptical doubts about clear and distinct ideas and about the existence and nature of the external world with his "proof" of a deity. As he, Descartes, said in his *Replies*, "once we have become aware that God exists. . . . since it is impossible that he is a deceiver, whatever we clearly and distinctly perceive must be completely accepted as true and certain."[5] And he tells us that he could not conclude that God was other than a deceiver if the ideas he has of material things had their "source other than corporeal things."[6] God, then, is the familiar block to scepticism about the possibility of knowledge, and specifically knowledge of the nature of the external world, for both Descartes and Paracelsus. Without the presumption of God's existence, there may well be mileage for sceptical intrusions about the possibility of knowledge in many areas.

The second feature of Paracelus's position that I noted was the special relationship between humankind and the deity. No other earthly creatures share our capacity for knowledge of the workings of nature, even though many of them clearly share our knowledge—are not deceived—about the existence of particular objects in the material world. And, perhaps more importantly for our purposes, though not so overt in Paracelsus, is our capacity for moral knowledge, which almost all were agreed was not open to the rest of the animal world.

And Paracelsus's third feature is the implied one of the wider price that would have to be paid if we were once to concede ground to the sceptic and allow his claims any credence. For if we were once to allow him a place then all would seem to be lost. We could not aspire to knowledge in any quarter. We could not know that there is a God or that we may obtain salvation; we could not make sense of moral knowledge or even the possibility of a science of nature. Scepticism, if it were once to gain entry, would be totally

---

[4]   These words are taken from the full title of the *Dialogues*.

[5]   In "Second Set of Replies" in *The Philosophical Writings of Descartes*, 3 vols. trans. J. Cottingham, R. Stoothoff and D. Murdoch (Cambridge: Cambridge University Press, 1984–91) 103.

[6]   *Sixth Meditation*, *Philosophical Writings*, 2. 55.

corrosive. Of course philosophers should not be intimidated by such threats. They should follow the argument, lead where it will. But it is never wrong to draw attention to the price that has to be paid, and if it is true that if scepticism comes in the door then salvation must flee by the window, we should know this before making the sceptical moves. Pascal, for one, well understood this in the seventeenth century!

Scepticism in Restoration England

If we turn now to the immediate context of English thought in the period leading up to Locke's writing the *Essay* we should note first that although the influence of Sextus Empiricus may certainly be detected,[7] scepticism was generally manifest in a mitigated form. Indeed, the word could be and was sometimes used in an entirely positive way. Glanvill could without embarrassment change the title of *The Vanity of Dogmatizing* in its second edition to *Scepsis Scientifica: Or, Confest Ignorance, the Way to Science*, thereby suggesting that a decent scepticism was the antidote to the dangerous game of dogmatics. And Boyle we know described himself as *The Sceptical Chymist*. In his *History of the Royal Society* Thomas Sprat explains in what sense the early fellows saw themselves as sceptically inclined: "To this fault of *Sceptical doubting*, the *Royal Society* may perhaps be suspected, to be a little too much inclin'd: because they always professed, to be so backward from *setling* of *Principles*, or *fixing* upon *Doctrines*."[8] But Sprat argues that the charge is not justified. They steer a middle course between the sceptics and the dogmatists, he tells us, neither rushing to hold opinions without evidence, but venturing after due consideration of the evidence "to give the advantage of probability to one Opinion, or Cause, above another" (ibid., 107). So the charge of scepticism, if it is to be made at all against the Royal Society and its fellows, looks to be at most of the mitigated variety.

But to leave an account of Restoration England at that point would not be to give a complete picture. And certainly it would distort the picture of the context in which Locke was to develop his philosophy because it ignores developments on the continent.[9] And it ignores, too, an important shift

---

[7]   See, for example, the quotation from Aubrey's "Life of Chillingworth" cited by Popkin, *History of Scepticism*, 67.

[8]   Thomas Sprat, *History of the Royal Society* (London: 1667) 106–7.

[9]   It is this territory in particular (though not of course exclusively) that Richard Popkin has done so much to map out, and where we now know the influence of sceptical thought was both wide and deep.

that had already taken place in the thought of leading theologians of the time, the move from claims of absolute, to those of only moral, certainty in central areas of theology. Both of these aspects of the contemporary scene are relevant to Locke, who was not only to become soaked in the writings of the continental thinkers but also in the theology of Chillingworth, Tillotson and the growing school of Latitudinarians, which rejected pretentious claims to infallibility in matters of theology.[10]

Locke's Intellectual Development in Relation to Scepticism

Through the whole of his mature life we have evidence that Locke held to a teleological view of man, his capacities and his knowledge. It is a picture which brings together his theology, moral theory and epistemology and which finds echoes in many, if not all, of his works. Essentially it is the belief that human beings have a purpose to fulfill in their lives and that God has provided them with the appropriate capacities to meet that purpose. He described it in his journal entry for Monday, 8 February 1677, written when he was staying in Montpellier:

> The business of men being to be happy in this world by the enjoyment of the things of nature subservient to life health ease and pleasure and by the comfortable hopes of an other life when this is ended: And in the other world by an accumulation of higher degrees of blisse in an everlasting security, we need noe other knowledg for the atteinment of those ends but of the history and observation of the effects and operations of naturall bodys within our power, and of our dutys in the management of our owne actions as far as they depend on our wills i.e. as far as they are in our power.[11]

Locke held, then, that we have been created with a purpose, and we have the required resources, in terms of knowledge and natural abilities, to fulfill that purpose. We have the potential for all the knowledge we require of how nature works and what the moral law is; it is substantially irrelevant that we cannot always reach the truth in other areas:

---

[10] See especially Van Leeuwan, chap. 2, R. R. Orr, *Reason and Authority. The Thought of William Chillingworth* (Oxford: 1967) chap. 3., and G.A.J. Rogers, "Locke and the Latitude-men: Ignorance as a Ground of Toleration" in R. Kroll, R. Ashcraft and P. Zagorin, eds, *Philosophy, Science and Religion in England 1640–1700* (Cambridge: Cambridge University Press, 1992), 230–52.

[11] R. I. Aaron and J. Gibb, eds., *An Early Draft of Locke's Essay. Together with Excerpts from his Journals* (Oxford: 1936), 88.

> Whilst then we have abilitys to improve our knowledg in experimentall
> naturall philosophy, whilst we want not principles where on to establish
> morall rules, nor light (if we please to make use of it) to destinguish good
> from bad actions, we have noe reason to complain if we meet with
> difficultys in other things which put our reasons to a non plus . . . . tis not
> to be wonderd if we have not abilitys given us to deale with things that
> are not to our purpose, nor conformable to our state or end.

He concludes the entry with a plea to recognize our weaknesses and not
to waste our time in the expectation of achieving knowledge in areas which
are beyond our powers. Rather, we should "apply the powers of our bodys
and facultys of our soules which are well suited to our condition in the search
of that naturall and morall knowledg which as it is not beyond our strength
soe it is not besides our purpose but may be atteind by moderate industry
and improved to our infinite advantage" (ibid., 90).

We might notice that in these words Locke shows himself, whilst in
the same stable as Paracelsus, somewhat more modest in his expectations
of achievement. He is a long way from the Faustian dream of all knowledge
being within our grasp. We should notice too that from this position he
rejects much of the optimism of the program that Bacon had charted for the
development of human knowledge. And, while he shares Bacon's hope of
improving the lot of man by the application of discovery for the benefit of
mankind, he could never have cited, as Bacon did, the text: "The spirit of
man is as the lamp of God, wherewith he searcheth the inwardness of all
secrets."[12] The Messianic optimism which some have found in Bacon, and
which was certainly present in England in the mid-century, never finds
expression in Locke's writings.

By the time that Locke made this journal entry he had already written
at least two early drafts of the *Essay*. Do they reveal similar positions? Or is
it that the journal entry reflects something new in his thinking, perhaps
encouraged by his reading whilst in France which almost certainly included
writings tending towards similar scepticism? Examples of these sceptical
works include Pascal's *Pensées* and Nicole's *Essais de Morale*.[13] Both of these

---

[12]   J. M. Robertson, ed., *Of the Advancement of Learning, The Philosophical Works of Francis Bacon* (London: 1905) 44. The text is Proverbs 20.27. Bacon's version is not that of the King James translation.

[13]   Cf. J. Lough, "Locke's Reading during his Stay in France (1675–79)," *The Library*, 5th ser. 8 (1953): 229–58 and especially the entry on 237. See also Lough, *Locke's Travels in France 1675–79. As Related in his Journals, Correspondence and Other Papers* (Cambridge: 1953), 111, where we find that Locke bought Nicole's *Essais* on Wednesday, September 30, 1676. Yolton has demonstrated Locke's impact on eighteenth-century

works were included in parcels of books which Locke sent home a month after the journal entry.[14] The *Pensées* lay much stress on man's intellectual infirmity, and one of Nicole's essays is entirely devoted to the limitations of the human mind. That Locke had considerable admiration for the work is testified by his translating three of the *essais*, including the one on the weakness of the intellect, into English for the benefit of Lady Shaftesbury, and in doing so he made his own additions and alterations. It includes much in close agreement with the journal entry and also with claims to be made later in the *Essay Concerning Human Understanding*. Thus Nicole, in Locke's translation, writes, "The sight of our minds and of our bodies are much alike: both superficial, both bounded. Our eyes pierce not to the inside of things: they stick at the surface. . . . Just after this manner is the view of things in our minds: we know nothing of most of them, beyond the shell and surface."[15] He constantly emphasizes the lack of certainty: "The discovery of truth, in most cases, depends upon our comparing probabilities together. And what is there more deceitful than such a comparison?" (ibid., 63). Pascal, too, constantly underlined the lack of sure knowledge inherent in the human condition: "We long for truth, but find only uncertainty within us"[16].

There can be little doubt that Locke's reading in France either brought home to him or reinforced his cautions about the extent of human knowledge. But we must also remember that he had already expressed important reservations in the early drafts of the *Essay* written in 1671, five years before his departure for France. It is to the extent of the sceptical content of these that we should now turn.

Scepticism and the Early Drafts

Study of the early drafts of Locke's *Essay* written in 1671 reveals what one might expect: namely, that whilst the general line of Locke's argument is

---

French thought (cf. his *Locke and French Materialism*, passim) but we must also remember Locke's debt to earlier French thinkers of whom Descartes was only the most important.

[14]   Cf. Lough, "Locke's Reading. . . . ," 237. See also W. Von Leyden, "Locke and Nicole. Their Proofs of the Existence of God and Their Attitude towards Descartes," *Sophia*, (January-March 1948): 41–55, and W. Von Leyden's "A Note on Translating Three of Pierre Nicole's *Essais de Morale*" in Von Leyden's edition of Locke's *Essays on the Law of Nature* (Oxford: 1954), 252–54.

[15]   "On the Weakness of Man," in *Discourse,* translated from *Nicole's Essays* by John Locke (London: 1828; reprint, Bristol: 1991), 60.

[16]   R. Pascal, *Pensées*, (Harmondsworth: Penguin, 1961), 102.

the same as in the final version, there are central claims of the mature work
which either find no place, or only exist in embryo, in these first formulations. It has been claimed, for example, that the primary-secondary quality
distinction does not appear in the early drafts.[17] Certainly, although he tells
us (in Draft B, Section 94) that he will offer us a proof of God's existence,
in the draft as we have it, it never materializes, and one might suspect that
Locke at this stage was not altogether sure of what that proof might be. It
has also been suggested that from the writing of the drafts in 1671 to the
writing of the final text in the late 1680's Locke became more conscious of
the power of sceptical argument against positions as he had at first proposed
them, influenced by the sceptical writers that he had in the interval been
reading.[18] I am not myself convinced about the source of this change.
Certainly there are changes in what Locke says, but how much they were
externally generated must be balanced against the fact that the argument
at almost all places becomes more sophisticated as we move from the early
drafts, through the version of 1685 (Draft C), to the first edition, and, in
important ways, more sophisticated still as we move through the four further
editions that Locke prepared in his lifetime. It seems to me, therefore, that
nearly all of the central claims of the finished *Essay* exist actually or in
embryo in the early drafts. Confining ourselves here to the issue of scepticism and its implications, I believe we shall see this to be true if we compare
the drafts with the printed text. Although there is scope for debate in some
matters, what I hope to demonstrate is that there is a general continuity in
his position, and although he does show increasing awareness of the logical
force of the sceptic's argument, he never sees it as so overwhelming as to
undermine his general conception of knowledge within the teleological
framework in which we have already seen his account is set.

In Draft A this teleological view first makes itself apparent in Sect. 10.
Locke is examining that sceptical problem which had arisen so powerfully
in Descartes's first Meditation as to whether there is an external world
which corresponds to our ideas. He writes:

> This certainty I say of a things existing when we have the testimony of
> our senses for it is not only as great as our frame can atteine too but as our
> condition needs for our facultys being suited not to the extent of beings
> and a perfect cleare comprehensive knowledg of them but for the preser-
> vation of us to whome they are given or in whome they are. . . . . for I

---

[17]   Cf. M. B. Bolton, "The Origins of Locke's Doctrine of Primary and Secondary
Qualities," *The Philosophical Quarterly*, 26, (1976): 305–16.

[18]   Cf. Bolton and Lamprecht, both cited in Note 2.

would fein see that sceptick, who did soe far doubt whether the fire he saw in a glasse furnace were any thing really existing without him soe far as to put his hand into it . . . [19]

Although the argument is elaborated in Draft B, the same claim is made, often with identical phrasing (*Drafts*, B.39.147). In the published work the position is exactly the same, but with the following addition:

Such an assurance of the Existence of Things without us, is sufficient to direct us in the attaining the Good and avoiding the Evil, which is caused by them, which is the important concernment we have of being made acquainted with them.[20]

Earlier in the same section sentiments entirely at one with those of the journal entry for 1677 are to be found, expressed in words which indicate irritation rather than sympathy with the sceptic's case. If anybody is so foolish as to doubt his senses and believes that all is a dream "then it is not much matter, that a Waking man should answer him," but if he wishes he may dream that he, Locke, replies thus:

That *the certainty* of Things existing *in rerum Natura*, when we have *the testimony of our Senses* for it, is not only *as great* as our frame can attain to, but *as our Condition needs*. For our Faculties being suited not to the full extent of Being, nor to a perfect, clear, comprehensive Knowledge of things free from all doubt and scruple; but to the preservation of us, in whom they are; and accommodated to the use of Life: they serve to that purpose well enough, if they will but give us certain notice of those Things, which are convenient or inconvenient to us (ibid., 634).

These hardly sound like the words of someone engaged in serious struggle with scepticism and fearful of being ensnared in its net! Rather, it would appear that Locke's famous common sense has dismissed the sceptic out of hand.

It would, however, be wrong to assume from this that Locke took all sceptical argument to be worthless. From the outset he held positions which have clear links with sceptical claims. Thus, in the first section of Draft A, and in open contrast with Descartes, he rejects the possibility of knowledge

---

[19] P. H. Nidditch and G.A.J. Rogers, eds., Draft A, sec. 10, in *Drafts for the "Essay Concerning Human Understanding" and Other Philosophical Writings*, (Oxford: 1989), 21.

[20] J. Locke *An Essay Concerning Human Understanding*, ed. P. H. Nidditch (Oxford: 1975), 4. 11. 8: 635. Cited by Book, Chapter and Section, followed by page number.

of the essence of both matter and spirit. But he does so while underlining the claim that we may still know that both exist even though we do not know their nature: "from our not having any notion of the essence of one we can noe more conclude its non existence then we can of the other" (*Drafts*, 2). And on causation he remarks that, although we come through experience to know many particular causes, "in universal propositions connecting causes and effects I cannot be assured they are true. . . . a comprehensive knowledg of causes and effects. . . . is I thinke out of the reach of humane understanding" (ibid., A.15.30). In general, the only knowledge we may have of the world is based on sense experience, which is always of the particular, and therefore "we must not expect a certain knowledg of any universall proposition" (ibid., A.31.61). At another place he links the certainty of propositions with their logical form: "all universall propositions are either Certain and then they are only verball but are not instructive. Or else are Instructive and then are not Certain" (ibid., A.29.55). Condensed in one sentence we have an anticipation of all the volumes of Viennese logical positivism!

Damaris Masham told Le Clerc that Locke valued knowledge as it was useful.[21] In many places in the *Essay* such a belief spills over into Locke's account of our faculties and their powers. One such is yet another anticipation of twentieth century philosophy in the text of the *Essay*, the issue of the possibility of a logically private language and the matter of the inverted spectrum. Locke is considering the potentially sceptical problem as to whether or not our ideas, compared with their causes in the world, may be judged true or false. He begins with an appeal to the by now familiar teleological argument. The simple ideas we have are produced in us by powers in objects which God has seen fit to give them "suitable to his Wisdom and Goodness." That is to say, God has decided that particular objects will produce the particular ideas that they do produce and thus enable us to distinguish things in the world by their constant effects on us: "God in his Wisdom . . . [has] . . . set . . . Marks of Distinction in Things, whereby we may be able to discern one Thing from another; and so chuse any of them for our uses as we have Occasion . . ." (2.32.14.388). Nor would it matter, Locke goes on to argue, if the idea of blue which the violet produces in my mind is matched in your mind by the idea produced by a marigold in another's. For, as we could never see into another man's mind and thus become confused about the causes, it could never make a practical difference, for it could never affect our public classifications: that is to say,

----

[21]   Masham to Le Clerc, Amsterdam Manuscripts 557a. From a transcribed copy passed to me by the late E.S. de Beer.

we would never be led by this fact into describing violets as yellow or marigolds as blue. Locke does not think such a thing does happen, because he thinks that there are reasons (which he does not give[22]) to think that qualitatively the same ideas actually occur in both minds. And anyway, "the contrary Supposition, if it could be proved, is of little use, either for the Improvement of our Knowledge, or Conveniency of Life; and so we need not trouble ourselves to examine it" (2.32.15.389).

The emphasis on the practical, the thesis that we possess faculties appropriate to our purpose—quite contrary to the suppositions of the sceptic who doubts or denies any such thing and even that we have a purpose of which we can know at all—is a theme returned to again and again. Thus, in his consideration of our knowledge of the existence of things other than oneself and God, the discussion of the certainty of our knowledge of material objects around us is premised on the supposition that our faculties are properly fitted to our needs. Locke once again dismisses the sceptic as absurd and continues: "As to my self, I think GOD has given me assurance enough of the Existence of Things without me: since by their different application, I can produce in my self both Pleasure and Pain, which is one great concernment of my present state."[23]

A few pages later he again makes the charge that the sceptic's position is absurd. It is foolish and vain, he says, for men to aspire to demonstration and certainty "*in things not capable of it.* . . . He that in the ordinary Affairs of Life, would admit of nothing but direct plain Demonstration, would be sure of nothing, in this World, but of perishing quickly" (4.11.10.636). But this does not imply that Locke sees argument against the sceptic as wholly pointless. He had, from the first draft onwards, always been prepared to argue that the consistency and coherence of our experience gives us reason to accept that the fire, for example, really exists—if the sceptic doubts his sight why does he not try putting his hand in it (4.11.7.633)! And he gives credence, too, to the fact that, for example, I cannot but see the sun if I turn my eyes towards it.

What, then, does my account of Locke's reponse to scepticism so far amount to? It is that from within a teleogical framework, often alluded to but less often spelt out, Locke advances a conception of the scope and limits

---

[22]   It is not absurd to assume that they are connected with the veracity of God.

[23]   4. 11. 3; 631. It is worth noting that Locke's appeal to God's purposes for man and nature is not confined to his epistemological and theological writings, but occurs in his political works as well. See, for example, the *Second Treatise of Government*, sec. 27. Patrick Day has pointed out to me the interesting fact that in this section Locke refers to God as "Nature."

of human understanding which rejects the sceptical arguments of the Pyrrhonists about the existence of the external world. At the same time, however, he realizes that his own claim that we have knowledge only as far as we
have ideas places large constraints on the power of the human mind to understand most of the natural world and much else besides. Locke finds this quite
consistent with man's place in the great design of things. We only need to
know certain kinds of things to have a chance of happiness in this life, and
to succeed to a perfect happiness in the next. But essential to this last requirement is knowledge of right and wrong, moral knowledge, for without
it our chances of obtaining eternal happiness are slim indeed, and it is to Locke's
account of the possibility of moral knowledge that we must soon turn.

Ayers on Locke and the Causes of Ideas

Michael Ayers has recently given an explanation of Locke's account of the
origin of simple ideas which he offers as Locke's bridge from the external
world to ideas. Ayers sees Locke as offering a consciously anti-Cartesian and
anti-Aristotelian analysis of simple ideas, which he holds, provides the key
to Locke's rejection of scepticism about the existence of external causes of
our ordinary perceptual experiences.

According to Ayers, Locke begins his account from "a pretended
scepticism" expressed thus:

> 'Tis evident the Mind knows not Things immediately, but only by the inter-
> vention of the *Ideas* it has of them. *Our Knowledge* therefore is *real*, only so
> far as there is a conformity between our *Ideas* and the reality of Things. But
> what shall be here the Criterion? How shall the Mind, when it perceives
> nothing but its own *ideas*, know that they agree with Things themselves?[24]

Locke's response to this pseudo-sceptical question, is, says Ayers, far from
sceptical and hinges on a very interesting theory of representation. Following Epicurus and Gassendi, Locke held that a simple idea is "a natural sign
of its cause." "Simple ideas must be taken to correspond to their natural
objects in regular and orderly ways, even if we are ignorant of the nature of
those objects and how they act on us" (Ayers, ibid., 38). Simple ideas have
a special role to play here precisely because they are simple and therefore
not the product of the mind, which has only the capacity to combine simple
ideas and never to create them.

---

[24]   4.4.3: 563,27; Ayers, *Locke*, 1: 38.

Ayers's reading of Locke emphasizes that whilst we can place full certainty in the fact of there being some natural cause of our simple ideas outside of us, they do not in themselves give us any certainy of the nature of their cause. Although Ayers gives us reason to read Locke (or a modified Lockean position) as providing a previously unnoticed argument to justify the claim that the senses provide us with knowledge of the existence of particular bodies without us, it is relevant to my earlier claims that in the passage cited by Ayers as providing the argument to bridge the gap between ideas and the world, the teleological element is again present. We can be sure, Locke says, that two sorts of ideas agree with things. The first are simple ideas "which since the Mind ... can by no means make to itself, must necessarily be the product of Things operating on the Mind in a natural way, and produced therein those Perceptions which by the *Wisdom and Will of our Maker they are ordained and adapted to*" (4.4.4.563,35) (emphasis added). They have "all the conformity which is intended" (by our Creator) "or which our state requires." The teleological reading is brought home again a few lines later: "For they represent to us Things under those appearances which they are fitted to produce in us. . . . and so to take them for our Necessities, and apply them to our Uses." And again, the idea of whiteness "as it is in the Mind exactly answering that Power which is in any Body to produce it there, has all the conformity it can, *or ought to have*, with Things without us." Thus, whatever merits Ayers's reading of Locke has, and it has many, it does some injustice to prize it apart from the teleological argument with which it is undoubtedly intertwined in Locke's text.

Locke and Moral Knowledge

Discussions of scepticism by philosophers have tended to focus on two main issues: (a) the power of reason, or (b) the power of the senses, to deliver knowledge. Although there is an obvious sense in which claims to moral knowledge might be subsumed under at least the first of these categories, the debate about morality in England in the second half of the seventeenth century was dominated not by issues raised by the traditional sceptics as such but by the philosophy of Hobbes. Hobbes himself, though not a follower of any of the classical sceptics, is nevertheless often accorded a place in the history of seventeenth-century scepticism for the alleged implications of his views.[25]

---

[25] On Hobbes and scepticism see R. H. Popkin: "Hobbes and Scepticism I" and "Hobbes and Scepticism II" in his *The Third Force in Seventeenth-Century Thought* (Brill: Leiden, 1992) 9–49.

Locke's relationship to Hobbes is a complex matter which we shall scarcely touch on here. But we can say that Locke was evidently keen to distance himself and his philosophy from charges of "Hobbism" and, although he is, I believe, much more influenced by Hobbes than he is willing to allow, there are differences in their intellectual positions on moral theory, and perhaps more important, their perceived positions were generally very different. Thus, whilst they both agreed with Aristotle in rejecting any account of knowledge, and therefore moral knowledge, based on an appeal to innate ideas, Locke's account of ethics was seen to make more direct and explicit links with religion, and specifically with the existence of God, than contemporary readings of Hobbes usually allowed. (I express myself in this rather cautious way because I happen to hold, with the late Arigo Pacchi, that Hobbes's moral position may be more closely linked to a theistic commitment than is usually supposed, but that is another matter which I argue elsewhere.)[26] In Locke's case, it is clear from many statements that he held to a close link between morality and religion such that without various theological premises no case could be made out for an objectivity in ethics. Thus we find that the early *Essays on the Law of Nature* begin from considerations of God's law which he sees as having been ordained by God's command and which he explains thus: " . . . this law of nature can be described as being the decree of the divine will discernible by the light of nature and indicating what is and what is not in conformity with rational nature, and for this very reason commanding or prohibiting" (*Law of Nature*, 112).

Having already rejected both innate inscription and tradition as possible sources of knowledge, Locke claims that we can come to a knowledge of this law through sense experience.[27] He first of all argues that we must concede the existence of God, for otherwise the world and ourselves are inexplicable. From this, he goes on, it follows by reason that "there must be some superior power to which we are rightly subject, namely God, who has

---

[26]   Cf. G.A.J. Rogers's "Religion and the Explanation of Action in the Thought of Thomas Hobbes," in *Thomas Hobbes. Le ragioni del modern tra teologia e politica*, ed. by G. Borrelli (Napoli: 1990), 35–50. See also M. Malherbe "La religion materialiste de Thomas Hobbes" in the same volume, and Arrigo Pacchi, "Hobbes and the Problem of God" in *Perspectives on Thomas Hobbes*, ed. G.A.J. Rogers and A. Ryan (Oxford: 1988), 171–87.

[27]   It is interesting that Locke in 1663 or 1664, when he wrote the *Essays on the Law of Nature*, remarks in the second of them that the issue of innate inscription "will perhaps be discussed in another place," anticipating the argument of Book 1 of the *Essay*. I know of no independent evidence that at this stage Locke was contemplating a major work such as the *Essay*.

a just and inevitable command over us and at his pleasure can raise us up or throw us down, and make us by some commanding power happy or miserable" (*Law of Nature*, 153, 155). God has right and authority over us just as the clay is subject to the will of the potter.

There may be deep problems in Locke's claims. But what those claims are is, I think, clear. Further, they fit well with the account of ethics that we find later in the *Essay*. By then, i.e. 1689, Locke has explicitly added revelation as a source of moral knowledge (it had not been relevant earlier) to the reason plus experience account of the earlier work. Of the "Divine Law," he says in the *Essay*, that it is a rule given by God:

> whereby Men should govern themselves. . . . .He [God] has a Right to do it, we are his Creatures: He has Goodness and Wisdom to direct our actions to that which is best: and he has Power to enforce it by Rewards and Punishments, of infinite weight and duration, in another Life: for nobody can take us out of his hands. This is the only true touchstone of *moral Rectitude*; and by comparing them to this Law, it is, that Men judge of the most considerable *Moral Good* or *Evil* of their Actions; that is, whether as *Duties, or Sins*, they are like to procure them happiness, or misery, from the hand of the ALMIGHTY (2.28.8.352).

The existence of God guarantees for Locke that rational self-interest and moral duty meet in one and provide precise answers to moral questions. But it is not just that there is a correct answer to moral issues: he also believes that human beings are equipped by God with the necessary intellectual and other attributes so that they may discover what those correct answers are. Nor is this something confined to the learned: it is a property of each adult member of the species (with the mentally sub-normal providing some few exceptions). As Locke sees it, there is a sharp contrast here between the possibility of knowledge of nature and knowledge of morality. Our faculties, he says, are not fitted to penetrate into the inner workings of nature—we cannot see the atoms of the creation—and therefore cannot know the essences of material objects. But all of us can "plainly discover . . . the being of a GOD and the Knowledge of our selves, enough to lead us into a full and clear discovery of our Duty" (4.12.11.646). Hence, he concludes "*Morality is the proper Science, and Business of Mankind in general,*" something for which we both have concern and "are fitted," i.e. have been created to be able to do. With these words I conclude this section with the claim that we can see in Locke's account of moral knowledge, as we did in his earlier response to scepticism about the senses, the same teleological framework which provides his answer to the sceptic.

Descartes, Locke and God

I have already mentioned, and in any case we are all familiar with, Descartes's answer to the sceptical problem, namely his discovery of a proof of the existence of God which ennables him to accept, if not exactly at face value, then at some quite easily identifiable level, the authenticity of our experience of a natural world around us and the reliability of a properly controlled reason. From what I have been saying so far it might appear that I am suggesting that Locke has a similar answer to the sceptic. I wish now to consider how far it is true that Locke merely repeats the moves already made by Descartes.

From the outset Descartes sets himself up as engaged in battle with the sceptic. He is seeking the certain and the indubitable and anything less is to be rejected; to find anything less than the certain will be failure. At the end of the *Fifth Meditation* we appear to have the strongest possible statement of the place of God in this program: "Thus I see plainly that the certainty and truth of all knowledge depends uniquely on my knowledge of the true God, to such an extent that I was incapable of perfect knowledge about anything else until I knew him" (Descartes, *Works*, 2.49). Knowledge of the existence of God becomes the key to knowledge of nature, or at least "the whole of that corporeal nature which is the subject-matter of pure mathematics." I think we may say, then, that for Descartes the failure to find a proof of the existence of God would inevitably lead to total epistemic disaster. On the other side, the success in the search has untold benefits. The position for Locke, however, is quite different. With regard to the natural world his goal is not certainty, though he is prepared, even happy, to accept it if he finds it. There is for him so little that counts as knowledge anyway that to be deprived of what there is would hardly be a major tragedy. We would still have probabilities, which would themselves be assessed without reference to theological preconceptions, based as they are on rules of evidence which he elaborates in book 4 of the *Essay*.

In another sense, however, the loss for Locke would be a major one in a way in which it would never be for Descartes. For the latter never offered us a moral theory nor, with the exception of some remarks in his correspondence with Princess Elizabeth, (ibid., 3:256ff) did he attempt to explain how such a theory might be related to theology. Whereas for Locke the rejection of God, or even simple agnosticism about God's existence, precipitates a major crisis in the rationale of his claims to moral knowledge.

Which of these philosophers, then, is better equipped to resist the sceptic? Which has more to lose from the sceptic's attack? The answer must surely be that for Descartes all must collapse if the sceptic is not defeated, and that he may only be defeated by the boot-strap operation of first establishing the existence of God. Locke, on the other hand, has a rather different position. Although it is nice for Locke to be able to prove that God exists, if he does not succeed, he has a fall-back position which is not nearly as vulnerable as that of Descartes. The fall-back position is that there are arguments of a probabilist sort which, even if they do not make God's existence certain, make it more likely than not, and that is all that he requires to make his whole picture more likely than not. Although in the *Essays on the Law of Nature* Locke treats the argument from design as if it leads to a certain conclusion—"it is undoubtedly inferred that there must be a powerful and wise creator of all these things, who has made and built this whole universe and us mortals" (*Law of Nature*, 153)—his position would not be much weakened if he allowed it only a matter of probability.

On the other hand, if it were to be established that there were no God, then Locke, like Descartes, would be in trouble. It looks as though atheism would indeed lead to scepticism, for with the knowledge that there were no God, then there would be no guarantee that there was any kind of match between our experiences and the way the world is. General epistemological scepticism would become irresistible. And, with regard to morality, without the sanction of eternal reward or punishment Locke pessimistically saw no alternative to unprincipled egotism.[28] In the remote possibility—remote because of its inherently paradoxical character—of the sceptic proving his case, then Locke's philosophical position looks doomed. I believe that Locke was aware of this and this partly accounts for the tone of annoyance that often creeps into his discussion of the sceptic's claims. Although he does not seriously entertain them, he realizes that they have great potential for destruction; they are weapons to be used sparingly, if at all, against one's enemies in case they are used in return. His position is not unlike a world leader contemplating nuclear war.

---

[28]   Thus Locke whilst extending toleration in religion to most sects (though, famously, not to Catholics) was not prepared to consider it for the atheist. As he puts it in *A Letter Concerning Toleration*: ". . . . those are not at all to be tolerated who *deny the being of a God*. Promises, convenants, and oaths, which are bonds of human society, can have no hold upon an atheist." M. Montuuori, *John Locke on Toleration and the Unity of God* (Amsterdam: 1983) 93.

Locke's Anti-Sceptical Arguments

Finally, I wish to make some comments both on the nature of Locke's arguments against sceptical claims and to say something about Locke and practicalities.

We have already seen that Locke dismisses worries about inverted spectra because they can have no practical consequences. In a section from which I have already quoted, where he is discussing and dismissing the possibility that somebody may be dreaming that there is a candle in front of him, he suggests that the putative dreamer might try putting his hand into the flame whence "he may perhaps be wakened into a certainty greater than he could wish, that it is something more than bare Imagination." I ignore temptations to consider whether Locke is here making an appeal to the Argument from the Paradigm Case, and go on to consider his following interesting words from the *Essay*: "So that this Evidence is as great, as we can desire, being as certain to us, as our Pleasure or Pain; i.e. Happiness or Misery; beyond which we have no concernment, either of Knowing or Being" (4.11.8.635).

Locke seems here to be saying that there is a practical dimension to certainty which takes us to the heart of the issue. Worries over certainty only have place where they may make some difference to what human beings may experience, ultimately in terms of their happiness and misery. Many of the disputes with the sceptics, as no doubt many of the disputes with and between the schoolmen, can make no practical difference to anything we actually do, and for that reason are idle speculations.

Whether or not we agree with Locke about this, I think we should see his claim for what it is. In so far as philosophical speculation has a bearing on practical matters, it has a point. Otherwise it does not. And for Locke the supreme practical question is: How may I achieve salvation? Contrary to those who wish to give him an entirely secular reading, it seems to me that Locke's philosophy, like that of the medieval schoolmen, was ultimately inextricably bound to his theology.

THE RECOVERY OF LOCKE'S LIBRARY

Peter Laslett, in conversation with John Rogers

[At the Locke Conference held at Christ Church, Oxford, in September 1990, Peter Laslett gave an unscripted talk about the recovery of Locke's Library. Later the substance of that talk was recorded in conversation with John Rogers in Laslett's room in Trinity College, Cambridge, and it is that which is printed here for the first time. The Locke Conference was sponsored by the Clarendon Locke Board of which John Yolton was at the time chairman and general editor. G.A.J.R.]

JR: Would you like to begin by telling me what exactly it was of Locke's literary possessions which you recovered?

PL: Yes, and I must insist at the outset that it was the *recovery* of Locke's library and not its *discovery*. By library is meant here a collection of bound volumes, nearly all of them printed books but some of them bound volumes of hand-written leaves, that is manuscripts. The recovery was not simply the location of about 660 of such items at a particular place, Ben Damph Forest House to be exact, on the shore of Loch Torridon in Wester Ross in the Highlands of Scotland. It consisted in fact in a search for the whereabouts of every single literary item which Locke had possessed at any time of his life and which was not already in one or other of the known collections of such things. By far the most important of these collections was of course the Lovelace collection in the Bodleian Library, which was already there in 1950 when the search began. Naturally I had previously made an exhaustive search in that archive.

 The intention was to survey and examine if possible every individual printed or hand-written page which was then extant and to decide what had happened to those which could be shown once to have existed but to have dropped from view. This meant tracing ownership and transfers over two centuries and more, inferring descents, identifying and tracking down possible purchasers and owners, writing to them, courting them, visiting them and keeping in as close touch with them as could be.

Every scholar is obliged of course to make a thorough survey of the available evidence as part of his or her plan of research, though many of them are evidently content with materials in print, and few of them prepared to search for possible sources outside libraries and other obvious places.[1] In 1950 moreover, I was under special necessity of making the most exhaustive survey of this kind. This was because I had just convinced myself that I might come across all or part of that major portion of the text of Locke's *Two Treatises of Government* which he himself said was "more than all the rest." Even a copy of one of the printings of the book issued in the lifetime of the author might yield valuable evidence and could do so even today, especially of course if that copy had ever been in the author's own possession. I had already established that a further copy corrected by Locke must once have existed in addition to that which had come to light at Christ's College, Cambridge, accepted for the nonce as "the master copy."[2]

JR: Did you actually find what you were seeking, or any part of it? Especially any part of *Two Treatises* in manuscript.

PL: In the event the huge missing portion of that exceedingly important book was not located during the search, nor was any fragment of it, nor has a trace of it appeared since in manuscript or in print. But the effort put forth finally succeeded in doing much to ensure that a goodly portion of the half of his library which Locke bequeathed, along with all his papers, to his King family heirs should stand where it now does in the Locke Room looking out over Broad Street in the Clarendon

---

[1] This unwillingness seems to me to have got stronger over the years except occasionally where the object is the editing of a text (not my original intention with Locke's political thinking). Even then few scholars other than historians seem anxious to become manuscript hunters, and historians often show reluctance. Of the dozens of research students in intellectual history I have known, and in many cases supervised, only two or three have had the urge to ferret out really novel unpublished sources, especially in the private houses where the materials often remain, and to negotiate with the owners, not shrinking from the taxing, intricate and delicate operations which this may entail.

[2] See Locke's preface to the book and for the particulars of the results of the survey, the introduction to P. Laslett's edition (Cambridge: Cambridge University Press, 1960, latest reprint 1991). See also an article by me in the *Journal of the Royal Society of Arts*, (May 1991).

Building of the Bodleian Library at Oxford. That portion, the King moiety as it will be called here, is now rather more complete than it was when I first saw it in the gunroom of Ben Damph Forest House on December 18th, 1951. It is more complete because some of the items which had escaped from the collection since the Kings were given it have been added to it since 1951, along with a scatter of volumes from the other half, which had never been with the King family but had gone to the Mashams (the Masham moiety). The whole assemblage stands today in the exact order in which it was ranged in the book boxes piled on top of each other in Locke's apartments in the manor house of Otes in Essex, owner Sir Francis Masham, baronet, when Locke died there in October 1704.

It is entirely owing to the munificence of the man who must be called the most generous and enlightened of living private patrons of scholarship of this kind, Mr. Paul Mellon, that this eminently satisfactory final result was brought about. All users of Locke's books and papers should be aware of this and of his role in the recovery we are discussing.

JR: The word recovery as opposed to discovery seems to imply that the existence of Locke's library was known before you came upon it. Was this so? Had anyone used the books and manuscripts which you came upon in 1951?

PL: Undoubtedly some scholars had worked on the Locke papers whilst they were in the possession of the King family alongside the King moiety of his books, especially in the later years. A.C. Fraser was one of them, as is plain from his little book *Locke* published in 1890. He showed scarcely any interest in the printed books there, however, nor did he in his annotated edition of the *Essay* appearing some years later. He also had access to what then still remained of the Masham moiety, which had been consulted at much earlier dates by interested scholars. Fox Bourne, Locke's Victorian biographer, also mentions the Masham archive, though he seems not to have worked in that held by the Kings. This was in spite of the fact that one of the successive heads of the line of King (created Barons of Ockham in 1725 and Earls of Lovelace in 1838) had exploited the family possessions to write a biography 45 years earlier. A generation after Fraser, Benjamin Rand worked at the principal Lovelace seat at East Horsley in Surrey. He counted himself a friend of the family, or at least of the then Countess. The 4th Earl of Lovelace told me, however, that he and his sister, Diana, once pushed the old man into the lake at East Horsley. Nevertheless in 1931 Rand published one of the outstanding manuscripts, what is now known as *Draft B* of the *Essay*, under the impression that it was the "original."

But it was not this literary event which drew widespread attention to the King holdings of Locke's papers and books. Rather it was an exhibition of them in the following year, 1932. This was the 300th anniversary of Locke's birth, and in celebration, so it was claimed, a large selection from the materials was displayed in London on the premises of Messrs. Bumpus. Considerable numbers of the books were shown there for all to see alongside the manuscripts.[3] It is no surprise therefore that five years later the more definitive "original" of the *Essay*, *Draft A*, was published by a ranking Locke scholar, R.I. Aaron. This does make some references to books owned by Locke.

What is a little unexpected is that Aaron had a co-editor, Jocelyn Gibb, a man of independent means, a publisher and a director of the firm of Bumpus for some time. He had literary interests, but no standing in studies of this kind. Jocelyn Gibb was a brother-in-law of the holder of the title, the recently succeeded 4th Earl of Lovelace, and had been put in charge of his literary inheritance. It could have been inferred that the object of the exhibition from the King point of view had been to find a purchaser or purchasers who would pay big money in favor of a lineage which had fallen on evil days.

JR: This must have been a period of great danger to the Locke archive from the scholar's point of view. The temptation to sell off particular items from the collection was surely very strong and a complete scattering at auction very likely. Why did things like this not happen?

PL: The absence of the bound volume containing the original of *Draft A* from the Lovelace collection now in Bodley, although it was present in the 1932 exhibition, is proof that individual sales had in fact begun to be made before ever I saw the library. This particular alienation has, I think, held up your own work on Locke's original texts. But the credit for preventing the whole of the King moiety, along with the Lovelace papers, from being sold at auction must certainly go to Jocelyn Gibb.

---

[3]   The facts about the descent of Locke's books and papers and about access to them are mostly to be found in J. R. Harrison and P. Laslett, *The Library of John Locke*, (Oxford: Oxford University Press, 1956, 2nd ed. 1971), hereafter referred to as H. and L. There is a copy of the catalogue of the 1932 exhibition in the Locke Room.

This came out at a meeting with him in the summer of 1951 which occurred at my instigation after I had got to know of his Lovelace links, a meeting the easier to arrange because of a manuscript discovery I had made which put something of a query on the work he and Aaron had published as *Draft A*.[4] He told me that he had intervened to stop Sotheby's selling the family's Locke possessions piecemeal. This must have been in 1931, two years after the 3rd Earl died and the estate had to face the usual crisis of death duties. A letter from the dowager Countess of Lovelace to Rand in February 1931 shows that a sale was then in prospect.[5] It seems that the materials were already in the hands of Sotheby's at that time, but with some exceptions, including the *Draft A* volume once again.

Its absence was due to the vagaries of the new holder of the title, and a story he told me himself hints at the reasons why some more responsible person was put in charge of the collections. The fourth Earl, Peter Lovelace, as everyone called him,—it is interesting that the name Peter descended from generation to generation from the original Peter King, Locke's second cousin and heir—had put the *Draft A* volume into his luggage on a trip to the Hotel Meurice in Paris. In bed there, a man from Sothebys wearing a bowler hat knocked on the door and demanded the volume to take to London and put back with the rest.

Gibb finally succeeded in getting Bodley to buy the papers, that is all Locke's manuscript materials, which he had arranged to have deposited in that Library during the Second War. He insisted to me that no interest was shown at that point by Bodley or anyone else in the printed books. These were presumably in store or at large in one or other Lovelace residence. In 1951 they had been lost from view, and those who might have been interested seemed to have supposed that they had gone to Bodley with the papers. This was not the case, and there was certainly no warrant for the extraordinary statement by Edmund Craster, Bodley's librarian, made when announcing in the *Times* in 1948 the acquisition of the Lovelace papers, that the rest of the collection had been dispersed.

---

[4] This was the identification of a partial draft of the *Essay* among the Shaftesbury Papers in the Public Record Office. See P. Laslett, "Locke and the 1st Earl of Shaftesbury," *Mind*, 241 (January 1952). See also P.H. Nidditch and Rogers, appendix 3.

[5] Countess of Lovelace to Benjamin Rand, February 1931, Rand papers, Houghton Library, Harvard University.

Gibb had relinquished responsibility for the library by the time of our meeting in July 1951. Still he was in touch with Lovelace and undertook to do what he could for my cause. But this was not the first move which I made towards getting access to Lovelace materials. I found when I checked the *Times* for Craster's assertion that ten issues later a Lady Diana de Hosszu, that same sister who had joined in Rand's discomfiture, had sent a letter contradicting Craster. That portion of Locke's library which he left to Lord King, she wrote, "has been preserved intact by his descendants and is still in the possession of my brother" (the *Times*, 22 January 1948).

I had sent a letter to her directly I saw that an opening had appeared, but no reply had come before my meeting with Gibb took place. In the end she did write and a meeting was arranged at her residence in Bedfordshire, where one of Locke's little diaries was handed round the tea-table, the first intoxicating glimpse of my quarry. This was in November 1951, and she finally offered to arrange for me to meet her brother. A point might be made here that in a quest of this kind more than one line of attack should, if possible, be mounted simultaneously. The more relevant people you know the better.

Both Lady Diana and Jocelyn Gibb informed me that Lovelace had recently returned from Tanganyika, rescued, Gibb said, by his family from a difficult situation and the effects of beriberi. To his sister's amazement he had married. His bride was the widow of a prominent Danish aristocrat, Blixen Finecke, of the family of Karen Blixen, the writer. When I met the Earl and Countess for the first time at the Station Hotel, Inverness, in December 1951, they had a baby son, Viscount Ockham, christened in his turn Peter John Locke King, and the present holder of the title as the 5th Earl of Lovelace. The infant Viscount was at Ben Damph House, whence Peter Lovelace was kind enough to send me in his car, driven by his chauffeur, to inspect the Locke books: a very handsome gesture.

JR: So the situation was pretty complicated with the family and its posses-sions when you managed to get access to all those Locke volumes in December 1951. What was it like dealing with the personalities in the drama? Did you believe you would succeed in what you were at, which I suppose must now have included an effort to get the collection, as a collection, into a scholarly haven?

PL: I happen to have been something of a naval diplomat during the War and a BBC producer after that, both of which tasks take a little finesse in personal relationships with difficult or potentially difficult people. But the *dramatis personae* in the Lovelace/Locke library affair were the knobbliest I have ever had to deal with, and this throughout the nine year continuance of the affair, especially towards the end. On my second visit in March, 1952, I near as a touch got exiled from Ben Damph Forest because the new Countess of Lovelace suddenly sus-pected that I was a Jew. For this reason she had taken against Mr. Robinson of Robinsons, a very prominent London dealer, when he had come to advise about the most saleable items a short while before I arrived. This must have been the occasion when he got hold of the volume containing *Draft A*, which you know so well, and there were other items too. During that expedition to the library I stayed in a small hotel some miles away and cycled to and fro along the highland tracks.

The house, its inmates, the people in the village and in the Station Hotel, Inverness (almost 80 miles away but the only place the Earl and Countess had to go to get away from the estate) hummed with stories of a scandalous, even a tragic, character. The Countess's husband, Blixen Finecke, had died while on a visit to Ben Damph Forest with his exceedingly attractive wife, and it was said that Lovelace was suspected of responsibility. Peter Lovelace himself told me that he, a ruined peer and a childless widower with so little to leave a successor, had never intended to perpetuate the line. But he had found himself marrying again, quite literally *noblesse oblige*. Such a confidence, made much later on of course, by a very likeable, eccentric, harum-scarum, irresponsible and ineffective man shows, I suppose, that I did succeed in getting on with him.

In fact we were to become friends, so far as that was possible given our very different positions. Unpredictable as he was, and as time went by rather wearisome as well, he showed unflagging generosity and unfailing hospitality. The Countess was rather more difficult, even after I had convinced her of my Aryan ancestry, though she was finally quite friendly too. My expedient with her was to be as useful as I could: to help for example to get successive companions for herself, nurses for her son, even governesses for the little boy's elder step-sisters. I had to undertake the task of putting Ockham's name down for Eton, which in her view anyway, had to be done pretty well at birth. I was soon made aware that I represented the possibility of some endowment descending to the child, since I came from the world of academic institutions which might buy the stuff I was there to study. As time went by, and you will infer that I found myself making several visits over a number of years to that magnificently sited Victorian sporting mansion, the transfer of the collection complete to a suitable institution did become as much an object as research amongst Locke's *reliquiae* to find anything, but anything, which bore on the text of *Two Treatises of Government*.[6] On my second visit my wife was generously invited to come along with our own infant son, who was Ockham's age, and she was a great help with the research.

A proper listing of the books was clearly necessary for my work, and I managed to persuade the Lovelaces that this would help their purposes too. Accordingly I found myself taking the late J. R. Harrison, of the University Library in Cambridge, a consummate bookman and outstanding cataloguer, with me to Ben Damph Forest to begin work on the catalogue which bears our joint names. Looking back I am astonished at the generosity and hospitality shown to a mendicant scholar. My general policy was to convince the Lovelaces that the better known and better preserved the books, the longer they were kept off the market, the more valuable they would be as an inheritance. They should be clung to at all costs for the sake of the little boy and the family line.

Nevertheless Ben Damph was a very long way from Cambridge, and John Harrison and I could not get up there often. On one of our returns we were told that a drunken cook had taken a dislike to the Locke library and had walked all the way down to the loch and flung in one of the copies of Pufendorf, *De Jure Naturale et Gentium*.[7]

JR: I have not inspected Pufendorf but the books in the Locke room show very few signs of the vicissitudes they must have gone through, and look to be in an excellent state of preservation. What were they like when you first handled them in 1951?

PL: The light was bad during the few days of my earliest visit to Ben Damph Forest house. It was mid-winter and the little hydro-generator which supplied the electricity was perpetually liable to have its water supply from the mountain stream attenuated by leaves in the entrance grill.

---

[6]   Details of what the Ben Damph library yielded in this direction will be found in the introduction to Laslett's edition. Though no fragment of a hand-written text ever made an appearance, it was a privilege to be able to work as editor with Locke's own copy of the first edition on my desk; it contains a few minuscule manuscript markings in his hand, nearly all inserted corrigenda—no more.

[7]   H. and L. 2401. Locke had two copies: one is at McGill, the other now in the Locke Room.

The books were in considerable disarray, though roughly shelved. Lots of bindings had been broken, loose papers were scattered about and many of the books were flecked with whitewash. I inferred that at one point they had been lying on the floor of a room being redecorated. Some of the vellum volumes had been nibbled by mice, but the damp-ness of the atmosphere had prevented them from drying out. It was exasperating to find the sticky remains of the rubber bands, which had been used on the books for the 1932 show, gumming pages together.

The collection was certainly not complete in the sense that it still contained all of the items left to Peter King, for that had numbered 1300 and more (see H. and L., page 56). I had difficulty in assessing the importance of the disappearance of a half of the collection during the two and half centuries which had passed whilst the family had the books. It was to be expected that losses would have happened, but I found myself perpetually badgering the Earl, the Countess, his sister and everyone else, asking if there were more books of Locke's; in another room? in another house? in store? with friends? This preoccu-pation continued till the end of the story, even with Mr Mellon. All I ever found out was that a book on Denmark had been taken to the Blixen Finecke Castle in that country. (Presumably H. and L. 950, Molesworth's *Account of Denmark*.) No doubt it is still there.

The reason why the Locke books in Bodley are now so different to look at and to handle than in 1951 is that they were meticulously repaired and reconditioned when Mr Paul Mellon acquired them. Evidently Peter Lovelace had decided to sell before I left for America in January 1959, in spite of everything which had been urged to the contrary, both in correspondence and during the further visits which John Harrison and I made to the house in the mid 1950s. The catalogue was fairly advanced by that time. We had even been permitted to carry some of the more important items down to Oxford for a while, for skilled attention and repair at the Bodleian Library.

Amongst them was Locke's master catalogue of his own books. There were also the two huge vellum bound folios containing the flowers gathered by Locke in the 1660s and pressed by him between the exercises submitted by his Christ Church undergraduate pupils, written mostly in Latin. These I had discovered at the bottom of a cupboard in the gun room smothered in the remains of a directory of Surrey of about 1910, a volume reduced to tatters by being shot through by a sporting gun.

It is for me a vivid memory, those three hundred year old flowers taken from the Oxford Botanic Garden, still yellow, red and blue, though faded of course with age, and lustreless in the uncertain light. As all users of them have discovered, Locke's books have few annotations in their margins, but they seem occasionally to have been used to press other blooms, to preserve letters and objects of various kinds. One book, added to the library after it had left Ben Damph, had a single hair carefully inserted between the pages. Some openings had strips of paper within them serving as bookmarks and cut from old letters. In fact several such letters were still present in complete form, prepared for their purpose by Locke's boy, presumably, and looking like limp combs, with very long teeth, to be torn off as required.

There were 20 odd bound manuscript volumes in the collection, though the one containing *Draft A* was not amongst them. Since the Bodleian Library had bought all of Locke's manuscripts, these volumes should not have been amongst the printed books and can only have remained there because little care had been taken to separate printed from manuscript books when the transfer to Oxford had been made. I remember coming across Locke's notes on reading Newton in the early hours of the morning—I did not go to bed at all during the few days of my first visit in case I should never see the library again—and being exasperated by the difficulty of understanding the text, some of it in hieroglyphics.

JR: What an experience for a scholar to have! But how did it happen that Mr Mellon was able to recover the condition of the books? Was it done whilst they were still at Ben Damph Forest House? Or where were they before they eventually got to Bodley?

PL: An account of how the transfer to the Locke Room finally took place can be followed, up to 1964 at least, in Harrison and Laslett. But there are some particulars which you might like to know about to do with personalities and personal events.

Peter Lovelace's domestic circumstances had changed by the late 1950s. When I last visited him in the summer of 1958, his wife and son were no longer there and everything was exceedingly unsettled. Nothing could have been more untoward from my point of view than for him to set about selling the books whilst I was on a year's sabbatical leave in the USA, during the following calendar year 1959. But this was just how it turned out. For the whole of those twelve months I found myself in perpetual correspondence with Lovelace, with his lawyers, with the firm of Robinson, with the Bodleian Library and of course with John Harrison, who kept me informed of what was going on at Ben Damph Forest. In the final weeks were added the requests of the would-be buyer, or rather of his ample entourage.

The Lovelace party wanted me to authenticate the goods for sale, to find a buyer, institutional or individual, to maximize the price. At the crucial point I was to try to talk to Mr. Mellon and cry the library up. The Bodleian Library wanted me to keep the price down, so that, if such a thing were possible, they could raise the money to acquire; to keep them informed of what Lovelace and his agents were at, to help if I possibly could to discover some source of patronage which might raise the wind. Why not Mr. Mellon himself? Mr. Mellon's agents had to be convinced that the library was all there. They had to ensure him against his "having his ears pinned back," which is precisely what the chief of them said that I personally had succeeded in doing when it was all over.

To find yourself on all sides of such an extraordinary, angular conjuncture is probably the worst ordeal for a scholar-researcher originally intent only on the complete mastery of his sources or hers. But it is important to recognize that such a thing can happen. Until the very last days of 1959 I found it impossible to expect an outcome which would leave no one with a grievance and yet to ensure the interests of future scholars.

The Bodleian Library had one resource in the position as it happened to be—that the most likely purchaser would be an American. The Board of Trade might refuse an export license, classing the collection as of truly national importance. The presence of this final sanction in the background did not let me off the hook. As the acknowledged expert on the matter my own opinion and advice might well be decisive.

As I reckoned it, sitting as a reader in the Folger Shakespeare Library in Washington D.C., picking up the threads to begin on *The World we have lost*, the future of the collection was uncertain whether or not the license was given. Its prospects in Lovelace's hands were decidedly unpromising, but who could tell what this, to me, completely unknown American purchaser might do with the books? The chances of help from a Maecenas, if small, would, I calculated, be strengthened if the books came up on the open market, which they were very likely to do should export permission be withheld.

What weighed most heavily with me was the intellectual relationship between Locke's printed books, his manuscripts and his writings. His "fractional" shelf marks, that is a figure (1–32) for the size of the book in inches above and the number of the book in the series he possessed of that size below, were used in his references in the published works, certainly in the *Essay*, and especially in his diaries, which were full of them.[8] He went from one to the other as he reflected, composed and published. There was no other example, as far as I know, certainly none in an author of this stature in England, where manuscripts and books had been preserved together as a structural whole. Both had to be kept in the closest proximity. I could not make any move which put the space of the Atlantic between them. I advised against any export license being granted.

It turned out that I was the one who would have to tell Mr. Mellon of this when I went to see him to describe the collection. Here was a diplomatic mission indeed, and I hope you will forgive the indelicacy of my mentioning that I was so nervous as I drove through Rock Creek Park, which runs through the center of Washington's residential area, on the way to Mr. Mellon's house, that I had to draw up and relieve myself behind a tree. The outcome was, however, a glorious surprise, a solution which gave everyone all that was wanted, except perhaps Mr. Mellon himself.

He had decided before ever we met or export permission was mentioned to buy the whole collection and give it to the Bodleian Library, making only one condition. All the manuscript books which I had found on the shelves at Ben Damph should go immediately to Oxford, but he would like to have the printed books in his private house at Oak Spring in Virginia, to be kept there in ideally regulated atmospheric conditions for long enough for him to enjoy their presence, though remaining the possession of the Bodleian Library. Meanwhile he undertook to refurbish the books up to the very highest standard. They were to stand in his residence in the order they had occupied in Locke's rooms, and John Harrison and I were to go over to set them up.

After some negotiation this amazingly generous plan was accepted on all sides, the Board of Trade included. Lovelace had got a substantial endowment for the family line, more I suspect than his advisers had realistically expected. The Bodleian Library had acquired the manuscript books, some of outstanding interest which would at last round off the collection acquired in 1948. There was now also the certainty

---

8   See H. and L. Plate 5 illustrates two books with press numbers on the spine: 7 for H. and L. 249; 71a for H. and L. 1218. These "fractional" press marks evidently bemused Benjamin Rand. During his retirement he collected as many as he could find from Locke's manuscripts and tried to puzzle out of them a numerical key to universal knowledge devised by Locke. See the Rand papers cited above.

of getting the printed books in due course. Paul Mellon had got the means to indulge his bibliophile's passion. As for myself, I had been given the satisfaction of knowing that future scholarly interest was finally secure, so far as that could be so. What is more, as time went by I found I had got a new friend in Mr. Mellon himself. This I believe was the largest individual gift made to the Bodleian Library up to that date. I doubt if it can have been exceeded in real terms since that time.

JR: You go a little far when you say that everyone gained. What did scholars living in Britain get in the way of access whilst the books continued to be separated from the papers, which is just what you say you would not have contemplated?

PL: This is rather a harsh judgment, I think. Though British scholars were unable to get access to Locke's books for a dozen years or so, they had the guarantee that after that they would be available to scholars in perpetuity. What is more, as you have noticed, the books would then be in splendid condition, and as it turned out would have had added to them all the Locke items which came onto the market during the interim and had been bought by Mr. Mellon. Most of the additions, which were also refurbished as they were acquired, belonged to the Masham moiety and so had not stood alongside those from the King moiety since they had been sorted out in the manor house at Otes by Pierre Coste and Anthony Collins in the last months of the year 1704.

JR: To this extent, then, the Masham moiety was recovered as part of the operation, though to a very, very much smaller degree.

PL: Yes, and the whole body of titles (as distinct from the books them-selves) ever possessed by John Locke had been brought to light and reduced to systematic, consultable order. The catalogue, based on Locke's own, which John Harrison and I had started in the early 1950s was further worked at and finally completed at Mr. Mellon's house. We stayed there as his guests, and this is why the entries for those items which are now in Bodley are marked in our catalogue with the words Oak Spring.
    It must be remembered that I was still engaged, now with Harri-son's help, on the recovery of literary items left behind him by Locke, which were not necessarily at Otes at his death, and which included of course the letters he had written to other people. We traced a collection to Nynehead Court, a house near Wellington in Somerset,

and determined that from there it had gone to Bembridge School on the Isle of Wight—the Clarke correspondence. No books went with the letters. We tracked down some more writings to a house in Suffolk: no books again. But we inspected many volumes which had been his but had escaped from either moity. They were mostly individual items, but some in twos and threes in private houses, like that of Sir Geoffrey Keynes near Newmarket.

The most important object of our search was naturally the Masham moiety itself. I finally determined that those books had been scattered far and wide about the world, after I had tracked down the last inheritor of the Masham/Locke possessions. This did not turn out to be a remote Masham descendant, but a distant cousin of the last of the direct family line of the Masham creditors. She was a wealthy old lady who lived at Sonning on the Thames, Mrs. Clement Williams.

Both of us got to know this charming dowager and to both of us she showed a friendliness and generosity which was as marked as that of other benefactors to Locke's memory, and from some points of view even more generous. Where Peter Lovelace had made me presents of a manuscript scrap or two rather as souvenirs, Mrs. Williams handed out complete manuscript items, even collections of them: to John Harrison a letter of Nelson's, to me a sizeable assemblage of Masham documents, including letters of the notorious Duchess of Kingston, who had been an associate at the Royal Court of the rather raffish last Lord Masham.

Though we got to know each other only in the last years and months of her life, my personal relations with Mrs. Clement Williams became rather close. Her liberality, however, raised a different set of the personal problems which can arise out of a quest of the type I am describing.

Our scholarly job with her as with Lord Lovelace had to be to make certain that every nook and cranny of the house in Sonning be searched for any scrap which came from Locke himself. This meant imposing on our relationship with her by poking into rooms and cupboards whenever the opportunity occurred, and relentlessly cross questioning her about what she had seen in earlier years, where things were, how people had behaved. Knowing what I did about her dealings with other people and institutions, this was a risky undertaking. The Essex County Record Office, for example, was interested in her literary possessions and had been pointedly snubbed. You can perhaps understand the jocular remark which I have sometimes made about the two most important skills required by the manuscript researcher, that of chatting up old ladies and that of being able to ride a bicycle in all weathers over difficult terrain.

Our friendship with Mrs. Williams fortunately survived the vicissitudes but, alas, not a single written or printed item which had been incontrovertibly owned by Locke or created by him ever came to light. It was a different matter with things like pictures.

We last saw Margaret Williams in her bed only a little while before the end. It turned out that she had altered the disposition of her possessions in my favour and had left to me the two portraits which you see on the wall behind you as we talk. One is a miniature, a splendid portrayal of Locke's great political patron, Lord Somers, drawn in pencil on vellum, so fine an example of its genre that it has been exhibited at the Victoria and Albert Museum. The other is my proudest possession. It is a contemporaneous variant of Kneller's last portrait of Locke, rendered in chalk on an oaken board, a boudoir portrait corresponding to the photographs of friends which are so often to be found in silver frames on the dressing-tables of comfortably placed ladies in our day. Its most likely original owner was Locke's closest friend of all, Damaris Masham. On the back is written "To be given to Peter Laslett of Cambridge 'some day.' The wish of Margaret E. M. Williams." She died in July 1966.

JR: The record then of conducting a "recovery" like that which you undertook for Locke's library turns out to be personal and concrete as well as intellectual and academic. The scattering of the Masham moiety has to be called a grievous loss even if what has ended in the Bodleian Library still comprises the most complete collection of the literary possessions of a great British intellectual which has ever come into existence. Did Mr. Mellon himself have a share in the planning of the outstanding monument which now stands in the Locke room?

PL: Certainly he did, and we discussed it on several occasions at Oak Spring on my later visits there, with the vellum and calf of Locke's bindings in the background. He was set on the library staying together and being put with the papers when it got to Oxford, and was quite prepared to include the items he had purchased since his acquisition from Lord Lovelace.

When he decided that the time had come to relinquish the books he had in his keeping, it was with Robert Shackleton, then Bodley's Librarian, that the arrangements were made. I was only a go-between by that time, caught up as I had become in other research enterprises of a quite different character. The Locke room was an achievement of Robert Shackleton, and it is quite proper that his own collection on Montesquieu should also be housed there.

I believe that he, and Mrs. Clement Williams, and even the 4th Earl of Lovelace, all of whom are dead, would have found some satisfaction in being told the complete story of the recovery of the library of John Locke. So perhaps will the dowager Countess of Lovelace and Mr. Mellon himself. I am sure that they would agree with me when I say that it represents an example instructive to the would-be researcher, an illustration of the principle that research is not simply a question of the catalogue-searching, bibliography-making and the pen and pencil or word processing tasks on which all of us are engaged. It is, and it has to be, a bold and risky venture into a set of personal relationships, going far beyond what is so easily and contemptuously referred to as The Ivory Tower.

In the case of the recovery of the library of John Locke it also turned out to be an exploration into the spontaneous kindness and generosity of many personalities, none of whom exactly shared my own interests and objects but nearly all of whom supported them to the full.

Natures and Laws from Descartes to Hume[1]

Michael Ayers

Introduction

Are universal laws reducible to the particular natures of things, or are natures reducible to universal relationships between types of events or states of affairs? In terms of the creation story, in the first case God creates and conserves things with the natures which make them what they *are*, but does not *also* have to impose laws or rules in order to determine what things *do*. I take it that, in general, Scholastic Aristotelians assumed that kind of model, while duly acknowledging God as First Cause of everything. To explain a regularity is to show how it flows necessarily from the essences, natures or powers of the created agents involved, at any rate in the case of natural agents lacking free will and so not subject to a moral "Law of Nature." According to various forms of "voluntarism," on the other hand, a theory going back at least to the eleventh century,[2] regularities in nature should be ascribed directly to the will of God, rather than to the naturally necessary actions of so-called "second causes." For the voluntarist, "second causes" are not really causes at all.

Both views existed in the seventeenth century but, as may sometimes have been intended, are not always easy to disentangle from each other. Boyle and Locke, for example, can both on some occasions seem to imply that laws are contingent additions to corpuscularian natures, and on others that events flow necessarily from those natures.[3] Nevertheless, there is a

---

[1] Earlier versions of the present paper were given at a symposium on "Natures versus Laws" at King's College, London, and the London School of Economics, on 3 November 1992, and at the inaugural meeting of the Australasian Society for the History of Philosophy at Canberra on 6 November 1993. I am grateful for comments received at both meetings.

[2] At that time it was advanced by Ghazali (Algazel), the Islamic sceptic and critic of Aristotelianism. The theory was criticized by Aquinas.

[3] For fuller discussion of this issue in Boyle, see M. Ayers, *Locke II: Ontology* (London: Routledge, 1991), chap. 11, 135–41. For the view of him as unequivocally voluntarist,

reasonably sharp division among early modern philosophers which cuts right across the more familiar distinction between "rationalists" and "empiricists" as it has ordinarily been applied to the canon from Descartes to Hume. This point is worth emphasizing insofar as the reduction of propositions about the natures of things to universal propositions about how things behave tends now to be regarded as an essential ingredient of consistent empiricism, if not to be attributed to Hume as its first inventor. Indeed, despite its medieval origins in a kind of sceptical empiricism, voluntarism was throughout the seventeenth century characteristically a position taken by Cartesian "rationalists" (although rejected by Spinoza and Leibniz), which "empiricists" characteristically opposed. Since that debate supplied a part of the background to the arguments of Hume, and they in turn have deeply influenced twentieth-century thinking, it seems worth the effort to try to understand it in terms of the participants's philosophical motives.

Laws over Natures: Mersenne and Descartes

It was Descartes who made voluntarism philosophically respectable in the seventeenth century, but even in his case it is open to dispute what his considered position really was. One question concerns the primary motive of his voluntarism. Was it theological (under which might be included a desire to make his materialist view of nature safe from the usual charge of atheism)? Was it general metaphysical or ontological considerations? Or was it a felt need for a *deus ex machina* to underpin particular features of his physics? Peter Dear's important recent book on Mersenne suggests a first approach to this question,[4] and a possible source of the view that the laws of motion have been created and maintained by God independently of the natures or essences of things, as something over and above those natures.

Mersenne's measured response to scepticism was primarily shaped by his desire to promote a mathematical approach to the physical world. The orthodox Aristotelian view was that mathematics is the purely abstract science of quantity: the object of geometry is bare, natureless matter abstractly considered as the subject of extension. In effect, mathematics is hardly a genuine science at all, in that it says nothing about natural or real

---

see J.E. McGuire, "Boyle's Conception of Nature," *Journal of the History of Ideas* 33 (1972), 523–42. Cf. E. McCann, "Lockean Mechanism," in *Philosophy, Its History and Historiography*, ed. A. J. Holland (Dordrecht: Reidel, 1983), 229–31.

[4] P. Dear, *Mersenne and the Learning of the Schools* (Ithaca: Cornell University Press, 1988).

essences: it is not knowledge *per causas*. Like others, Mersenne tried to improve the standing of mathematics by drawing on the Christianized Platonism of St. Augustine. He conceded that pure mathematics is not directly concerned with natural essences or with change, but its objects exist as ideas, archetypes or eternal truths in God's mind, known by us insofar as human reason resembles divine reason.[5] The crucial metaphysical claim, however, was that God employed mathematics in the creation and conservation of the natural world. Mathematical knowledge empowers us to explore, at the level of appearances, a "universal harmony" between things which is built into nature as a whole. The "mixed mathematics" of sciences such as harmonics, mechanics, astronomy and geometrical optics reveals this harmony to us, although not with the absolute certainty of pure mathematics. Because their principles involve some general assumptions about their natural objects, the conclusions of these sciences should be subject to strict observational checks. So it seems that the mathematical laws of the universal harmony are not entirely independent of the unknown natures of things. Nevertheless Mersenne's model would seem liable to drive the two apart.

Like Mersenne's, Descartes' explanation of scientific knowledge, its possibility and its application to the world is constructed around the supposed triangular relationship between eternal truths in the Creator's mind, things created according to those eternal truths, and at least some of those eternal truths imprinted on human minds. In effect, Descartes avoided Mersenne's scepticism simply by denying the presumption of unknown essences beyond the knowable eternal truths of mathematics, thus closing the gap between mathematics and nature. Bodies, "in so far as they are the subject-matter of pure mathematics,"[6] constitute, as such, a substance capable of separate, concrete existence independent of all but its Creator. In other words, mathematics reveals the very essence of things. With this proposal Descartes drove teleology out of physics more decisively than Mersenne. Yet he seems to have followed Mersenne in regarding the laws of mechanics as the principles of a universal, divinely ordained harmony *between* things. It is as if he could not after all believe that a "nature" in the full sense, a nature which determines what happens to its possessor, could

---

[5] So far from accepting that mathematics is not a genuine science, Mersenne seems to have favored the strongly Platonist argument that, just because it deals with change, *physics* is not a science in the full sense. Cf. Ibid., 54

[6] R. Descartes, *Meditations* 6: *Oeuvres de Descartes*, ed. C. Adam and P. Tannery 10 vols., (Paris: J. Vrin, 1973–4), 7:71. All translations of Descartes are from *The Philosophical Writings of Descartes*, trans. J. Cottingham, R. Stoothoff and D. Murdoch (Cambridge: Cambridge University Press, 1985).

be captured by a purely mathematical description. He implicitly denied matter even the kind of agency traditionally ascribed to "second causes," since he employs this term, not for bodies or their attributes and powers, but for the specific laws or rules according to which God conserves bodies and their motions[7]—a fairly striking way of emphasizing the primacy of laws over natures.

Descartes did not hide his debt to Plato. His God, like the form of the Good in the analogy of the sun in Plato's *Republic*, is both the conserving cause of the objects of knowledge and the source of the light by which we know them—the dual theme of the *Third Meditation*.[8] His physics, however, seems Epicurean rather than Neoplatonic—witness his notorious proposal that all the wonders of creation, from the system of heavenly bodies to the species of living things, could have arisen out of chaos simply in accordance with the laws of mechanics, without specific design or ordering principles.[9] The Cartesian God creates neither Aristotelian substantial forms nor Neoplatonic plastic natures as causal intermediaries to do his ordering for him. Nor is He a wise architect or craftsman structuring, as means to his ends, an antecedently created material which then naturally operates in such a way as to fulfil the divine purpose. Yet Descartes avoided the "atheism" of Epicurus by finding an acceptably Christian, equally traditional, alternative role for God as the omnipotent ground of all being and change. This conception he developed in terms of a notion of continuous recreation according to which the act of recreating a body necessarily involves the creation of its motion or rest. For a body to move is for it to be recreated at a place different from (and in a certain relation to) the one it occupied a moment before.[10] Yet in that case, it seems, in itself the body could just as well have been recreated elsewhere. Its "nature" can offer no constraint, so that the actual motion depends, not on the body or its nature, but on God's will.

---

[7]   Cf. R. Descartes, *Principles of Philosophy* 2.37: "certain rules or laws of nature, which are the secondary and particular causes of the various motions which we see in particular bodies."

[8]   I take it that the point of the "hyperbolical" doubt about reason itself was to reveal God as the source of light. The later part of the Meditation was concerned to show, as Descartes put it to Gassendi (using the metaphor of light to make a different point), that as "the sun is the cause of the light which proceeds from it, [so] God is the cause of created things, not just with respect to their becoming, but with respect to their being" (Fifth Replies, AT 7: 369).

[9]   R. Descartes, *Discourse on the Method*, 5: (AT 6: 42f).

[10]   For discussion of the details of Descartes's model (which are irrelevant to the present point) see D. Garber, *Descartes' Metaphysical Physics* (Chicago: Chicago University Press, 1992), 266–73, 286–8.

So a first explanation of Descartes's voluntarism might be as follows. He favoured Augustinian Platonism because of its philosophy of mathematics, but wished to purge it of teleology and its teleological theology. He was then led, in developing an alternative theology, to postulate bodies which are inert, i.e. which are in themselves capable of being subjected to an indefinite variety of laws, even if actually ruled by the one system of laws agreeable to the immutable will of God. This conception, in effect if not in intention, was a development of Mersenne's view of mixed mathematics as concerned with a general harmony in nature. There was, it should be said, a further Platonic dimension to Cartesian voluntarism. For when Plato argued for teleological explanation against materialism and empiricism in *Phaedo*, he praised the Anaxagorean view of the world as inert matter moved by mind. Although Descartes excluded teleology from physics, his world is after all one in which, as Plato put it, "the ordering mind orders everything and places each thing as it is best." It seems likely that a main motive for his standing so ostentatiously on the side of Plato's gods, against the giants, was to preempt the charge that a mechanistic physics went hand in hand with atheistic materialism.

Laws and Powers in Descartes

Some have attributed Descartes's voluntarism to a general problem in his physics. They start from the assumption that his spare, geometrical conception of matter emerged precisely because it does not ascribe to bodies the forms, natures, qualities and powers which both Aristotelians and Neoplatonists employed in their teleological pseudo-explanations. Unfortunately, as (on this view) he came to realize, physics needs forces. By postulating direct divine agency, however, he could get the best of both worlds, by allowing that matter moves *as if* it possessed powers over and above its geometrical properties. As Daniel Garber has recently put it, "Descartes seems less a precursor of later occasionalism than the last of the schoolmen, using God to do what substantial forms did for his teachers."[11]

If that proposal does capture Descartes's motive, then his system might seem open to the criticism that ascribing things to God's will simply replaces one kind of pseudo-explanation by another. As Boyle remarked in one of his less voluntaristic passages, "when we give such general answers, we pretend not to give the particular physical reasons of the things proposed,

---

[11]　Cf. ibid., 305; cf. G. Hatfield, "Force (God) in Descartes' Physics," *Studies in the History and Philosophy of Science* 10, 1979, 113–40.

but do in effect confess we do not know them."[12] Indeed, postulating voluntaristic correlations and postulating arbitrary, ad hoc powers might seem to come to much the same thing. Leibniz (in my view, wrongly) took Locke's notion of divine "superaddition" of powers to be voluntarism,[13] and criticized him for supposing that "God [gives] things accidental powers which [are] not rooted in their natures and [are] therefore out of the reach of reason in general." This line of thought, Leibniz believed, would open a backdoor to Aristotelian occult qualities.[14] Descartes might have replied that his voluntarism is not, after all, Boyle's "general answer," since in identifying the laws of motion and showing how they flow from God's immutability in *Principles* he is giving a fully specific account of what he called "the secondary and particular causes of the various motions we see in particular bodies" (2.37). He might equally have claimed that these laws, since they flow intelligibly from the immutability of God, are not in fact "out of the reach of reason in general." Nevertheless, Leibniz's criticism has some force.

There is a more serious obstacle to our ascribing Descartes's voluntarism to his recognition of the need for forces in physics, and that is his own explicit account of force. Some have argued that his explanations of the rules of impact in particular involve a notion of force which is irreducibly dynamic.[15] Hence the need for God's continuous agency. Yet Descartes himself states expressly in *Principles* that force or power consists "simply in the fact that everything tends, so far as lies within itself, to persist in the same state, as laid down in our first law," i.e. the law of inertia (2.43). Such a claim appears both to be emphatically reductive with respect to force and, by the same token, to limit God's "dynamic" role to that of upholding the first law from which the laws of impact are derived. In so far as the first law looks like a metaphysical truism anyway, the task would hardly seem worthy of omnipotence. Certainly, at least, some of Descartes's contemporaries had no difficulty in regarding the law of inertia as a metaphysical condition of the mobility of body which stands to reason in its own right, reducing to

---

12 R. Boyle, *A Free Enquiry into the Notion of Nature* (London: 1685–6), 18.

13 For an extended discussion of this issue, see Ayers, op.cit., 142–53.

14 G.W. Leibniz, *New Essays on the Human Understanding*, trans. P. Remnant and J. Bennett (Cambridge: Cambridge University Press, 1981), 382.

15 See M. Gueroult, "The Metaphysics and Physics of Force in Descartes," in *Descartes: Philosophy, Mathematics and Physics*, ed. S. Gaukroger Cf. A. Gabbey, "Force and Inertia in the Seventeenth Century: Descartes and Newton," in ibid., and D.Garber, op.cit., ch.9, esp. 293–9.

16 Cf. I. Beeckman, *Journal tenu par Isaac Beeckman de 1604 à 1634*, ed. C. de Waard, 4 vols. (The Hague: Nijhoff, 1939–53), 1: 24f

the principle that every change requires a cause of that change.[16] So when Descartes prefers one rule of impact to another on the ground that it is "easier," he does not have to mean that less real force is required, just that less change is involved: i.e. the rules of impact are supposed to follow from the first law.[17] So it is difficult to see how any of the arguments for specific rules of impact could supply a reason, independent of the first law, for moving to a view of all activity as God's activity. Yet the first law itself seems to supply little ground for calling on the omnipotent will.

Powers and the Ontology of Substance and Accident

All this might seem to confirm the first suggestion, that Descartes adopted voluntarism as part of a defensive theological strategy. Yet there seems to have been another, perhaps crucial motive in the attractions of a purely geometrical conception of corporeal substance from the point of view of ontology. For that conception seemed to give a perspicuous explanation of what it is for an accident to exist "in" a substance, and of what an "accident" is anyway, that it can do so—questions to which Aristotle had notoriously failed to give clear and satisfying answers.[18] The issue was, in effect, whether there are so-called "real" accidents existing in a peculiar metaphysical relation to substances, or whether accidents are no more than some kind of "beings of reason," only distinguished from their substances by a mental act of abstraction. Two antecedent lines of thought cast some light on the form taken by the debate in the seventeenth century. One can be exemplified by the

---

[17]   The point can be exemplified with reference to the third rule of impact. This states that, if (in an ideal, impossible state of separation from the rest of matter) a perfectly "hard" body, B, struck another, C, of the same size moving less rapidly in the opposite direction, then C would bounce back from B, and B would continue in the same direction, both travelling at the intermediate speed (i.e. an appropriate proportion of the excess of B's motion over that of C would be transferred to C). In other words, the bodies would behave much as (according to Descartes) they would have done if B had been larger than C, rather than as they would have done if, being the same size, they had been travelling at the same speed (when both would have bounced back at that speed). This result is preferred because it is "easier" (i.e., less force is required) for B to communicate some of its motion to C than for C to turn back all B's motion. Here it might seem that Descartes avoids an ontology of powers by interpreting the language of quantitatively determinate forces in terms of a voluntarism according to which God chooses ad hoc between rules on the basis of their easiness or simplicity. Yet for Descartes the "easier" outcome is simply the one which involves less change. Consequently all God needs to do here too is to uphold the first law.

[18]   A famous discussion of the relation is Aristotle, *Categories* 1a 16–1b 9.

discussion of abstract terms by that ace ontologist, William of Ockham (in part
1 of *Summa Logicae*), the other by a passage from Epicurus's *Letter to Herodotus*.

Ockham set out to consider whether abstract terms denote entities in
either their universal or their particular uses—i.e. whether we need to
postulate such abstract objects as humanity or whiteness in general, or as
this particular human being's humanity or whiteness. Real universals are
rejected in the first part of the argument, but it is the second part, relating
to abstract particulars, which is relevant here.

Ockham's strategy is to pass through the Aristotelian categories in turn,
razor in hand. Unsurprisingly, he has no truck with abstract entities in the
first category, *substance*. When we say that John is a man, "man" does not
signify an attribute distinct from, and present in, John (i.e. John's "humanity"). It is a general term the function of which is simply to signify all
particular men, and the abstract term only has a function in universal
propositions.[19] Moving on to the second category, Ockham offers some
ingenious argument for the view that *quantity* is similarly "not an absolute
thing really and totally distinct from" what is quantified.[20] Roughly speaking, his thought is as follows: When a body is divided, its quantity is divided.
So if the quantity were a distinct thing, the body in which it inhered would
have to be present to it in such a way as allowed each part of the body to be
present to a part of the quantity (since when the body is divided, the
quantity is divided). And for that the body would have already to be
quantified (1.44). Another thought is that God could not annihilate a
thing's quantity without annihilating the thing. So there aren't bodies *and*
quantities, just quantified bodies.

Relation is another category which proves to contain no "real" or really
distinct beings, on the ground that relations are nothing other than, nothing

---

19   William of Ockham, *Summa Logicae* 1.42. See *Ockham's Theory of Terms*, trans. and introd.
by Michael J. Loux (South Bend, IN: Notre Dame, 1974), 131–188. In universal propositions it seems that the abstract term (as Michael Loux puts it, ibid., 11–62) "provides
us with an abbreviated way of making claims about what is necessarily true of men *qua* men."

20   For example, those who hold that the quantity of a body is distinct from, and inheres
in, the body, must suppose that a body is, as Ockham put it, a substance having parts
"one of which lies beneath a part of the quantity inhering in the whole and another of
which lies beneath another part of that quantity." But if a thing's quantity is a distinct
entity, and given that the substance is prior to what inheres in it, God could destroy the
quantity while conserving the substance. Supposing that He does so, either the parts of
the body are spatially arrayed or they are not. If they are, then the body is quantified,
and the supposed entity, its quantity, turns out to have been superfluous. If they are not,
then the quantity cannot be destroyed without the body changing place (presumably,
as its parts shrink to a point), which is absurd.

external to, the absolute beings which are related. When he arrives at the category of *quality*, however, Ockham draws a distinction between qualities such as shape, straightness and curvedness on the one hand and qualities such as whiteness, knowledge and light on the other. The former are not distinct beings, but the latter are. The test is this:

> [Any two] predicables which, while incapable of being truly applied to one thing at the same time, can successively hold true of an object merely as a result of local motion, need not be construed as signifying distinct things.

Accordingly, the predicates "curved" and "straight" are such that the abstract terms "curvedness" and "straightness" signify nothing apart from the things which are curved or straight. The same goes for all shapes, for rarity and density, and for thinness and thickness and the like. On the other hand, it is different in the case of terms like "whiteness", "blackness", "heat" and "cold". For it is not simply because a thing or its parts undergo local motion that the thing becomes hot or cold. Consequently, these terms do designate things distinct from substance.

Ockham's view was rejected by Suarez, who at the beginning of the seventeenth century stated that a thing's quantity, as well as such purely qualitative attributes as colors or heat and cold are distinct beings. He postulated a special modal relation, and modal distinction, between accidents and their substances—called "modal" because *inherence* is a mode of the accident joining it to its substance. Accidents are naturally dependent on substances but, in virtue of their ontological status as distinct entities, they are capable of miraculous existence apart from their substance. Indeed, accidents do exist so separated, and a substance exists without its quantity in the sacrament of the Eucharist.[21]

Let us turn to Epicurus, who asserts in his Letter to Herodotus[22] that what exist "in themselves" as independent natures are bodies and the void. Shape, size, weight and resistance are permanent attributes of *body* as such. Color is a permanent attribute of *visible body* (i.e. body as seen or visualized) and is relative to observers. We can also think of an attribute as permanent in relation to a *kind* of body (i.e., a complex of atoms) "as heat to fire, liquidity to water". "Accidents" are impermanent, and include mental and moral states and specific qualities. Epicurus apparently did not count

---

[21] *Disputationes Metaphysicae* (Hildesheim: G. Olms, 1965, facs. ed. of C. Berton, Paris, 1866, vol. 5, 25–6) 2, 255ff.

[22] Esp. secs. 68–73. For Epicurus's Letter to Herodotus, I use the translation of A.A. Long and D.N. Sedley, *The Hellenistic Philosophers* (Cambridge: Cambridge University Press, 1987), 1: 33f.

determinate shapes among the "accidents" of bodies as such, presumably because they are at any rate permanent attributes of the immutable atoms. He did not deny, but was eager to emphasize the reality of accidents, which would have been held doubtful in the context of much ancient philosophy because of their fleeting nature (it had, indeed, been denied by the earlier atomist, Democritus) (1.34). It seems that, although accidents are neither intrinsic nor permanent, we should grant them reality as individualized by sensation. ("They are viewed in just the way that sensation itself individualizes them.") We should recognize their relativity to the perceiver, but not deny their reality—indeed, the Epicurean Polystratus remarked that we should not deny that something is really poisonous just because it is poisonous only to some.[23] Yet it is clear that for Epicurus accidents *belong* to bodies solely in virtue of the permanent attributes which give rise to them— roughly, what Locke came to call "the primary qualities of the minute parts."

No attributes, however, whether permanent or impermanent, exist per se or in themselves. The nature of a body or per se entity, whether an atom or complex of atoms, can be said to consist in the sum of its attributes, but it does so in a special way. Attributes are not parts and can in no way exist in separation from the whole. They are rather, Epicurus seems to have meant, aspects of things on which we can focus whether perceptually or in thought. Permanent attributes are simply those abstract aspects of bodies through which we conceive of bodies as such, and without which bodies are inconceivable.

These two very different arguments, of Epicurus and Ockham, together reveal clearly why mechanistic corpuscularianism should have been seen as a means of sweeping away the doctrine of "real accidents" and solving the metaphysical problem of the inherence and unity of accidents in their substance. Following Epicurus, the New Philosophy simply reduced the qualities which had resisted Ockham's razor to those that it had successfully shaved off. All qualitative change, they claimed, does after all depend solely, in the object, on the movement of its parts. Given that thesis, there is no reason to regard any accident as an entity distinct from the substance in which it inheres. As Hobbes remarked, everyone understands the relation between an extended thing and its shape or limits, a moving thing and its motion. For Hobbes, an accident (as Epicurus had proposed in general and as Ockham had concluded in these cases) is nothing but "the manner by which any body is conceived."[24] The apparent variety of qualitative accidents is merely, as Hobbes put it, "a diversity of seeming";[25] or, as Digby argued at about the same time, "what is but one entire thing in itself,

---

23   Polystratus, "On Irrational Contempt," chap. 26 in ibid., 36.

24   T. Hobbes, *De Corpore* 2.8.3.

seemeth to be many things in my understanding."[26] Descartes's treatment
in *Principles* of "modal distinctions" and "distinctions of reason" carries a
similar message, i.e. that the many-one relation of transitory modes to the
corporeal substance in which they inhere is to be understood as the relation
of determinates to the determinable properties of extension and mobility,
while these and other permanent attributes are not really distinct from their
substance or from one another (1.61ff.). To have introduced other kinds of
quality or power into this pure material world in which *every* accident fails
Ockham's test for a really distinct entity would have wrecked its pretensions
to special ontological intelligibility.

Ontology and Voluntarism

It is, then, easy to understand why Descartes (rather like Epicurus) should
have been attached to a spare, purely geometrical "nature" of matter simply
on general grounds of ontology: it makes sense of the relation between
substance and accident. All this, however, suggests a general reason why
Descartes might have preferred divinely upheld laws over natural interactions even with respect to his first law. For if the motion of A, as a mode of
A, is nothing really distinct from A, but is simply an aspect of A through
which A may be conceived, then it is clear that a motion cannot really pass
from one body to another.[27] Thus no *entity* is conserved when the quantity
of motion in the world is conserved: naturalistic talk of the transference and
conservation of motion is just a way of saying that, as Descartes put it,
"whenever the motion of one part [of matter] decreases, that of another
increases by the same amount" (2.36). What could maintain this universal
harmony between bodies but God?

There are only hints of an argument along these lines in Descartes, but
it was explicitly developed by his followers in a way which linked it to the

---

[25] T. Hobbes, *Leviathan* chap. 34.

[26] K. Digby, *Two Treatises: Of Bodies and Of Man's Soule* (Paris: 1644), 3.

[27] Since Descartes favored a geometrical, relational account of motion, it might seem
inconsistent of him to have treated it as a mode of particular bodies. For discussion of
this problem, see Garber, op.cit., 157–75. If all motions could be viewed as relative
modifications of one substance, matter, (as seems consonant enough with the Cartesian
plenum), then it might seem that the problem of transference would not arise. Perhaps
because he felt that it would threaten the principle that every bit of matter is really
distinct from every other bit (and the substantial status of individual bodies), Descartes
avoided this solution, but it was probably a motive for Spinoza's monism.

question of the ontological status of powers. Cordemoy and La Forge, for example, both support the conclusion that, strictly speaking, no body moves another, by appealing to the principle that "motion is nothing but a mode, which can no more pass from one subject to another than the other modes of matter."[28] The thought behind La Forge's argument seems to be that, since the cause of "transferred" motion cannot be that same motion occurring earlier in another subject, the event cannot be interpreted in terms of a motion's tendency to maintain itself. The cause of any body's motion must therefore be distinguished from the motion itself. Let us then suppose (this somewhat Ockhamesque argument continues) that this separate cause of motion lies in bodies themselves. In that case it would have to do so as an active power or force in addition to motion. Since this power would have to be supposed to increase and diminish along with motion, the same problems would arise over its transference as arise for motion itself. Since, taken as a mode, it could not conceivably be transferred, the only alternative (if that made sense) would be to suppose that it causes motion in another body on impact by a kind of creative act, creating a cause of motion like itself in the body struck. The absurdity of these suppositions establishes, for La Forge, that the cause of motion is nothing in bodies, but is God, the only thing capable of creation.[29]

Malebranche appealed to similar considerations, but only after establishing that God maintains everything in being by a constant creative act. Since He cannot create a body without creating it somewhere and in some state, it follows that the "moving force of body is nothing but the activity of God's will which conserves it successively in different places". It is this principle of Cartesian theology which makes it clear that no body moves another,

> for a body cannot move another without communicating to it its moving force. But the moving force of a body in motion is nothing but the will of the Creator. . . . It is not a quality which belongs to the body itself.

---

[28]   L. de La Forge, *Traitté de l'esprit de l'homme* (Amsterdam: Abraham Wolfgang, no date), 250f; cf. G. de Cordemoy, *Le discernement du corps de l'ame*, in *Oeuvres Philosophiques*, ed. P. Clair and F. Girbal (Paris: Presses Universitaires de France 1968), 138. Both passages are cited by T.M. Lennon in N. Malebranche, *The Search after Truth*, trans. T.M. Lennon and P. Olscamp (Columbus: Ohio State University Press, 1980), 813. Lennon sees "nominalism" as a fundamental element in the argument, but interprets it here as the rejection of universals, which, as we have seen, is not quite right. At the same time, he claims that "Cartesian nominalism has as its consequence that to cause a new mode is to cause a new substance"—i.e. entails recreation of the substance, a connection with nominalism which is obscure to me.

[29]   Cf. Lennon's commentary in Malebranche, op.cit., 814.

Nothing belongs to it but its own modifications; and modifications are inseparable from substances.[30]

So much for the various reasons for voluntarism which seem to have weighed with Descartes and his followers. To recapitulate, the three lines of his thought which I have tried to disentangle from, and relate to, the others are (1) the employment of Augustinian Platonism as a metaphysical basis for applied mathematics, (2) the rejection of teleology, and of forms and powers, in physical explanation, and (3) the concern for the ontology of substance and accident. His primary motive throughout was a desire to make sense of the physical world in terms of a quantitative, mathematical mechanics, and to construct an epistemological and metaphysical framework within which such a mechanics has a place. The Augustinian rationalism, the theology centered on omnipotence, and the reductive ontology of accidents, as well as the rejection of teleological and ad hoc explanatory concepts, was embraced by that fundamental purpose. Malebranche, on the other hand, despite his deployment of the Cartesian dialectic and undoubted interest in mechanics, was primarily motivated by theology. It is characteristic of him to claim that the self-evident principle that a body cannot move itself, maintain itself in motion or determine the motion of another body exemplifies the more general point that the whole idea of a force or power or efficacy in created things is self-contradictory. The only intelligible "necessary connection" is between the will of an omnipotent being and the object of that will. Correspondingly, he was even clearer than Descartes that, if we consider only bodies as they are in themselves, how in general they behave has to be learned from experience. Only if we turn to God, and to the principle that He achieves the most perfect world by the simplest means, will the laws of mechanics become intelligible to us. That is about as close as this dialectic, as so far described, approaches anything which could be called "empiricism."[31]

If the arguments for voluntarism were metaphysical rather than epistemological, so were the arguments against it. Leibniz has already been

---

[30] *Elucidation 15* of *The Search after Truth.*

[31] An interesting antivoluntarist argument is that of Fontenelle, who argued in effect that, even if we grant that the rules of impact are arbitrary creations of God, we must recognize at least one constraint on them which is due to the nature of body. For, if two bodies collide, God simply cannot maintain both in being without ensuring that each resists penetration by the other. The implication of the argument is that, since the impenetrability of body constitutes one ineluctable constraint on the laws of motion despite God's omnipotence, we might as well concede the possibility that events are altogether determined by the created nature of body. Cf. Lennon in Malebranche, op. cit., 819ff.

mentioned as an anti-voluntarist, but his position was not a simple one. Despite his expressed scorn for scholastic powers, he insisted against Descartes and Malebranche that there is force or efficacy in created things, and that laws are merely abstractions from created individual natures. Voluntarism, for Leibniz, turns the natural into the miraculous. Mere repetition or universality is not enough to render miracles natural: "properly speaking, God performs a miracle when he does something that surpasses the forces he has given to creatures and conserves in them."[32] He offered a famous physical demonstration that force must be distinguished from motion, arguing that it is force, not quantity of motion, which is conserved.[33] Nevertheless he allowed that the possession of force by bodies is not intelligible in itself, but only becomes so if we recognize that the apparently material subject of force is really immaterial or spiritual. Behind the phenomenon of force lies the reality of appetition. This reduction of the material to the spiritual meant that his ontology or theory of substance is centered on Descartes's other paradigm of the substance-attribute relation—the thinking thing's reflexive awareness of itself as the continuing subject of a variety of perceptions, desires and volitions. Leibniz also accepted the principle that a mode cannot be transferred from one substance to another, agreeing that there is therefore no real interaction between finite substances. Yet he avoided the conclusion that God does everything by postulating a preestablished harmony between individual substances such that each is determined to undergo changes corresponding to the changes in the others. It seems that, just because of the ontological principles he shared with the voluntarists, voluntarism could be excluded from Leibniz's system only in virtue of other dramatic changes in the metaphysical scenery.

Anti-voluntarism and Empiricism in the Seventeenth Century

Another kind of opposition to voluntarism was represented by constructive empiricists, i.e. those seventeenth-century "new philosophers" who drew on the Epicurean and Stoic theories of knowledge developed in opposition to various ancient forms of scepticism. From Bacon to Locke, whether or not they supposed that a systematic "science" of nature is possible, such

---

[32] G.W. Leibniz, Letter to Arnauld, 30 April 1687, *The Leibniz-Arnauld Correspondence*, ed. and trans. H.T. Mason (Manchester: Manchester University Press, 1967), 116.

[33] Cf. G.W. Leibniz, *Discourse on Metaphysics* sec.17.

empiricists were dedicated to the view that, insofar as knowledge is possible, it is so in virtue of our direct confrontation with nature, through the causal mechanisms of the senses, and our consequent employment of the sensory imagination. Broadly, the empiricists were the philosophical naturalists of seventeenth-century epistemology, eschewing supernaturalism and therefore eschewing anything like a pure intellect directly enlightened by God.[34] It is therefore not surprising if they rejected voluntarism, and favoured natures over laws. For seventeenth-century voluntarism, as we have seen, was part and parcel of an attempt to find metaphysical foundations for the new science in a view of the relationship between divine and human reason. Leibniz was unusual in his embodying a supernatural epistemology in a strongly anti-voluntarist metaphysics.[35]

The constructive empiricists did not, however, reject the intuitive basis of philosophical mechanism, i.e. the thought that mechanical change is intelligible in itself as qualitative change is not. That is true even of Locke, for whom mechanical change as we know it is only intelligible given certain assumptions, and within narrow limits. Indeed, empiricist mechanists were free from a certain difficulty here. For, as Malebranche's pronouncements on the inertness of matter bring out with particular clarity, a very odd thing about voluntaristic mechanism is that the voluntarism works against just the kind of natural intuition as makes the mechanism attractive. Consider the example given in the Port Royal *Logic*: if we see an axle, sections of which are shaped to fit the holes in two millstones, one hole round and the other square, we can predict with certainty which millstone the axle will turn.[36] The authors of the *Logic* say that we employ "reason" in making our "infallible" prediction, but it is implausible to suppose that our immediate realization that it is the stone with the square hole which will turn involves reflection, as on a premise, on the immutability or perfection of the Creator,

---

[34] I do not mean that a rhetorical notion of enlightenment was entirely cast aside, but (e.g.) when Locke characterized "reason" (which here includes and presupposes sense perception) as "natural revelation," the significant word is "natural" (*Essay concerning Human Understanding* 4.19.4). Where Malebranche explained the ordinary operation of sense and reason in supernatural terms, Locke emphasized that God ordinarily enlightens us through natural means and mechanisms, the "candle, that is set up in us" (*ibid.* 1.1.5).

[35] Cf. Leibniz's comments on Malebranche in his *Conversation of Philarete and Ariste*, in G. W. *Leibniz: Philosophical Essays*, trans. R. Ariew and D. Garber (Indianapolis: Hackett, 1989), 267f. Leibniz would no doubt have rejected my characterization of his innatism as a "supernatural" epistemology, since it explains knowledge in terms of the forces created with us.

[36] A. Arnauld and P. Nicole *Logic, or the Art of Thinking* 1.1.

or on the divine tendency to produce the richest outcome by the simplest means. Empiricists, on the other hand, could hold that the superior intelligibility and predictability of mechanical processes lies with just those features which are open to view. Their problem as mechanists was to account both for that intelligibility and for mathematical necessity without postulating a pure intellect with divine intimations of the eternal truths. Epicurean and, in particular, Stoic theory of inference or "signs" supplied a model, with its suggestion that systematic abstraction from clear and distinct sense impressions could lead us to conceptually evident hypotheticals, such as "Where there is motion, there is empty space," or "If sweat flows through the skin, then there are ducts." That theory probably influenced Bacon,[37] but for present purposes Hobbes provides a more striking development.

For Hobbes, systematic "science" is possible through the analysis of the objects of sense-perception conducted with the aid of language. The propositions of science are analytic, either definitions or consequences of definitions.[38] They are therefore verbal. Yet they are not trivial, because well-chosen names and definitions enable us to analyze the objects of experience and focus on those of their aspects which matter for the purpose of understanding them through their causes. Sensory knowledge takes things in as wholes: by sense we know what the thing is before we turn to its particular attributes or accidents. This is "*cognitio quod est.*" "*Cognitio causarum,*" knowledge of causes, on the other hand, requires analytic abstraction, since "the cause of the whole is compounded from the causes of the parts." As for Epicurus, a "part" is here not literally a part, but an abstract aspect or "way of conceiving of a body"—Hobbes's definition of an *accident.* Analysis and abstraction will bring us eventually to the most general or simple concepts (i.e. the basic concepts of geometry and mechanics), a level at which causal principles are, Hobbes claimed, "manifest in themselves."[39] The definitions which constitute the explications of these simple concepts are the first principles of natural philosophy (including "moral philosophy" or psychology). In other words, laws are firmly grounded

---

[37]   For Bacon the progressive analysis of experience leads towards "what is prior and better known in the order of nature," establishing "progressive stages of certainty." The ultimate aim is "certain and demonstrable knowledge." *Novum Organum,* ed. T. Fowler (Oxford: Oxford University Press, 1878), 181–84, 195–99; *The Works of Francis Bacon,* ed. J. Spedding, R.L. Ellis and D.D. Heath (London: Longmans, 1858–61), 40–3, 50.

[38]   *De Corpore* 1.2.9: "every true universal proposition is either a definition, or part of a definition, or demonstrated from definitions."

[39]   *De Corpore* 1.6.5: "*Causae . . . universalium . . . manifestae sunt per se.*"

in natures which are perspicuous to sense. Allegedly, if we treat sensible objects abstractly enough, physics just falls out.

It will already be clear that Hobbes endorsed an ontology of substance and accident much like that of Epicurus and Descartes. He also endorsed the principle of nontransference: as he put it in *De Corpore*, "when a hand, being moved, moves a pen, the motion of the hand does not migrate into the pen, . . . but its own new motion is generated in the pen" (2.8.21). Yet he saw no problem in allowing genuine interaction without genuine transference of motion, taking it that the laws of inertia themselves simply spell out the self-evident necessity that any new accident in a body must be the effect of some accident of another adjacent body (ibid. 2.9.7). The motor power which figured in the arguments of the Cartesians he simply identified with motion itself: "a power is not some accident distinct from all action, but is a certain action, namely a motion, which is called a power insofar as another action is later produced by it" (ibid. 2.10.6).

If it seems strange that an empiricist epistemology should purport to ground a dogmatic physics, it may seem less so if we bear in mind, not only the ancient sources, but that Hobbes's hostility to Descartes was not to his dogmatic mechanism, but to the theological framework on which Cartesian epistemology and physics was hung. The intuition Hobbes was pursuing and purporting to explain, the seeming intelligibility of mechanical processes by comparison with qualitative change, was wholly neutral with respect to the issue between empiricism and theories of direct or innate illumination by God.

Some constructive empiricists, of course, were anti-dogmatic. Gassendi instigated this approach, but it was taken in terms more directly allusive to the question of voluntarism by Locke, although his pronouncements raise a tangled issue of interpretation which I will not rehearse now.[40] In general Locke claimed that, because we lack access to mechanical structure, different in each sort of thing, and even to the general nature of the matter which composes them, we are unable to expand our glimmering comprehension of mechanical processes into "a science of bodies." What may seem to support a Leibnizian interpretation of Locke as a voluntarist is his repeated suggestion that, when faced with an "inconceivable" connection (i.e. one we cannot understand), "we are fain to quit our Reason, go beyond our *Ideas*, and attribute it wholly to the good Pleasure of our Maker." Sometimes he seems ready to assign all universal connections to God's will, but that suggestion (so I would argue) is made in the context of an assumption that there are intelligible connections, possible objects of universal knowledge

---

[40]   Examined in Ayers, op.cit., chap. 12, 142–153.

or science, behind the apparently brute facts we observe. In *Essay* he certainly contrasts mechanical processes, in which antecedent and consequent "seem to us to have some *connexion* one with another", with qualitative processes in which there is no "discoverable connection" (4.3.12). With respect to the latter "we are . . . left only to Observation and Experiment," and "can reason no otherwise about them, than as effects produced by the appointment of an infinitely Wise Agent, which perfectly surpass our Comprehensions" (ibid. 4.3.28). Locke's references to God's will constitute a sceptical comment on the philosophical voluntarism of the time, rather than an endorsement of it.[41] Voluntarism, he implies, is the product of ignorance.

Another apparent allusion to voluntarism in *Essay* occurs in his account of our idea of power:

> Whether Matter be not wholly destitute of *active* Power, as its Author GOD is truly above all *passive Power*; and whether the intermediate state of created Spirits be not that alone, which is capable of both *active* and *passive Power*, may be worth consideration. I shall not now enter into that Enquiry, my present Business being not to search into the original of Power, but how we come by an idea of it (2.21.2).

Locke goes on to suggest that our idea of agency comes primarily from "reflection on the Operations of our Minds," in particular on willing. Impulse, on the other hand, gives "but a very obscure *Idea* of an *active Power* of moving in Body." A billiard ball struck by a cue exhibits only passion in moving, and in impelling another "it only communicates the motion it had received," and so gives us only an idea of "the Continuation of the Passion." The hypothesis that matter is inert is redolent of Cartesian voluntarism, but the very *un*-Cartesian argument that we observe the body "only to transfer, but not to produce any motion" suggests that the theological speculation Locke regards favorably is not voluntarism, but his own express thesis that, at the beginning of the world, God had not only to create matter, but also to give it a push, since matter could not be supposed to put itself into motion.[42]

---

41   There are admittedly other considerations which may encourage an interpretation of Locke as a voluntarist. For discussion of what are probably the strongest of them, see Ayers, op.cit., 148–52.

42   Cf. *Essay* 4.10.10. The point has to do with the important theological difference between Descartes and Locke as to the logical status and theological respectability of the various proofs of God's existence. Locke assimilated the argument from the existence of myself as a thinking thing to arguments from design, a move which made it compatible with his neutrality on the question of whether the thinking thing is immaterial or material. Cf. Ayers, op.cit., chap. 14, 169–183.

All this helps to explain Locke's view of the relation between substance and accidents. He shaped his epistemology around the usual contrast between the real unity of a substantial thing on the one hand and, on the other, the multiplicity consequent on the plurality of the senses together with any further mental distinctions we can draw—a multiplicity of aspects, Hobbes's "diversity of seeming."[43] Where Locke differed from Hobbes and Descartes was in sceptically suggesting that we lack the knowledge necessary to reduce this phenomenal and conceptual multiplicity to an intelligible unity, and so to understand the relation between substance and accidents. He questioned the corpuscularian solution of the ancient problem, claiming it still to be the case that "of *Substance*, we have no *Idea* of what it is, but only a confused obscure one of what it does."[44] Descartes's account of matter fails to distinguish matter from empty space; that of the atomists merely presupposes the cohesion of the postulated particles (ibid.2.23). Locke took over the Epicurean preference for a conception of bodies pared down to certain permanent attributes, i.e. those primary qualities "such as . . . the Mind finds inseparable from every particle of Matter"(ibid.2.8.9); but he could not agree that this conception captures the full explanatory nature of matter.

The Voluntarism of Berkeley

The link between empiricism and naturalism was not totally firm. Boyle may have been a voluntarist; Newton did not rule out an explanation of gravity in terms of direct divine agency; and Newton's admirer Bentley took

---

[43]　Cf. *Essay* 2.2.1: / *Though the Qualities that affect our Senses, are, in the things themselves, so united and blended, that there is no separation, no distance between them; yet 'tis plain, the Ideas they produce in the Mind, enter by the Senses simple and unmixed. For though the Sight and Touch often take in from the same Object, at the same time, different Ideas; as a Man sees at once Motion and Colour; . . . Yet the simple Ideas thus united [sc. as qualities] in the same Subject, are as perfectly distinct [sc. in the mind], as those that come in by different Senses.*

[44]　The sentence comes from the anti-Aristotelian sally of *Essay* 2.13.19: / *we take it for a sufficient Answer, and good Doctrine, from our European Philosophers, That Substance, without knowing what it is, is that which supports Accidents. So that of Substance, we have no Idea of what it is, but only a confused, obscure one of what it does.* / The same point is, of course, a central theme of 2.23, and in 2.23.2 there is the explicit claim that corpuscularianism (i.e. the theory that "the subject wherein Colour and Weight inheres" is "the solid, extended parts" or particles) simply puts the problem off in the same way as "the Indian . . . who, saying the World was supported by a great Elephant, was asked, what the Elephant rested on; to which his answer was, a great Tortoise."

the need for such an explanation to be an argument for God's existence.[45] In Berkeley, however, we seem to have the first modern philosopher to present a worked-out connection between empiricism and voluntarism, a system in which the former underpins the latter. Yet several commentators[46] have questioned the significance of this connection, suggesting that Berkeley's voluntarism, together with other central doctrines, was simply taken over from Descartes or Malebranche. Certainly his system bears some of the most characteristic marks of the Platonic-Cartesian tradition. First, minds are very firmly placed higher than bodies on the scale of being, and in this connection Berkeley expressly alludes to Plato's battle between giants and gods.[47] Secondly, our knowledge of the natural world is attributed to a kind of divine illumination, as God "exhibits" his ideas to us.[48] Thirdly, De Motu again echoes Plato in praising Anaxagoras as a proto-voluntarist who recognized that mind is the principle of motion of inert, mobile matter. "Of the moderns," Berkeley continues, "Descartes has put the same point most forcibly. What was left clear by him others have rendered involved and difficult by their obscure terms."[49] Berkeley also alludes approvingly to the principle of conservation or continuous creation employed by both Descartes and Malebranche: "For no other cause of the successive existence of the body in different parts of space should be sought, it would seem, than that cause whence is derived the successive existence of the same body in different parts of time"(ibid. 34).

A clear, radical difference from Descartes and Malebranche, however, is that divine ideas are for Berkeley sensible particulars rather than universal archetypes, and that God makes us acquainted with them in ordinary sensation rather than in abstract thought. The fact is that Berkeley is

---

[45]   Richard Bentley, A Confutation of Atheism from the Origin and Frame of the World (the first Boyle Lectures, of 1691), reprinted in Isaac Newton's Papers and Letters, ed. I.B. Cohen (Cambridge: Cambridge University Press, 1958).

[46]   A.A. Luce, Berkeley and Malebranche (Oxford: Oxford University Press 1934); H. Bracken, Berkeley (London: Macmillan, 1974); L. Loeb, Descartes to Hume (Ithaca: Cornell University Press, 1981).

[47]   Berkeley, Siris, sec. 263.

[48]   Cf. G. Berkeley Three Dialogues between Hylas and Philonous 2, Works of George Berkeley, ed. T.E. Jessop and A.A. Luce (London: Nelson, 1964), 2: 214f: "They must exist in some other mind, whose will it is they should be exhibited to me." Compare the use of "exhiberet" at Descartes, Principles 2.1, in the context of the question as to whether sensory ideas are caused by matter or immediately by God.

[49]   Berkeley, De Motu 30. The "obscure terms" perhaps include "occasion," a Malebranchian use of which Berkeley criticizes at Principles 1.69.

ostentatiously both nominalist and empiricist. Analysis of his argument reveals, I believe, that his main purpose is to show that the empiricism of the giants leads, not to their traditional materialism, scepticism and athe-ism, but to the anti-materialism and theism of the gods. Again I must leave the argument to other occasions. But I would point out that Berkeley's voluntarism is founded on utterly different principles from those of Des-cartes and Malebranche. Cartesian voluntarism stemmed from a programme of mathematizing physics based on a geometrical, mechanistic conception of matter as a substance, together with a metaphysical theory of the substance-accident relation, all of which was in Berkeley's eyes gross error. Berkeley's own voluntarism is a direct consequence of his denial that sensible things are substantial, and it hardly needs saying that he ascribed the great philosophical mistake of elevating matter to the status of a substance above all to the epistemological distinction between things as they are perceived and things as they are in themselves. Properly regarded as ideas, he held, it will be evident that bodies are "visibly inactive":

> whoever shall attend to his ideas . . . will not perceive in them any power or activity; there is therefore no such thing contained in them. A little attention will discover to us that the very being of an idea implies passiveness and inertness in it . . . : neither can it be the resemblance or pattern of any active being.[50]

Berkeley's claim is that "bare observation" or "experience" will assure us not only that the things or attributes we review are inert, but that they are so just because they are ideas. Where Malebranche contrasts the impotence of the creature with the intelligible efficacy of an omnipotent will,[51] Berkeley compares inert ideas with efficacious volitions reflexively apprehended in our own case. Again the appeal is to experience: "This making and un-making of ideas [in imagination] doth very properly denominate the mind

---

[50] *Principles* 1.25, which begins: "All our ideas, sensations, or the things which we perceive, by whatever names they may be distinguished, are visibly inactive, there is nothing of power or agency in them."

[51] It is true, as Loeb points out (op. cit. 230), that Berkeley presents such a contrast at *Philosophical Commentaries* 107, yet this section reads as a reflection on the implications of his thesis that bodies are ideas (already presented) rather than as a motivating preconception. Berkeley rejects the consequence that we are not agents in the world at *Commentaries* 548.

[52] Ibid., sec. 28. Cf. *De Motu* 25, where the example is of bodily movement: "that there is [in thinking things] the power of moving bodies we have learned by personal experience, since our mind can stir and stay the movements of our limbs."

active. Thus much is certain, and grounded on experience."[52] Our experience of our own successful willing is "immediate knowledge"[53] of action,
and the word "action" gets its meaning from this experience. This claim is
directly reminiscent of Locke's account in *Essay* of our idea of active power,
which "we have only from what passes in our selves, where we find by
Experience, that barely by willing it, barely by a thought of the Mind, we
can move the parts of our Bodies"(2.21.4). So Berkeley's voluntarism is
firmly grounded on his concept empiricism with respect both to the inertness of matter and the activity of mind.

Hume's constant conjunctions

Although Berkeley's aim was to break the traditional links between empiricism and both materialism and scepticism, his arguments struck Hume as
"the best lessons of scepticism, which are to be found either among the
ancient or modern philosophers."[54] How we understand Hume on natures
and laws depends very much on how we interpret his whole argument. If,
like his Positivist admirers, we suppose that his purpose is reductive ontology, it might be tempting to read his account of causation as voluntarism
without God. We might take him to be saying that there are no natures out
there, just contingent regularities or constant conjunctions. These prompt
the imagination to form misleading conceptions of power, necessity and
efficacy in things, but are in themselves just brute facts. Alternatively,
following some recent commentators,[55] we may take him to be, not an
analytic, reductive ontologist, but a sceptical realist. On such an interpretation, he joins with Hobbes and Locke in assuming that observable
regularities do indeed flow necessarily from the natures of things, but
advances a more profound scepticism than Locke's in denying us even a
glimmering comprehension of mechanical processes. Any ideas which we

---

53   Cf. *Dialogues* 3, *Works* 2, 232.

54   D. Hume, *An Enquiry concerning Human Understanding*, ed. L.A. Selby-Bigge.
(Oxford: Oxford University Press, 1975), 10.2: (marginal sec. 122).

55   See J. Wright, *The Sceptical Realism of David Hume* (Manchester: Manchester
University Press, 1983), D.W. Livingston, *Hume's Philosophy of Common Life* (Chicago:
University of Chicago Press,1984) and G. Strawson, *The Secret Connexion* (Oxford:
Oxford University Press, 1989). Strawson's argument is criticized in D. Pears, *Hume's
System: an Examination of the First Book of his Treatise* (Oxford: Oxford University Press,
1990), K.P. Winkler, "The New Hume," *Philosophical Review* 100.4 (1992): 541–79 and
J. Broackes, "Did Hume Hold a Regularity Theory of Causation?" *British Journal for the
History of Philosophy* 1.1 (1993): 99–114.

may suppose ourselves capable of forming of things' natures, their efficacy
or the necessity with which they act are illusory constructs of an imagination
driven by habit and and other principles still more irrational and absurd.
We mistake the subjective certitude of our natural beliefs for the perception
of intelligible necessity. Nevertheless, the constructed, naturally inescap-
able world of the imagination is sufficiently related to the unknowable
things as they are in themselves for all our practical purposes. If it were not
so, we would quickly end in disaster.

Here I want only to point out that the interpretation of Hume as a
sceptical realist for whom unknown natures underlie regularities gains
some, perhaps considerable, support from his direct consideration of voluntarism in the *First Enquiry*.[56] The discussion starts with the consideration of a
form of the tentative proposal of Locke's (without alluding to its endorsement and employment by Berkeley) that we receive an idea or, in Hume's
terms, an impression of action or power in voluntary action and thought.
It passes on, first, to Cartesian voluntarist physics, and then to the Malebranchian proposal that we can understand all causality, including seem-
ingly voluntary action and imagination, only in terms of the efficacy of an
omnipotent will. Hume's strategy with respect to all these lines of thought
is to agree that we have no impression of power or agency in purely physical
sequences, but to deny that things are any different in the case of volition,
whether human or divine.

First, if we were immediately aware of the power of our volitions we
would be able to predict infallibly when the willed outcome, physical or
mental, would follow. That, however, is something we have to learn from
experience—and by "experience" Hume meant, of course, neither
Berkeleyan reflexive awareness nor simple trial but repeated observation of
similar volitions followed by similar outcomes.[57] Why the outcomes often
match the volitions is utterly mysterious to us:

> Is there not here, either in a spiritual or material substance, or both, some
> secret mechanism or structure of parts, upon which the effect depends,
> and which, being entirely unknown to us, renders the power or energy of
> the will equally unknown and incomprehensible?[58]

Voluntary imagination appears to us as an unintelligible creation of ideas,
while "we learn from anatomy" that there must be a long sequence of

---

56   *Enquiry* 7.1, marginal secs. 51–57.

57   Cf. nn. 52–3, above.

58   *Enquiry* 7.1, marginal sec. 53.

unknown and unintended physiological events coming between the volition and any willed bodily movement. As for Malebranche's occasionalism,
it is self-evidently a thesis which goes beyond the scope of human understanding: "We are got into fairy land, long ere we have reached the last steps
of our theory." Besides, we "have no idea of the Supreme Being but what
we learn from our own faculties."[59] If our own agency is unintelligible, then
so is divine agency.

The argument against Locke's proposal as to our idea of active power,
and therefore the whole argument against voluntarism, presupposes an
explicit formal notion of what it would be like to understand a causal
sequence. As he had put it in the *Treatise*:

> for a causal sequence to be intelligible, we must distinctly and particularly
> conceive the connexion betwixt the cause and effect, and be able to
> pronounce, from a simple view of the one, that it must be follow'd or
> preceded by the other. This is the true manner of conceiving a particular
> power in a particular body. . . . [60]

This is not a common-sense account of what it is to understand a sequence,
but just that formal notion, made explicit by Arnauld, which a dogmatic
naturalistic mechanist (such as Hobbes) would have claimed is satisfied by
a suitably abstract conception of observable mechanical processes, and
which the anti-dogmatic or sceptical naturalistic mechanist (such as Locke)
would have claimed is at best only partially satisfied by any conception of
ours of any process. There is no obvious sign that Hume's account of this
notion is ironical or hostile. Here the argument continues:

> Now nothing is more evident, than that the human mind cannot form
> such an idea of two objects, as to conceive any connexion betwixt them, or
> comprehend distinctly that power or efficacy, by which they are united.[61]

---

[59] Ibid., marginal sec. 57.

[60] D. Hume, A *Treatise of Human Nature* 1.3.14. Cf. *Enquiry* 7.1, marginal sec. 50: /
"were the power or energy of any cause discoverable by the mind, we could foresee the
effect, even without experience; and might, at first, pronounce with certainty concerning it, by mere dint of thought and reasoning." / Compare too the well-known passage
in Locke's *Essay*, 4.3.25: / "I doubt not but if we could discover the Figure, Size, Texture,
and Motion of the minute Constituent parts of any two Bodies, we should know without
Trial several of their Operations one upon another, as we now do the Properties of a
Square, or a Triangle."

[61] Ibid., marginal sec. 52.

This looks like what might be called an extreme Lockean scepticism.[62] At any rate, in the *Enquiry* it is by applying just this mechanistic conception of intelligibility to volition that Hume finds it no exception to the rule:

> if by consciousness we perceived any power or energy in the will, we must know this power; we must know its connexion with the effect; we must know the secret union of soul and body, and the nature of both these substances.[63]

The (not particularly persuasive) claim is that, as in all other cases, we are reliant on "experience" of observable conjunctions for our belief in, and indeed our idea of, our own power. Our belief that our thoughts are having an effect on the world, our subjective sense of our own agency, is as much a result of custom and habit as any other causal belief. It is difficult to see how this argument could have had force for Hume, if he in fact rejected the mechanist ideal of intelligibility which is stated as its premise.

Conclusion

Our interpretation of historic philosophical arguments and theories tends both to determine, and to be determined by, our view of particular philosophical issues. The philosophical issue of laws *versus* natures, regularity *versus* necessity, has throughout the twentieth century been colored by a standard reading of Hume's argument together with standard assumptions about the "rationalism" which he was opposing and the "empiricism" which he was allegedly making more rigorous or consistent. The inadequacy of this view of Hume's purposes and achievement has begun to emerge in the last ten years or so. Whether or not the new interpretation of Hume as a "sceptical realist" is satisfactory as so far presented, its very possibility has brought into prominence features of his argument which had previously been more or less ignored. It is unlikely that we shall do them justice or settle the issue of Hume's intentions except in the context of a detailed and structured account of the positions and controversies to which he was responding. John Wright has drawn attention to the influence on Hume of

---

62   Contrast ibid., marginal sec. 50 ("We only find, that the one does actually, in fact, follow the other. The impulse of one billiard-ball is attended with motion in the second") with *Essay* 2.8.11 (" . . . impulse, the only way which we can conceive Bodies operate in") and other passages in which Locke allows at least a dim comprehension of mechanical processes (e.g. 2.4.1 and 5, and 4.3.13).

63   Ibid., Marginal sec. 52.

some earlier theories of the imagination and imaginative belief, including mad belief. In considering Hume's error theory of both everyday and philosophical beliefs, it is unsurprisingly illuminating to consider the theories of error with which he was familiar. Similarly, it will hardly be possible to enter usefully into the question of Hume's attitude towards "the true manner of conceiving of a particular power" without also investigating seventeenth-century mechanism and voluntarism, theories to which he openly alludes. If we want to know where Hume stood, it is important to keep in mind when he stood there.

COMMON SENSIBLES AND COMMON SENSE IN LOCKE AND BERKELEY

Geneviève Brykman

An observation about Aristotle could well be applied to Locke and Berkeley. In Aristotle's development of the notion of "common sense," there is a blind spot: Aristotle provides no elucidation whatever of how "common sense" passed from meaning a sensing faculty common to several senses to meaning something like common rationality,[1] the only meaning it retains today. I shall here leave aside the use of "common sense" to mean "common rationality." That use of the term, to be sure, is—practically speaking—strongly entrenched in the thinking of both Locke and Berkeley, and will later be taken as basic by the Scottish "common-sense philosophers." But I shall here confine my attention to the role played by "common sense" in the compass of external sensory experience, a compass in which both Locke and Berkeley developed an original ontology and epistemology.

I

If we stick to the search for a *koine aisthesis*, we shall see that Locke establishes, in various ways, that "common sense," considered as a faculty capable of synthesizing impressions got from several senses, can be dispensed with. Nonetheless he maintains, in a tradition that can be traced back to *De Anima*, the existence of "common sensibles." As for Berkeley, denying even the existence of "common sensibles," he has no need at all for a faculty of "common sense:" he finds the unifying principle of sensory data in experience itself. So the "common sense" of my title will paradoxically turn out to be a thing not to be found.

Is there, according to Locke, a sensory faculty common to several senses? To answer this question, we have to go back to the early sections of

---

[1]   Aristotle. *De Anima* 3.1–5; *De Interpretatione* 16a.

the *Essay 2*, which, in the account of "ideas of sensation,"[2] draws the
essential distinction between primary and secondary qualities, the ideas of
both kinds of qualities being there understood to be effects of qualities
themselves. Locke offers an analysis of ideas of sensation that provides
Boyle's corpuscularian philosophy with the atomistic epistemology it calls
for.[3] What Locke argues for, as early as chapter 2, is the existence of simple
ideas of sensation that are the building blocks of our knowledge of the
external world. He recognizes that "though the Qualities that affect our
Senses, are, in the things themselves, so united and blended, that there is
no separation, no distance between them; yet 'tis plain, the Ideas they
produce in the Mind, enter by the Senses simple and unmixed" (2.2.1).
Where and how, then, is this synthesis of simple ideas effected?

A little further along, we learn that our ideas of primary qualities
resemble these qualities, whereas our ideas of secondary qualities are wholly
relative to the power of the primary qualities to produce them in our sense
organs (2.8). But Locke's philosophy puts primary stress on the necessity,
in an examination of human knowledge, of a radical analysis that issues in
the simple idea as the atom of knowledge. For, Locke tells us,

> though the Sight and Touch often take in from the same Object, at the
> same time, different Ideas; as a Man sees at once Motion and Colour; the
> Hand feels Softness and Warmth in the same piece of Wax: Yet the simple
> Ideas thus united in the same Subject, are as perfectly distinct, as those
> that come in by different Senses. The coldness and hardness, which a Man
> feels in a piece of Ice, being as distinct Ideas in the Mind, as the Smell
> and Whiteness of a Lily; or as the taste of Sugar, and smell of a Rose: And
> there is nothing can be plainer to a Man, than the clear and distinct
> Perception he has of those simple Ideas; which being each in it self un-
> compounded, contains in it nothing but one uniform Appearance, or Con-
> ception in the mind, and is not distinguishable into different Ideas (2.2.1).

When Locke has finished with this resolution of the datum into its simple
components, it must be acknowledged that he hardly poses the question

---

[2] J. Locke, *Essay* 2.1.2: "In that [experience], all our Knowledge is founded; and from that
it ultimately derives itself. Our Observation employ'd either about external, sensible
Objects; or about the internal Operations of our Minds, perceived and reflected on by
ourselves, is that, which supplies our Understandings with all the materials of thinking."
And 2.1.4: "These two, I say, viz., External, Material things, as the Objects of SENSATION;
and the operations of our own Minds within, as the Objects of REFLECTION, are, to
me, the only Originals, from whence all our Ideas take their beginnings."

[3] P. Alexander, "Boyle and Locke on Primary and Secondary Qualities," in *Locke on
Human Understanding*, ed. I. C. Tipton (Oxford: Oxford University Press, 1977).

how the synthesis of sensible ideas is carried out. After analysis of our experience as a whole, simple ideas are presented as the irreducible components of our knowledge; and Locke, setting out an imaginary genesis of this knowledge, posits that the understanding, once furnished with simple ideas, has the power to repeat, compare and unite them (Essay 2.2.2). Experience presents itself as a continuum of simple ideas of sensation and reflection, even if the corresponding physical and mental realities, taken in themselves and apart from appearances, are discrete. Thus, Locke attributes to the understanding, without emphasising it, the faculty of reproducing, comparing and uniting simple ideas, presupposing the *resemblance* of the ideas of primary qualities to those qualities. But the understanding is not sensory in origin and so cannot be considered a "common sense."

In a spirit that seems directly inspired by Aristotle's *De Anima* (425a–427c), Locke adds that—although it is not impossible for God to make a creature with different senses or with more than the five senses a human being ordinarily has—we are not capable of imagining or knowing a sensory experience that differs from our own: we cannot imagine bodies' having qualities other than those conveyed to us by hearing, taste, smell, sight and touch (*Essay* 2.2.3.) And if man had been dealt but four senses, the qualities that are the object of the fifth sense would have been as much beyond our imagining and knowledge as are the qualities that belong to the sixth, seventh, or eighth sense we must suppose possible in other beings (*Essay* 2.2.3). In the same vein, Locke ends chapter 2, on simple ideas, with a touch of scepticism. He observes,

> He that will not set himself proudly at the top of all things, but will consider the Immensity of this Fabrick, and the great variety, that is to be found in this little and inconsiderable part of it, which he has to do with, may be apt to think, that in other Mansions of it, there may be other, and different intelligent Beings, of whose Faculties, he has as little Knowledge or Apprehension, as a Worm shut up in one drawer of a Cabinet, hath of the Senses or Understanding of a Man . . . .' Locke admits: "I have here followed the common Opinion of Man's having but five Senses; though, perhaps, there may be justly counted more . . . " (2.2.3).

A note Pierre Coste appends to the French translation of this passage makes it obvious that what Locke was alluding to here was not a possible "common sense" whose task is the perception of common sensibles. Coste suggests that it is instead—as Montaigne puts it,[4] and as accords with Aristotle's

---

4 The passage of Montaigne (*Essais* 2.2.12) cited by Coste: "La première considération que j'ai sur le sujet des sens, est que je mets en doute que l'homme soit pourvu de tous

argument—a matter of recognizing that none of our senses lets us imagine or know what a different sense could do, nor lets us deny the possibility of another sense by which we could perceive what we, in our present condition, are wholly ignorant of.[5]

The inventory offered, in chapter 3, of different simple ideas, wherein Locke classifies the several kinds of simple ideas of sensation, somewhat advances our understanding of the matter. Four categories are presented:

1) ideas that come into our minds by one sense only,
2) ideas that come into the mind by more senses than one,
3) ideas that are had from reflection only, and
4) ideas that are suggested to the mind by all the ways of sensation and reflection.

The third category—simple ideas from reflection—can be left aside. But in the fourth, one might be tempted to see in the expression "all the ways of sensation and reflection," the locus par excellence of a common sense. Locke here gives, as different simple ideas, some unitary experiences: pleasure or pain (uneasiness); power; existence; unity (2.7.1). But instead of what Locke calls ideas, can we substitute the more synthetic notion of consciousness? Then the concept of common sense would have a change of tenor. We would no longer be dealing with the *koine aisthesis*, but with the experience of the *internal sense*[6] that is at once *conatus*, succession, and unity.

---

les sens naturels. Je vois plusieurs animaux qui vivent une vie entière et parfaite, les uns sans la vue, les autres sans l'ouie; qui sait si a nous aussi il ne nous manque pas encore un, deux, trois ou plusieurs autres sens? Car s'il en manque quelqu'un, notre discours ne peut en découvrir le defaut. C'est le privilège des sens d'être l'extrême borne de notre apercevance; il n'y a rien au-dela d'eux qui puisse nous servir a les découvrir: voire ni l'un des sens ne peut découvrir l'autre [. .]. Nous saisissons la pomme quasi par tous nos sens: nous y trouverons de la rougeur, de la polissure, de l'odeur et de la douceur; outre cela, elle peut avoir d'autres vertus, comme d'assècher ou de restreindre, auxquelles nous n'avons point de sens qui se puisse rapporter. Les propriétés que nous appelons occultes en plusieurs choses, comme l'aimant d'attirer le fer, n'est-il pas vraisemblable qu'il y a des facultés sensitives propres a les juger et a les percevoir, et que le défaut de telles facultés nous apporte l'ignorance de la vraie essence de telles choses?"

[5]   Berkeley does not do Locke justice when he remarks, in the *Philosophical Commentaries*: "Incongruous in Locke to fancy we want a sense proper to see substances withal" (601); or, "There is a Philosopher who says we can get an idea of substance by no way of Sensation or Reflection. & seems to imagine that we want a sense proper for it. Truly if we had a new sense it could only give us a new Idea" (724).

[6]   Locke incidentally uses "internal sense" to designate the experience each man has of the succession of ideas of reflection, and this experience, he says, is formed by analogy

As for the unity of the outer sensible world, Locke, as we have seen, gave to the understanding a power to synthesize simple ideas.[7]

To the indication—very slight indeed—of this synthetic power of the understanding in the *Essay*, must be added two other presuppositions that somewhat complicate the answer to my initial question: (1) the power of primary qualities and (2) the power of sight to explore the data of the other senses.

1) It is in the first two categories of simple ideas cited above that Locke remains most faithful to Aristotles's inquiry in *De Anima*. In the same way that, for Aristotle, there are "proper sensibles" and "common sensibles," there are, for Locke, ideas proper to one sense alone and ideas common to several senses. The two philosophers agree in saying that sensible ideas or 'proper sensibles' are correlated with the five sense organs considered as independent of one another. About what makes a community of certain sensibles and the perception we have of them, Locke gives an original explanation, one resting on Boyle's description of reality that puts into play the distinction between primary and secondary qualities. It is not because we are endowed with a common sense that we can perceive by sight and touch together something's size and shape: It is because the material things themselves objectively have a shape, a size, solidity and mobility, that we perceive them as having such, by several modes of sensation. Here, let us recall that Locke describes the ideas of primary qualities as resembling those qualities (2.8.15); so that if the shape I feel and the shape I see each resembles the shape of the external object, these two shapes—that seen and that felt—will resemble each other; and there is every reason to think that we will speak of them as a single shape and ignore the several different sensory means by which we perceive them. It is thus not the existence of a common sense, but the very nature of the primary qualities, and the fundamental presupposition of a resemblance between our ideas and the qualities themselves, that accounts for our impression of a unity in the object and of a regularity of the world. Here is the "empiricist" dimension of Locke's theory of knowledge, an empiricism that holds its own with the understanding's power of synthesis noted above.

2) By the question he put to Locke, Molyneux opened yet another way that seems to have proved an impasse for Locke. Could Locke still believe

---

with external experience: "This Source of Ideas, every Man has wholly in himself: And though it be not Sense, as having nothing to do with external Objects; yet it is very like it, and might properly enough be call'd internal Sense" (2.1.4).

[7] See note 1, above, and *Essay* 2.2.2.

that color and light are not the only objects perceived by sight? Could shape-as-seen and shape-as-felt be spoken of as if the primary qualities were really common to the two senses? Conceding that the ideas that come to us by the senses are often changed by judgment (2.9.8), Locke ingeniously brings up the problem Molyneux put to him:

> Suppose a Man born blind, and now adult, and taught by his touch to distinguish between a Cube, and a Sphere of the same metal, and nighly of the same bigness, so as to tell, when he felt one and t'other, which is the Cube, which the Sphere. Suppose then the Cube and Sphere placed on a Table, and the Blind Man to be made to see. Quaere, Whether by his sight, before he touch'd them, he could now distinguish, and tell, which is the Globe, which the Cube.

Following Molyneux, Locke answers in the negative, without much consideration of his previous discussion, which had been more favorable to a sort of *priori* activity by the understanding:

> I agree with this thinking Gent. whom I am proud to call my Friend, in his answer to this his Problem; and am of opinion, that the Blind Man, at first sight, would not be able with certainty to say, which was the Globe, which the Cube, whilst he only saw them: though he could unerringly name them by his touch (2.9.8).

Locke thus introduces a development about the synthetic capacities of the organ of sight that is worthy of Malebranche and his analysis of "natural judgments:" sight is the most synthetic but, at the same time, the most deceiving of all our senses (2.9.9). So,

> because Sight, the most comprehensive of all our Senses, conveying to our minds the ideas of Light and Colours, which are peculiar only to that Sense; and also the far different Ideas of Space, Figure, and Motion, the several varieties whereof change the appearances of its proper Object, viz. Light and Colours, we bring ourselves by use, to judge of the one by the other.

Here, it is sight that does the work of a common sense, without Locke ever expressly according it such a function.

II

Berkeley's *Essay towards a New Theory of Vision* has its source in precisely this passage. Locke draws a comparison between the data of sight and the signs that are perceived by someone who reads or hears a message.[8] On this point, Berkeley had every reason to say that he was, in relation to Locke, as a pigmy to a giant (*Commentaries*, 678). This is just where Berkeley stands in the comparison for he took, as his jumping-off point, Locke's comparison of the givens of sight to a message read or heard. From Locke's plain comparison of the objects of sight to a language, these objects will become, with Berkeley, a genuine language: and the common sensibles maintained by Locke will, with the collapse of the distinction between primary and secondary qualities, disappear.

1) Throughout his work, Berkeley will be strictly faithful to the thesis of the heterogeneity of the sensible series, relating each to one of our five sense organs. This is what, in particular, he recalls to his correspondant in his *Theory of Vision Vindicated*, in twice calling to his attention (*T.V.V.* 15 & 41) that the opinion that there are common sensibles was what the *New Theory of Vision* was directed against. And he observes that the thesis of the heterogeneity of objects of sight and objects of touch was really the pillar of his own theory.[9] One could go further and say that the heterogeneity thesis is the keystone of his immaterialist ontology.

An avid reader of Bayle's *Dictionaire*, Berkeley had found, in the articles *Pyrrhon* and *Zénon*, that primary qualities were not to be treated differently

---

[8] *Essay* 2.9.8; & 2.9.9: "Because Sight, the most comprehensive of all our Senses, conveying to our Minds the Ideas of Light and Colours, which are peculiar only to that Sense; and also the far different Ideas of Space, Figure, and Motion, the several varieties whereof change the appearances of its proper Object . . . we bring our selves by use, to judge of the one by the other. This . . . in things whereof we have frequent experience, is performed so constantly and so quick, that we take that for the Perception of our Sensation, which is an Idea formed by our Judgment; so that one, viz., that of Sensation, serves only to excite the other, and is scarce taken notice of it self; as a Man who reads or hears with attention and understanding, takes little notice of the Characters, or Sounds, but of the Ideas, that are excited in him by them."

[9] *T.V.V.* 41: "As to light, and its several modes or colours, all thinking men are agreed that they are ideas peculiar only to sight; neither common to the touch, nor of the same kind with any that are perceived by that sense. But herein lies the mistake, that, beside these, there are supposed other ideas common to both senses, being equally perceived by sight and touch, such as extension, size, figure, and motion. But that there are in reality no such common ideas, and that the objects of sight, marked by those words, are intirely different and heterogeneous from whatever is the object of feeling, marked by the same names, hath been proved in the Theory, and seems by you admitted. Though I cannot conceive how you should in reason admit this, and at the same time contend for the received theories, which are as much ruined as mine is established by this main part and pillar thereof."

from secondary qualities.[10] Bayle observed (*Pyrrhon*, Remarque B) that the "new philosophers"—the cartesians—used a language still more positive (that is, more radical) than the ancient pyrrhonists:

> Personne, parmi les bons philosophes, ne doute plus que les sceptiques n'aient raison de soutenir que les qualities des corps qui frappent nos sens ne sont que des apparences [. . .] la chaleur, l'odeur, les couleurs, etc. . . ne sont point dans les objets de nos sens; ce sont des modifications de mon âme; je sais que les corps ne sont point tels qu'ils me paraissent. On aurait bien voulu en excepter l'étendue et le mouvement, mais on n'a pas pu; car si les objets de sens nous paraissent colorés, chauds, froids, odorants, encore qu'ils ne le soient pas, pourquoi ne pourraient-ils point paraître étendus et figurés, en repos et en mouvement, quoiqu'ils n'eussent rien de tel?"[11]

In the *Dictionaire* Berkeley had likewise found something to shore up his understanding of Locke (*Essay* 2.23), by his reading of Malebranche and Nicole, holding, as they did, that our eyes are "natural glasses" and that the recent use of microscopes no longer allowed us to know whether extension as it appears to us corresponds to a real extension.[12] The *Philosophical Commentaries*—in particular Notebook B—show the decisive importance, for Berkeley, of the ontological and epistemological consequences that can be drawn from microscopic observations.[13] Malebranche and Locke hold

---

[10]   On the immaterialism of these articles, see G. Brykman, *Berkeley, philosophie et apologétique* (Paris: Vrin, 1984), 75–85.

[11]   Bayle, recalling in a note that Simon Foucher had proposed this objection to Malebranche, continues: "Le Père Malebranche n'y repondit pas. Il en sentit bien la force."

[12]   Locke, *Essay* 2.23, and Malebranche, *Recherche de la verité* 1.6 Bayle's "Zénon" (Remarque G) gives full treatment to this chapter of the Recherche, which corresponds to the observations of the "Messieurs de Port-Royal" that he recalls thus: "Il n'y a qu'a considérer que si tout le monde n'avait jamais regardé les objets exterieurs qu'avec des lunettes qui les grossissent, il est certain qu'on ne se serait figuré les corps et toutes les mesures des corps que selon la grandeur dans laquelle ils nous auraient ete representés par ces lunettes. Or nos yeux mêmes sont des lunettes, et nous ne savons point précisement s'ils ne diminuent point ou n'augmentent point les objets que nous voyons. . . . On ne sait point aussi si nous voyons de la même grandeur que les autres hommes; car encore que deux personnes, les mesurant, conviennent ensemble qu'un certain corps n'a, par exemple, que cinq pieds, néanmoins, ce que l'un concoit par un pied n'est peut-être pas ce que l'autre conçoit: car l'un conçoit ce que ses yeux lui rapportent; et un autre de même; or peut-etre que les yeux de l'un ne lui rapportent pas la même chose que les yeux des autres leur représentent, parce que ce sont des lunettes autrement taillées."

[13]   *Philosophical Commentaries* 63: "Ignorance of Glasses made men think extension to be in bodies"; 91: "Qu: whether if (speaking grosly) the things we see were all of them

that size is wholly relative. Beyond this relativity, the microscope shows, according to Berkeley, that there is no common measure nor any common nature between the data of sight and touch.

In this matter Bayle again may have pointed the the way to immaterialism: the *Dictionaire* showed the young Berkeley that he could take for his own some observations of Sextus Empiricus. Sextus, explaining the third trope by which the ancient sceptics attempted to lead us to the suspension of judgment, supplies the thesis that will be the "pillar" of Berkeley's whole work: the heterogeneity of data of the senses.[14] The third trope rests, says Sextus, upon "the diversity of our sense organs." By all evidence, he argues, the senses are different.

> So, to sight, a picture seems to present hollows and protrusions; to the touch, it does not. Honey is pleasing to the tongue of some, but unpleasant to their eye. Likewise, perfume: it pleases the sense of smell but is disagreeable to the taste.

This paves the way for the thesis of the heterogeneity of the sense organs. And Berkeley found as well in Sextus the thesis of their relativity, which were to be used by Montaigne, Malebranche and Locke. For Sextus continued with the paradigmatic example of an apple, a traditional figure in the sceptical argument:[15] "Each of the sensations that comes to us seems to present itself to our senses in different ways," Sextus recalls; "an apple to us is smooth, has a good smell, is sweet and yellow; but clearly we do not know whether an apple has only these qualities." Sextus adds that it might have others, or else might have only a single quality that our sense organs make an erroneous analysis of, and this leads him to a view freely developed after the invention of eyeglasses:

> Let us imagine a man who had, since birth, the sense of touch and of taste but not hearing and sight. This man will believe that there is nothing perceivable by sight and hearing, and that there are only the three sorts of qualities that can be perceived.

---

too small to be felt we should have confounded tangible & visible extension & figure?" On Berkeley's particular interest in microscopes, see Geneviève Brykman, "Microscopes and Philosophical Method in Berkeley," in *Berkeley: Critical and Interpretive Essays*, ed. C. Turbayne (Minneapolis: University of Minnesota Press, 1979), 69–82.

[14] Sextus Empiricus, *Outlines of Pyrrhonism* 1.14.

[15] See Berkeley, *Principles* 1, Sec. 1. Berkeley, who reduces "things" to collections of sensible ideas, uses the example of the apple but is always careful to underscore its dubious pedigree. He had to fight against scepticism by turning the adversary's weapons against him.

For Berkeley, the way was clearly marked: "to be is to be perceived," on the one hand, and, on the other, the data of the senses are heterogeneous in that the five sense organs are not commensurable with each other.

2) Molyneux's blind man, like the heterogeneity thesis, runs through the whole of the *N.T.V.* So one may be surprised to see that not until section 132 does Berkeley explicitly cite the passage of the *Essay* about the blind man made to see (2.9.8).[16] The observations above seem to say that, to establish an immaterialist ontology, the young Berkeley relied on sources other than this blind man, still hypothetical in 1709, and that the heterogeneity thesis does not depend wholly on him. But Berkeley, having shown that we do not perceive distance by sight, and having at the same time established that the data of sight reduce to patches of light and color, considers that establishing what is involved in perceiving size and location is helpful in circumscribing the proper objects of sight. However, the root of the matter for immaterialism is already planted in sections 41–45 of the work, and all Berkeley's other observations pertaining to the optical controversies of his time, go back to this original ontology. Thus he says, at the end of the examination of distance perception, that

> From what hath been premised it is a manifest consequence that a man born blind, being made to see, would at first have no idea of distance by sight; the sun and stars, the remotest objects as well as the nearer, would all seem to be in his eye, or rather in his mind. The objects intromitted by sight would seem to him (as in truth they are) no other than a new set of thoughts or sensations, each whereof is as near to him as the perceptions of pain or pleasure, or the most inward passions of his soul (Sec. 41).

However, Berkeley remarks, the supposition common to writers on optics is that men judge distance by the angle of the optic axes, just as a blind man can judge it by the angle of two sticks held one in each hand; and this supposition would lead to the admission that a man born blind would have need of no new experience to perceive distance by means of sight (Sec. 42).

In all this, Berkeley seems essentially to be attacking geometrical optics. He has, however, a more ambitious metaphysical objective, which is openly displayed only in the very last part of the *N.T.V.* As he himself suggests,

---

16   M. Atherton, *Berkeley's Revolution in Vision* (London: Cornell University Press, 1990), chap. 10.

when he announces the plan of this work,[17] his final aim was to refute the most current opinion of the writers on optics: that common sensibles exist. This is why he returns to it more directly in the last part, recalling *in extenso* the passage in Locke about the blind man made to see. This time he does not directly use the blind man to support the *N.T.V.*, but to underscore that Locke and Molyneux, given their ontological presuppositions, really have no right to respond negatively to the question Molyneux raised. They took it that the objects of sight and touch differed only numerically, when they must in fact be different in kind.[18] It might be said that the distinction Berkeley makes (*N.T.V.* 132) between the "numerically distinct" and the "specifically distinct" is not altogether clear.[19] And it should be said that his earlier argument that the data of sight and touch are numerically different was already a way of showing that they are specifically different. The data of touch present themselves in three-dimensional space—that measured by the motions of our body,[20] whereas the data of sight, which

---

[17] *N.T.V.* 1: "My design is to shew the manner wherein we perceive by sight the distance, magnitude, and situation of objects. Also to consider the difference there is betwixt the ideas of sight and touch, and whether there be any idea common to both senses."

[18] *N.T.V.* 131: "It is, I think, an axiom universally received that quantities of the same kind may be added together and make one intire sum. . . . Now let any one try in his thoughts to add a visible line or surface to a tangible line or surface, so as to conceive them making one continued sum or whole. He that can do this may think them homogeneous: but he that cannot, must by the foregoing axiom think them heterogeneous . . . ." In Section 132, Berkeley cites at length the passage in the Essay about Molyneux's blind man, and in section 133 goes on: "Now, if a square surface perceived by touch be of the same sort with a square surface perceived by sight, it is certain the blind man here mentioned might know a square surface as soon as he saw it: It is no more but introducing into his mind by a new inlet an idea he has been already well acquainted with. Since, therefore, he is supposed to have known by his touch that a cube is a body terminated by square surfaces, and that a sphere is not terminated by square surfaces: upon the supposition that a visible and tangible square differ only in numero it follows that he might know, by the unerring mark of the square surfaces, which was the cube, and which not, while he only saw them. We must therefore allow either that visible extension and figures are specifically distinct from tangible extension and figures, or else that the solution of this problem given by those two thoughtful and ingenious men is wrong."

[19] On this problem in the *N.T.V.*, it is fruitful to consult the harsh but thought-provoking commentary of D. M. Armstrong, *Berkeley's Theory of Vision* (Melbourne: Melbourne University Press, 1960), 23–28.

[20] *N.T.V.* 45: "Whoever will look narrowly into his own thoughts and examine what he means by saying he sees this or that thing at a distance, will agree with me that what he

are only coloured patches—not even "surfaces"—are always only two-dimensional, neither flat nor raised: in the conceptual apparatus of the *N.T.V.*, they correspond to a certain number of visible points on the visual field, metaphorically called "extension," after proper extension, which is tangible extension. In the *N.T.V.*, what is basic is the affirmation of heterogeneity of sense data and, before section 132, it is already implied that there are no common sensibles. The last part is only another way of arguing more directly against common sensibles, with a means proper to Berkeley's philosophy (a means Berkeley had just discovered): the critique of abstract ideas. The major ontological conclusion consists in the affirmation that the apparent connection between the given of sight and of touch, although regular, is not at all necessary: the objects of sight are the language that Nature (or God) uses to inform our eyes about the objects of touch (Secs. 59, 140, 142–44, 147, 152). The image Locke uses in comparing the perception of the tangible by the visible to the words of a language (*Essay* 2.9.9) is, at this very place, transformed by Berkeley into a real language by which God speaks to us through Nature.[21] Though Berkeley had started by saying that he was, in relation to his predecessor, as a pigmy is to a giant, he developed from a modest analogy of Locke's, altogether original ontology.

A question remains: how the divine language is acquired by men, and what the faculty required in this acquisition is. In other words, what exactly is the nature of these quick shifts from sight to touch that make us believe that the objects seen have the dimension of depth outside of ourselves? Here is a problem that finds no solution in the *N.T.V.* and seems not to have much bothered Berkeley: on the one hand, up to section 41, he keeps on declaring that these shifts between sight and touch are "entirely the result of experience" (Secs. 20, 41); on the other, he asserts later in the *N.T.V.*

---

sees only suggests to his understanding that after having passed a certain distance, to be measured by the motion of his body, which is perceivable by touch, he shall come to perceive such and such tangible ideas which have been usually connected with such and such visible ideas." Some corresponding passages, on this organization of space by its relationship to the perceiving subject's own body, are to be found in *Principles*, secs. 3, 44, 58.

[21]   *N.T.V.* 147: "Upon the whole, I think we may fairly conclude that the proper objects of vision constitute the (an) universal language of (the Author of) nature, whereby we are instructed how to regulate our actions in order to attain those things that are necessary to the preservation and well-being of our bodies, as also to avoid whatever may be hurtful and destructive of them." *N.T.V.* 152: "Hence it is that the voice of (the Author of) nature, which speaks to our eyes, is not liable to the misinterpretation and ambiguity that languages of human contrivance are unavoidably subject to." (I have put in parentheses the words added in 1732.) See also *Alciphron* 4, secs. 11–12.

(66, 74, 126), then in the *T.V.V.* (50–52), that such shifts are the fruit of "suddain suggestions of fancy." Finally, one cannot fail to note the various indications that attribute a power of suggestion to visual ideas themselves, according to a conception not elaborated by Berkeley, that tends to unsettle the dualism usually imputed to him of the activity of spirits and the passivity of ideas.[22] Leaving these problems unresolved for the present, we can say that, for Berkeley, it is the relative stability of the divine language that plays the part of a "common sense."[23]

---

[22] G. Brykman, "Passivité des esprits et passivité des idees dans l'immaterialisme de Berkeley," *Bulletin de la Societe Francaise de Philosophie*, (Jan.-Mar. 1986).

[23] We cannot dogmatically say that God's creation will last as it is: "By a diligent observation of the phenomena within our view, we may discover the general laws of Nature, and from them deduce the other phenomena, I do not say demonstrate; for all deductions of that kind depend on a supposition that the Author of Nature always operates uniformly, and in a constant observance of those rules we take for principles: which we cannot evidently know" (*Principles*, sec. 107).

Note: All my thanks to Katherine McCracken for the kind help she gave in translating this paper (published in *Revue de Métaphysique et Morale*, Octobre, 1991).

Abstraction and Representation in Locke, Berkeley and Hume

M. A. Stewart

I

In seventeenth– and eighteenth–century philosophy, an abstract idea is typically an idea that has been abs-tracted in something close to the etymological sense, that is, drawn off or separated out from an idea that was initially not abstract, or was at least less abstract. Thus Locke defines abstraction as the separating of ideas "from all other *Ideas* that accompany them in their real existence," and speaks of an abstract idea as "removed in our Thoughts from particular Existence, (that being the proper Operation of the Mind, in Abstraction, to consider an *Idea* under no other Existence, but what it has in the Understanding)" (*Essay*, 2.12.1; 4.9.1).[1] Abstraction as separation is possible only where there are other attendant ideas from which to separate. Although we can form abstract simple ideas, we cannot form them by abstracting *from* simple ideas, but only by abstracting from a multiplicity.[2]

---

[1] For references to standard authors and direct quotations from them, the following editions are used: J. Locke, *An Essay concerning Human Understanding*, ed. P. H. Nidditch (Oxford: Clarendon Press, 1975); G. Berkeley, *Manuscript Introduction*, ed. B. Belfrage (Oxford: Doxa, 1987); id., *Works*, 9 vols., ed. A. A. Luce and T. E. Jessop (Edinburgh: Nelson, 1948–57); D. Hume, *A Treatise of Human Nature*, ed. L. A. Selby-Bigge, rev. P. H. Nidditch (Oxford: Clarendon Press, 1978); id., *Enquiries concerning Human Understanding and concerning the Principles of Morals*, ed. L. A. Selby-Bigge, rev. P. H. Nidditch (Oxford: Clarendon Press, 1975).

[2] In Locke there is a three-step sequence: one first distinguishes, then compares, then abstracts (2.11.12). Descartes was speaking of abstraction in a different sense when he spoke of the concept of limit as something "more general" but not "simpler" than shape, and as "compounded" out of a number of different simple natures, shape being one (*Regulae* 12, in *Oeuvres de Descartes*, 11 vols., ed. C. Adam and P. Tannery (Paris: Vrin, 1974–83), 10. 418–19). This is the process Pierre Gassendi called "aggregation" and distinguished from abstraction. The same process is at work in forming the "simple," or indefinable, idea of color from the ideas of green, blue, red, etc.

One route through which abstract ideas come into early modern philosophy is through Cartesianism. Descartes wrote in *Regulae*, at rule 13:

> We can abstract a problem which is well understood from every irrelevant conception and reduce it to such a form that we are no longer aware of dealing with this or that subject-matter but only with certain magnitudes in general and the comparison between them (AT 10. 431, trans. Cottingham et al.).

Algebra is a study in which abstraction, so conceived, is endemic; and just as "problems" can be abstracted, so can specific ideas.

> Thus, when I consider a shape without thinking of the substance or the extension whose shape it is, I make a mental abstraction. I can easily recognize this abstraction afterwards when I look to see whether I have derived the idea of pure shape from some richer idea within myself, to which it is joined in such a way that although one can think of the one without paying any attention to the other, it is impossible to deny one of the other when one thinks of both together. (To Gibieuf, AT 3. 472, trans. Kenny.)

The seventeenth century could have known Descartes's position through *Replies to Objections*, 1 and 5, and *Principles of Philosophy*, 1.61–2. But their main source for a Cartesian theory of abstract ideas would have been book 1 of the Port-Royal *Logic*. Here it is even plainer that the separation involved is a mental artifice. That which is considered apart in thought does not exist separately in reality, neither do we suppose it does. We have no difficulty in considering the length of a line or road without also considering its width, but we do not suppose it has no width.

> In the same way, having drawn on paper an equilateral triangle, if I confine myself to the consideration of it in the place where it is, with all the accidents which determine it, I shall have the idea of *that triangle alone*; but if I detach my mind from the consideration of all these particular circumstances, and consider only that it is a figure bounded by three equal lines, the idea which I form of it will, on the one hand, represent to me more accurately that equality of lines; and, on the other, will be able to represent to me *all equilateral triangles*. And if, not restricting myself to that equality of lines, but proceeding further, I consider only that it is a figure bounded by three right lines, I shall form an idea which will represent *all kinds of triangles*. If, again, not confining myself to the number of lines, I simply consider that it is a plane surface, bounded by right lines, the idea which I form will represent all rectilineal figures; and thus, step by step, I am able to ascend to *extension itself*. (*Logic*, 1.5, trans. Baynes)

Though the etymology is still genuinely assumed, its application is from an early date metaphorical. Abstraction becomes a form of selective attention to one or more aspects of something more complex; and the role of what is selectively considered—whether it be the whole or the selected parts—is to "represent" all those things of which the selected features are joint aspects, thereby making "the ideas of singular things become common."

Cartesian abstraction involves a distinction of reason, not of imagination. There is also a Gassendist tradition. Everything that affects our senses, says Gassendi, is particular, but we do not have enough individual names to go round. We therefore form general ideas, which we can do in either of two ways.

One is by aggregation. We form the idea of a collection of similar things to which we apply the same name. Where an aggregation of species forms a genus, there is a combining of differences, illustrated from the Tree of Porphyry. The general idea of *animal* collects together the ideas both of rational and of brute being; that of *living thing* collects the ideas both of animal and plant; that of *body* collects the ideas both of living thing and of inanimate thing; and so on, progressively, to the most general (and non-Porphyrian) idea of *being*.

His other route to general ideas is by abstraction. This involves separating out the common features of similar things and forming an idea of those, discarding the details in which they diverge. The result, in the case of *man*, is an idea which represents not this, that or the other man, but man "in general or in common." And although the imagination may not be able to form an idea of man who is neither large, small nor middling, neither young, old nor in between, neither black, white nor any other color, etc., the *mind* can avoid such discriminations (*Institutio Logica*, 1.4–8).[3]

Locke seems to have come to this or other comparable literature quite late. He was to be disparaging about "this whole *mystery* of *Genera* and *Species*, which make such a noise in the Schools" (*Essay*, 3.3.9). In the extensive discussion of definition and of the imperfection and abuse of words in Draft B, sections 64–93, the language of "abstraction" is plainly absent; but the concept might seem to be not far below the surface of sections 69, 73 and 91–2. He writes occasionally of ideas of our own compounding which "represent" many particulars (sections 69, 82, 83, 86), so the function that abstract ideas will go on to serve has already been identified. But once the abstracting mechanism is fully in place, in Draft C

---

[3] Howard Jones muffs this in his translation of Gassendi's *Institutio Logica* (Assen: Van Gorcum, 1981), 92, but in his introduction (li–liv) he notes Gassendi's distinction elsewhere between the roles of *phantasia/imaginatio* and of *intellectus/mens*.

and the final text, Locke too sets limits to our powers of actual mental separation. A distinction is possible, through "partial Consideration," between light and heat, but this should not be mistaken for separation; while motion cannot so much as be "conceived" without space, "and yet," he says, "Motion is not Space, nor Space Motion" (*Essay*, 2.13.13, 11).

But the concept of abstraction, without the attendant psychology of ideas, is much older. It goes back at least to Aristotle's account of mathematics as a study of the formal features of things abstracted from their matter (*Physics* 2.2, 193b). When abstraction comes to be tied in with the way of ideas in the seventeenth century, these ideas are conceived to be in some way representative—that is, presentational—of something beyond themselves;[4] so that abstract ideas are thought of as representative in some special or distinctive way. Their distinctive mode of representation is most often worked out in relation to debates on the origin and operation of language, out of a half-formed but none too clear conviction that, if we understood the workings of language, we would understand also something about human thought and, ultimately, about knowledge. Even if abstract ideas precede language, as Locke and others supposed, the main interest is in using an account of abstraction to show both how it is possible to acquire language, and how it is possible to use language once acquired. The account is also employed to explain what is going on in the minds of those who are actually using it, both as speakers and as hearers.

That a single doctrine should satisfy all these different needs—indeed, that there should be a homogeneous class of phenomena at all that constitute the media, vehicles and content of human thinking—is not plausible, and I shall not spend time trying to argue its merits or lack of them. What interests me here is the way that the debate about the existence and nature of abstract ideas enters into and affects the tradition of seventeenth– and eighteenth–century British and Irish philosophy; in particular, what happened between Locke and Hume, as a result of the intervention in the debate by Berkeley. In spite of the great burgeoning of English writing on language from John Wilkins to James Harris, the debate on abstraction and the nature of general ideas remains the preserve of the philosophers. In Berkeley and Hume the philosophical interest is quite profound, since both thought that the acceptance or rejection of Locke's account of the possibilities for abstraction had implications for metaphysics. But apart from Hume, only Chambers took much notice of Berkeley's critique until the time of Reid

---

[4] This was the common meaning of the Latin *repraesentare*—to manifest or present, and hence, to make present to the mind. On seventeenth-century English usage, see *Oxford English Dictionary*.

and Monboddo, and only they took much notice of Hume's. When textbook writers like Hutcheson and Duncan discussed abstraction, they by-passed both Berkeley and Hume, and followed the same tradition as Locke.[5]

II

In section 12 of the first *Enquiry*, Hume cites as an argument conducive to scepticism—this is scepticism with regard to the senses—Berkeley's argument that primary qualities cannot be conceived without secondary, and must, therefore, have the same mind dependence that secondary qualities allegedly have. Conception is here equivalent to imagination, and the attempt to imagine primary qualities independently of secondary is a case of misguided abstraction. We cannot do it because of the necessary determinateness of all ideas. Berkeley, Hume thinks, has hereby shown the notion of matter to be unintelligible—that is, beyond the reach of our ideas. But he does not see him as having refuted the existence of matter, which may still survive as "a certain unknown, inexplicable *something*, as the cause of our perceptions" (*Enquiry*, 155).

Hume cites as a second argument conducive to scepticism—this time, scepticism with regard to reason—the fact that the same geometry which produces clear demonstrations of familiar theorems generates also the paradoxes of infinite divisibility which are "big with contradiction and absurdity" (157). This sceptical argument may, he thinks, be defeated, by recognizing that all mathematical ideas are particular (he seems to mean determinate), because all ideas are particular. There are no distinctively abstract or general ideas, but "all general ideas are, in reality, particular ones, attached to a general term, which recalls, upon occasion, other particular ones, that resemble, in certain circumstances, the idea, present to the mind" (158, n.). We reason as if these other ideas, which can be recalled, are successively recalled and used. But each particular idea is reducible to minimum points, and it makes no sense to try to conceive or speak about infinite divisibility.

---

5   E. Chambers, *Cyclopaedia* (1728), s.v. "Abstraction"; J. Burnett (Lord Monboddo), *Of the Origin and Progress of Language* (1773), 1.1.6–9; T. Reid, *Essays on the Intellectual Powers of Man* (1785), 5.6. For the textbook tradition, see I. Watts, *Logick* (1725), 1.3.3; F. Hutcheson, *Synopsis Metaphysicae* (1744), 2.1.4; id., *Logicae Compendium* (posthumous, 1756), 1.3; W. Duncan, *Elements of Logick* (1748), 1.4.2; *Encyclopaedia Britannica*, first edition (1771),   s.vv. "Abstract ideas" and "Abstraction"; E. Bentham, *Introduction to Logick* (1773), 1.4.

In the earlier *Treatise*, there is an alternative formulation of this account of general ideas, and the view is there ascribed to Berkeley. It is again used to undermine the alleged (but strictly impossible) belief in infinite divisibility.[6] The argument is continued into Book 1, Part 2, where Hume identifies the Port-Royal *Logic* of Arnauld and Nicole as one casualty (*Treatise*, 34, 43). He is here in no doubt that there are "general ideas"— ideas "general in their representation"—and he considers Berkeley to have given a definitive account of the nature of such ideas (17, 20, 22). But he gives two different formulations, corresponding to the phrasing just quoted. His best known formulation is that at the beginning of the section "Of Abstract Ideas", where he says that "all general ideas are nothing but particular ones, annexed to a certain term, which gives them a more extensive signification, and makes them recall upon occasion other individuals, which are similar to them" (17). Here it is *ideas* which signify and recall other ideas.

The alternative account has the *terms* recall other ideas: "A particular idea becomes general by being annex'd to a general term; that is, to a term, which from a customary conjunction has a relation to many other particular ideas, and readily recalls them in the imagination" (22). Under the scope of the general term, the particular idea is then said not to signify, but to "represent," other individuals, which he illustrates with one of Berkeley's own examples: "the general idea of a line, notwithstanding all our abstractions and refinements, has in its appearance in the mind a precise degree of quantity and quality; however it may be made to represent others, which have different degrees of both" (19). It is the latter account that survives in the *Enquiry*; and, to the extent that it was present in the *Treatise* too, one might conclude that it is Hume's preferred view, and that the first formulation was an unconscious deviation.

Was it a simple slip of the pen—or, at least, no more than a momentary excess of associationist zeal? That depends on how we read the activation of the "custom," or disposition, which enables us to correct errors in mathematical reasoning: "The word raises up an individual idea, along with a certain custom; and that custom produces any other individual one, for which we may have occasion" (20–21). In a careless distortion of Berkeley's phrasing, Hume says that it is the mind or imagination—even, at one point, the "attendant custom"—which "suggests" the additional ideas (21, 23–4).

It is the first formulation that Hume explicitly ascribes with fulsome praise to Berkeley, and in this he is plainly wrong. Later, he refers to "the

---

[6]   For a fuller exposition of this difficult passage, see J. P. Wright, *The Sceptical Realism of David Hume* (Manchester: Manchester University Press, 1983), sec. 9.

hypothesis I have propos'd concerning abstract ideas, so contrary to that, which has hitherto prevail'd in philosophy" (24). That may be consistent with his believing he was following Berkeley, and with Berkeley's being as much out on a limb as Hume himself. But it suggests a claim to originality in Hume's own position, a suggestion reinforced by his identifying the role of custom as its distinguishing feature. If he claims originality for that, all he can have intended to ascribe to Berkeley is the thesis that ideas are "particular in their nature, but general in their representation." Both were agreed on what they considered the particularity of all ideas. Berkeley's view is "that a word becomes general by being made the sign, not of an abstract general idea but, of several particular ideas, any one of which it indifferently suggests to the mind." So the word "line" owes its generality to "the various particular lines which it indifferently denotes." "[T]here is no such thing as one precise and definite signification annexed to any general name, they all signifying indifferently a great number of particular ideas" (*Principles*, Introd., sections 11–12, 18).

In place of Berkeley's "indifferent suggestion," Hume has a piece of associationist psychology. For Berkeley the same word suggests now one, now another idea, varying from occasion to occasion;[7] and he is notoriously inexplicit on how the whole class of these ideas is to be defined. For Hume, more alive to the restlessness of human thought, it is applied now to one, now another, recalling them successively on the same occasion. They are associatively linked by resemblance "as we may be prompted by a present design or necessity" (*Treatise*, 20), a process which serves—if only slightly— to locate less random individuals than Berkeley's account.[8] It is helped by the fact that "Before those habits have become entirely perfect, perhaps the mind may not be content with forming the idea of only one individual, but may run over several, in order to make itself comprehend its own meaning, and the compass of that collection, which it intends to express by the general term" (22).

---

[7]   Cf. T. Hobbes, *Elements of Philosophy*, 1.2.9: "for the understanding of the extent of an universal name, we need no other faculty but that of our imagination, by which we remember that such names bring sometimes one thing, sometimes another, into our mind."

[8]   Hume effectively redefines abstraction, as a matter not of separation but of implicit comparison, and uses the same notion to explain what others have called "distinctions of reason" (24–5). Hutcheson, either because he still conceived abstraction in terms of Lockean separation or because he disliked the consequences derived from the rejection of that view, appears to have criticized Hume on this score. We have to guess the nature of the criticism from Hume's reply, summarized in a letter to Hutcheson of March 1740 and partly amplified in the appendix to the *Treatise* (637). Hume there denies that our awareness of the resemblances in things involves us in a traditional sort of abstraction, and uses simple ideas to prove the point.

Though Berkeley himself does not usually explain the signification of words through the association of ideas, he does use the association of ideas (he calls it "suggestion") and develop the role of custom in important ways, notably in his theory of vision. Furthermore, he describes the association in semantic terms—in terms of one idea's being a sign of, or standing for, another, so that signifying and signified ideas may trigger each other in the mind. Hume, with wider interests in association, may therefore have fallen naturally into construing Berkeley's theory of association-as-signification as a theory of signification-as-association.

In the *Enquiry*, however, this association is scaled down. It is now consistently the general term, no longer the particular idea, which "upon occasion" (i.e. other occasions) recalls other resembling ideas to mind.

> [W]hen the term Horse is pronounced, we immediately figure to ourselves the idea of a black or a white animal, of a particular size or figure: But, as that term is also usually applied to animals of other colours, figures and sizes, these ideas, though not actually present to the imagination, are easily recalled; and our reasoning and conclusion proceed in the same way, as if they were actually present. (*Enquiry*, 138, n.)

The "as if" here is an indication that the putative association is not actually made. And this is a counterpart to Berkeley's account of the proof of the sum of the angles of a triangle. The triangle I envisage may be right-angled and isosceles, but no use is made of the information, "which sufficiently shews that the right angle might have been oblique, and the sides unequal, and for all that the demonstration have held good" (Introd., section 16).

In spite of this, we are no closer to finding in Hume an authentically Berkeleyan account of signification. It was never Berkeley's intention to suggest that general words signify representative ideas, as Hume understands representation; that is, ideas representing more than one individual. So no mechanism to account for the representation can constitute a legitimate extension of Berkeley's doctrine. On the contrary: the doctrine that Hume claims to find in Berkeley is Locke's rather than Berkeley's, and is precisely that doctrine in Locke which Berkeley so strenuously opposed.

III

Berkeley does, to be sure, say something in defense of representative ideas. They figure in the introduction to the *Principles*, immediately after his attack on general ideas as "formed by *abstraction*," and again, soon after, in his account of universality.

Now if we will annex a meaning to our words, and speak only of what we can conceive, I believe we shall acknowledge, that an idea, which considered in it self is particular, becomes general, by being made to represent or stand for all other particular ideas of the same sort. (Introd., section 12)

Thus when I demonstrate any proposition concerning triangles, it is to be supposed that I have in view the universal idea of a triangle; which ought not to be understood as if I cou'd frame an idea of a triangle which was neither equilateral nor scalenon nor equicrural. But only that the particular triangle I consider, whether of this or that sort it matters not, doth equally stand for and represent all rectilinear triangles whatsoever, and is in that sense *universal.* (Introd., section 15)

These will suggest to any well-bred scholar certain parallels in Locke's *Essay.*

This [sc. considering ideas separate] is called ABSTRACTION, whereby *Ideas* taken from particular Beings, become general Representatives of all of the same kind; and their Names general Names, applicable to whatever exists conformable to such abstract *Ideas.* . . . Thus the same Colour being observed to day in Chalk or Snow, which the Mind yesterday received from Milk, it considers that Appearance alone, makes it a representative of all of that kind; and having given it the name *Whiteness*, it by that sound signifies the same quality wheresoever to be imagin'd or met with. (*Essay*, 2.11.9)

Words are general, as has been said, when used, for Signs of general *Ideas*; and so are applicable indifferently to many particular Things; And *Ideas* are general, when they are set up, as the Representatives of many particular Things: but universality belongs not to things themselves, which are all of them particular in their Existence, even those Words, and *Ideas*, which in their signification, are general. When therefore we quit Particulars, the Generals that rest, are only Creatures of our own making, their general Nature being nothing but the Capacity they are put into by the Understanding, of signifying or representing many particulars. (3.3.11)

Universality is but accidental to it [Knowledge], and consists only in this, That the particular *Ideas*, about which it is, are such, as more than one particular Thing can correspond with, and be represented by. (4.17.8)

It would look from these quotations as if Locke and Berkeley may have disagreed on how representative ideas are set up, but did not disagree on the fact of their existence; and the second passage from Locke is prefaced with a remark which shows that they are at least agreed that general words are "applicable indifferently" to many particulars. Let us note the parallels, but not rush to assume that we know what they are doing there.

It is inconceivable that Berkeley was not familiar with the relevant passages in Locke and their attendant contexts. His discussion is saturated with phrasing drawn from these contexts. The first of the passages just quoted occurs only one paragraph before other passages from which Berkeley himself quotes extensively in section 11 of the introduction, and he follows those quotations with another which occurs only five paragraphs before the second passage of Locke cited above. The details of the formation of the abstract ideas of *man* and *animal* in sections 9 and 10 of the introduction are directly modelled on phrasing in Locke's account at 3.3.7–9. Berkeley knew these contexts inside out. So it will not do to assume that, in his zeal to attack what he took Locke to be saying on abstraction, he simply overlooked that his own positive account of representation is present in Locke too. The question is, rather: given that Berkeley knew that the representation thesis was a feature of the Lockean account, how does he come to turn this thesis against Locke, and to promulgate a theory of general ideas as representative ideas as part of an attack on his source?

To show precisely how much Berkeley understood of Locke's position, it is helpful to go back to the early manuscript of his introduction to the *Principles*. This was recently republished in a definitive stratified transcription by Bertil Belfrage, which enables us to see clearly for the first time not just the development of Berkeley's thought on these matters, but, arising from that, the correct historical interpretation of his mature views. Although there is less development between the manuscript and published doctrines than Belfrage has claimed, Berkeley's engagement with Lockean notions is fuller and clearer in the manuscript than in the more polished final text.[9]

The decisive passage begins on folio 3 of the manuscript, and first read like this:

> By Abstract Ideas, Genera, Species, Universal Notions all which amount to the same thing, as I find those terms explain'd by the best and Clearest Writers, we are to understand Ideas which equally represent the Particulars of any Sort, & are made by the Mind which observing that Individuals of each Kind agree in some things, & differ in others, takes out & singles from the rest, that which is common to all, making thereof one Abstract, General Idea; Which General Idea contains all that Idea wherein the Particulars do agree & partake separated from & exclusive of all those other concomitant Ideas, whereby the Individuals are distinguish'd one

---

[9]   On the wayward exegesis which accompanies Belfrage's exemplary text, see M. A. Stewart, "Berkeley's Introduction Draft," *Berkeley Newsletter* 11 (1989–90): 10–19. Belfrage's response in the following issue does not address anything I said.

from another. [to *added*] This abstract, general Idea, thus framed the Mind gives a General Name & lays it up & uses it as a Standard whereby to judge what Particulars are & what are not to be accounted of that Sort; Those only which contain every part of the General Idea having a right to be admitted into that Sort & called by that Name. (folios 3–4)

Berkeley followed this with an example, the supposed abstract idea of *man*, and after that the examples of *animal* and *line* (folios 4–5), before tracing the motivation to believe in such ideas to Locke's views on the reason of animals and on human language (folios 7–10). In the printed version, the introductory characterization of abstract ideas is reduced and the examples are better organized. The example of a line is dropped from this position, and Berkeley treats first of the abstraction of simple ideas (extension, color, motion), as a lead-in to the other former examples of complex ideas constructed from them (Introd., sections 7–9).

In both versions Berkeley aimed to be paraphrasing the same received view. The manuscript account of this view, "as I find those terms explain'd by the best and Clearest Writers," gives a three-part account of what are called indifferently "Abstract Ideas, Genera, Species, Universal Notions."[10] First, they have a certain *function*: they "equally represent the Particulars of any Sort." Secondly, they have a distinctive *origin* in the workings of the mind: the mind "observing that the Individuals of each Kind agree in some things, & differ in others, takes out & singles from the rest, that which is common to all." Thirdly, they have a specified *content*: the general idea "contains all that Idea wherein the Particulars do agree & partake separated from & exclusive of all those other concomitant Ideas, whereby the Individuals are distinguish'd from each other." If we include the rest of the paragraph, which was cut at an early stage, we have to add further components: the idea thus formed is *called* by a general name and *used* as a standard for sorting particulars. In the elaboration of the examples, the content is further specified, in terms which less directly echo the account of origin and more directly echo Locke's account of non-particular features.

---

[10] In Notebook A, entry 688, Berkeley records his intention of using Locke as his example in the introduction, "he being as clear a writer as I have met with." He adds, more hopefully than perceptively, "Such was the Candour of this great Man that I perswade my self, were he alive, he would not be offended that I differ from him seeing that even in so doing I follow his advice viz. to use my own Judgement, see with my own eyes & not with anothers." One example of Berkeley's more extensive use of Locke's language in the manuscript draft than in the published text is the term "concomitant ideas," used to refer to those particularizing details which are not included in the general idea (fol. 4; *Essay*, 2.11.9).

Turning with these clues to the printed account, we can detect Berkeley specifying first the supposed origin and then the supposed content of abstract ideas. (That it is still being presented as the received view is plain from sections 6, 7 and 9.) The supposed origin lies in the ability of the mind to "consider each quality singly, or abstracted from those other qualities with which it is united" (section 7). The content is "something common and alike in all"; for example, in extension it is "neither line, surface, nor solid, nor has any figure or magnitude but is an idea entirely prescinded from all these" (section 8). The function of such ideas is spelt out in relation to motion: it "equally corresponds to all particular motions whatsoever that may be perceiv'd by sense." There is a reference to "representation" tucked away in section 16 (echoing folio 15 of the manuscript), in Berkeley's reconstruction of the rationale behind Locke's account of the triangle "in which all the particulars do indifferently partake, and by which they are all equally represented." So the pieces of the story are still there, just more scattered.

In both versions Berkeley considers the received view, taken as a package, reprehensible, though it remains to be seen how far he saw himself as rejecting each detail. He argues against the package, and offers an alternative account of how particular ideas operate in relation to general knowledge, and of the use of general words. At the heart of his attack is the conviction that no ideas can represent by being abstract, since the very process involved in abstraction destroys their capacity to represent. This is especially clear in the manuscript because of what Berkeley there requires a representative idea to do, namely, *copy* or reproduce its original. In a nutshell, he equates being a representative with being a representation.

IV

Conceding for argument's sake that ideas cannot be communicated without words, Berkeley notes that general words are general only because they "mark a Number of particular Existences," that each is "made the sign of a great number of particular Ideas, between which there is some likeness," and that having general names "does not imply the having of General Ideas, but barely the Marking by them [the names] a Number of particular Ideas" (folios 10–11). He never shifted from this view, which is found again throughout the printed introduction: "a word becomes general by being made the sign, not of an abstract general idea but, of several particular ideas, any one of which it indifferently suggests to the mind" (section 11; cf. 18, 24). There is no mention of representative ideas. Berkeley achieves Locke's own avowed purpose, of having general words be "applicable indifferently to many particular Things" (3.3.11), precisely by not invoking representative ideas.

The point is reinforced in the manuscript by a distinction between two kinds of representing, replaced in the printed text by an account of the function of diagrams in geometry. Let us look at the manuscript first. Berkeley's first inclination was to say, after making the point that general names do not require general ideas: "Which will be made yet more manifest, if we consider the different manners wherein Words & Ideas do stand for & represent things" (folio 11).

It is arguable that he did believe that words represent things in one way and that ideas represent things in another. Almost immediately afterwards, he leaves uncorrected the statement, "The Word Man may equally be put to signify any particular Man I can think of." Note: a particular man, not a particular idea of a man. "But I cannot frame an Idea of Man, which shall equally represent & correspond to each particular of that Sort of Creatures, that may possibly exist." However, recalling the Lockean context of the debate, and the two-tier theory of signification that goes with it, he amended the earlier sentence, to read: "Which will be made yet more manifest, if we consider the different manners wherein Words represent Ideas, & Ideas things."

Berkeley uses this "difference," as he considers it, to trace out and criticize the logic of the received view. Having stated that "there is no Similitude or Resemblance betwixt Words & the Ideas that are marked by them," and that "any Name may be used indifferently for the Sign of any Idea, or any number of Ideas" because it is not "determin'd by any likeness" to represent one more than another, he contrasts this with what is "supposed" to be so and "thought" to be so with ideas:

> But it is not so with Ideas in respect of Things, of which they are suppos'd to be the Copies & Images. They are not thought to Represent them any otherwise, than as they resemble them. Whence it follows, that an Idea is not capable of representing indifferently any Thing or number of Things, it being limited by the likeness it beares to some particular Existence, to represent it rather than any other. (folio 11, later restyled)

Who makes the "supposition" from which this "follows"? Whatever Locke is supposed to have meant in claiming that some ideas are "resemblances" of what they represent, he constantly confined it to the small class of ideas of primary qualities. Berkeley knew those passages well enough. What did he read in Locke that led him to extend the account?

In his chapter "Of Adequate and Inadequate *Ideas*", Locke distinguishes ideas which "perfectly represent" their archetypes from those which are "but a partial, or incomplete representation." The problem cases are complex ideas, but from these we can exclude complex ideas of modes "because they not being intended for Copies of Things really existing, but for Archetypes made by the Mind, to rank and denominate Things by, cannot want any thing."

> But in our *Ideas* of *Substances*, it is otherwise. For there desiring to copy Things, as they really do exist; and to represent to our selves that Constitution, on which all their Properties depend, we perceive our *Ideas* attain not that Perfection we intend: We find they still want something, we should be glad were in them; and so are all *inadequate*. . . .

> Now those *Ideas* have in the Mind a double reference: 1. Sometimes they are referred to a supposed real Essence of each Species of Things. 2. Sometimes they are only design'd to be Pictures and Representations in the Mind, of Things that do exist, by *Ideas* of those qualities that are discoverable in them. In both which ways, these Copies of those Originals, and Archetypes, *are* imperfect and *inadequate*. . . .

> Those who, neglecting that useless Supposition of unknown real Essences, whereby they are distinguished, endeavour to copy the Substances, that exist in the World, by putting together the *Ideas* of those sensible Qualities, which are found co-existing in them, though they come much nearer a likeness of them, than those who imagine, they know not what real specifick Essences: yet they arrive not at perfectly adequate *Ideas* of those Substances, they would thus copy into their Minds: nor do those Copies, exactly, and fully, contain all that is to be found in their Archetypes. (2.6.3, 6, 8)

Summarizing his view in sections 12–14, Locke says that simple ideas are *ektupa* or copies, explicitly instancing ideas of secondary qualities which even in the previous chapter he has stressed are not "the Images, or Representations of what does exist." Complex ideas of modes and relations "are not Copies, nor made after the Pattern of any real Existence," because they are not distinct from their own archetypes. Ideas of substances "*are Ectypes, Copies* too; but not perfect ones, not *adequate*" (cf. 3.4.17).

In the following chapter, "Of True and False *Ideas*", Locke writes that the mind "makes a tacit Supposition" of the "Conformity" of ideas to things. The supposition is chiefly prevalent in relation to abstract complex ideas, and only a serious problem in relation to ideas of substances. These are to be considered "as Collections of simple *Ideas* in the Mind, taken from Combinations of simple *Ideas* existing together constantly in Things, of which Patterns, they are the supposed Copies" (2.32.4, 6, 18). He then shows the sense in which such ideas may be true or false, but it is a mode of speaking which (contrary to Gassendi) he thinks misleading and to be avoided.

Although Locke leaves his metaphors uninterpreted, it is at least clear that he distinguished resemblances from copies, and that Berkeley in assimilating the two has mixed up two separate discussions. For Locke, not all ideas are "supposed" to copy; still fewer succeed in copying; not all of these are representations, and few actually "resemble" their sources. An idea is a copy of anything to the extent that there corresponds to it a specific external power to cause it, and it is caused directly by the exercise of that power; and a complex idea is—*per impossibile*—a perfect copy to the extent that its constituents not only emanate from a single complex cause but reflect all the powers embodied in that cause. An idea is a resemblance to the extent that the power to cause it lies in the cause's having the quality that it is perceived to have, and not some other quality or qualities in virtue of which the idea occurs. Locke's—cautiously qualified—accounts of copying occur most often in relation to general ideas of substances, and it is those that are particularly, and less cautiously, under examination in Berkeley's manuscript.[11]

The manuscript retains the same ordinary distinction between ideas and things that we have in the *New Theory of Vision*, and not even in the printed text does the ontological status of things enter the discussion in the introduction. So long as this ordinary distinction is maintained, it is easy enough for Berkeley to appear to be handling a Lockean theme. If it can be rejected on what he believed to be its own terms, then he is in that much stronger a position to develop the rest of an anti-Lockean philosophy. But Berkeley's misreading of Locke, and the refutation based upon it, are traceable to his *own* belief that ideas represent their originals by resemblance. For Locke, as John Yolton has forcefully argued, the representation of things by ideas was all along a "semiotic" representation (*Essay*, 4.21.5), not an iconographic one.[12] It was Berkeley, not Locke, who took the

---

[11] I am assuming here the account of complex ideas of substances given in M. A. Stewart, "Locke's Mental Atomism and the Classification of Ideas: 2", *Locke Newsletter* 11 (1980): 25–62. Locke's account of the properties of ideas has been relatively little studied, and then almost entirely in relation to simple ideas. See J. L. Bermúdez, "The Adequacy of Simple Ideas in Locke—A Rehabilitation of Berkeley's Criticisms," *Locke Newsletter* 23 (1992): 25–58; T. Heyd, "Locke's Arguments for the Resemblance Thesis Revisited," *Locke Newsletter* 25 (1994): 13–28.

[12] J. W. Yolton, *Locke and the Compass of Human Understanding* (Cambridge: Cambridge University Press, 1970), chap. 9. That Berkeley, even in his published work,

terminology of copying literally, believed systematically that ideas copy-resemble their originals, and saw that if they do, then they cannot copy-resemble other individuals to the same, or any, degree. This belief survived the completion of his move to immaterialism. The evidence is not in the introduction, but in the body of the text:

> The ideas imprinted on the senses by the Author of Nature are called *real things*, and those excited in the imagination being less regular, vivid and constant, are more properly termed *ideas*, or *images of things*, which they copy and represent. (*Principles*, section 33)[13]

But they can only copy and represent their own kind (cf. section 8). Berkeley repeated the distinction in his second letter to Le Clerc of 1711, where he distinguished between firsthand tactual perception and a creation of the imagination "in the likeness of" the ideas perceived by touch. In section 45 of *A Defence of Free-thinking in Mathematics*, he said, "To me it is plain there is no consistent idea the likeness of which may not really exist." That ideas copy their originals is likewise an essential premise of his refutation of the thesis that there can be ideas of spirits: for if there were, they would have to "represent unto us, by way of image or likeness, that which acts," and no image can act (*Principles*, section 27; cf. ms. introduction, folio 27).

There is an ambiguity in the term "idea," which was used both of original perceptions and of subsequent thoughts. This gives it an extended and confusing scope in Berkeley's philosophy, once the distinction between perception and things is branded as an improper abstraction. In the manuscript he uses "Thoughts" interchangeably with "Ideas" (folio 10). Locke was seen to have claimed that in speaking we communicate what we are thinking, and that our thoughts in the appropriate way mirror their objects. Berkeley, accepting and stressing Locke's own insight that all thought is in some sense particular, found that this mirroring could not be done if Locke then destroyed the particularity of the thoughts. They would lose the only

---

continued to associate representation with resemblance has been noted by K. P. Winkler, *Berkeley: An Interpretation* (Oxford: 1989), 14.

[13] Cf. Notebook A, entries 657a, 823. In a letter of 8 December 1709 to Samuel Molyneux (Luce, no. 5), Berkeley concedes that his recollection of a house or city "do's very rudely resemble the Thing it represents, and not in each Circumstance accurately correspond with it. And yet it may serve to most Interests and purposes as well as if it did." This is presumably saved from being a Lockean abstraction by the retention of some particularizing detail. A similar view was to be taken by Hume (*Treatise*, 3). Elsewhere, in discussing matter and mind, Hume says that if an impression were to "represent" a substance, it would have to resemble it (233).

content by which they could function as copies, and so, in order to function, had to retain the particularity of the content even if some of it did not on occasion concern us. It becomes irrelevant whether we say that thoughts represent things or that they represent the perceptions of things, once that whole distinction is abandoned.

V

We see, then, that several theses strikingly concentrated in Berkeley's manuscript survive, dispersed, as a permanent part of his philosophy—that there are no abstract ideas as there construed, because the kind of abstracting involved cannot be done and it would not help if it could; that in so far as words signify ideas, they always signify particular ideas; and that the ideas which occur in discursive thinking represent their particular originals by resemblance, regardless of the metaphysical status of the originals.

The general strategy of the published introduction is as follows. Berkeley says that scepticism about the world owes less to the world than to mistaken beliefs about ourselves. But before correcting those mistakes, we should at the outset be alive to "the nature and abuse of language," because this will be a recurring theme. Preparatory to that, it is appropriate to lay to rest one particularly vicious piece of nonsense about our mental faculties—this doctrine of abstract ideas. The doctrine is spelt out and illustrated. Of course, there is a harmless sense in which an idea can be abstract on the one hand, or general or universal on the other. Both are illustrated from geometry, in terms very different from those used by Locke of his triangle. This confusion between the harmlessly general and the abstract has arisen from mistaken views about the signification of general words. People have thought they could separate, for example, motion from matter, because they have supposed they actually do it every time they talk about it. But when general words signify ideas, they signify different particular ideas on different occasions. However, they do not always signify ideas, and some words never or virtually never do so. There are other ends of language, which are itemized. So let us not be tricked by words, but on those occasions where they are or can be used to represent ideas, let us keep our minds as far as possible on the ideas.

Notice that in this sequence the demolition of abstract ideas precedes and is independent of the positive account of the signification of words. The latter comes in to help explain the belief Berkeley has just refuted. Why would anyone believe in abstract ideas? Because they are mixed up about words. As Berkeley says, he wanted to say something about the use of words by way of preface to a general study of human faculties, but he found himself "anticipating his design," having to nail a particular thesis about our faculties first to sell his message about the use of words (Introd., section 6). To someone brought up on Locke, this is an odd division of labor: deal with abstraction first and language second, and keep them apart. But that is Berkeley's point. Locke is in the scrape he is because he tried to run together topics which do not belong together.

The organization of the published introduction is already implicit in the manuscript, but there is one major difference. In folio 11 of the manuscript, as we have seen, Berkeley explored the implications of the view that there is a difference in the "manners wherein Words represent Ideas, & Ideas things." He spelt out the manner in which ideas (thoughts) represent things (their originals). This drops out of the printed text, not because he no longer believes it, but because it does nothing to help us understand how words represent ideas. Studying the relation of ideas to things had a negative value, helping to eliminate abstract ideas; but it has no positive value, since there is a total *difference* between the "manners wherein Words represent Ideas, & Ideas things." Instead, he now writes:

> By observing how ideas become general, we may the better judge how words are made so. (Introd., section 12)

This is a shift of the first importance. We are now to be told something which will help us understand better how words represent ideas, something we never fully understood before. In the manuscript we had only the relatively negative information that words do not resemble ideas, and represent many of them indifferently, as signs (folio 11). The new explanation is an analogy from the way in which *ideas* may be general without abstraction. But let me repeat the importance of seeing the order of exposition. Berkeley's discussion of the operations of language comes only after abstract ideas have already been killed off. It is a move to a new stage of discussion, and in this new stage his account of the representative character of general ideas precedes and explains his semantic theory; it does not assume or depend on it, let alone constitute it.

The doctrine of section 12 of the introduction is repeated in sections 126–28 of the main text, and at *Alciphron* 7.7 in the early editions. This time there is no reference to the way the words of a language suggest non-resembling ideas or anything else: it is about the way one particular line may represent or signify others. This is the positive development of a doctrine otherwise hidden in a throwaway remark of the manuscript: "how are signs of any sort render'd Universal, otherwise than by being made to signify, or represent indifferently, a Multitude of particular Things?" (folio 10). In the manuscript this is worked out exclusively in relation to words as "Signs of our Thoughts." Berkeley was there confining himself to attacking the received view on general or universal ideas, first as being invalidated by what he considered a hopeless conception of abstraction or separation, and secondly as motivated by wild notions about the actual signification of words. But if that were still his sole concern, the account of general ideas in the published text need never have seen the light of day. It is not integral to the attack on abstract ideas, or to an account of what any words signify. Unfortunately, many readers since Hume have run away with the idea that Berkeley's published doctrine is that general words signify representative ideas, and that he supports this with examples.[14]

Berkeley published no such doctrine, and the whole trend of his discussion is against it. He says often enough and plainly enough that general words signify nothing but particular ideas, and any of a number of those indifferently. And after introducing his new-found "general ideas" in a new, non-abstractionist, sense, he never says or suggests that general words stand for general or representative ideas so defined. The function of these new-found ideas is something different. In saying that words become general in the way that ideas do, he is trying to explain the less intelligible by the more intelligible, the unfamiliar by the commonplace. The one contemporary who read Berkeley correctly on this was Chambers. So what are these supposedly familiar general ideas, if they are not the significations of words, but rather an analogy to help us see something *about* the significations of words?

Berkeley's examples are of visible designs on paper. Here we have particular ideas of the usual kind. When geometers do a proof, they prove something of the figure in front of them (or of an imaginary figure in front of them). Berkeley then shows the sense in which they can be said to have proved the same thing of other figures which resemble the first in salient respects, but of which the first is in no way a *copy*. (He does not mean the tangible figures which are suggested by the visible figures: it is perhaps unclear what tangible figure corresponds to a visible circle inscribed on a page as distinct from the visible edge of a circular page; but in any case Berkeley has told us elsewhere that there is only one tangible circle

---

[14]   The correct logic of Berkeley's argument has been seen by G. J. Warnock, *Berkeley* (Harmondsworth: Penguin, 1953), 69–70; and J. Dancy, *Berkeley: An Introduction* (Oxford: Blackwell, 1987), 30. The traditional interpretation lingers on in I. C. Tipton, *Berkeley: The Philosophy of Immaterialism* (London: Methuen, 1974), 155; J. L. Mackie, *Problems from Locke* (Oxford: Clarendon Press, 1976), 120; and J. O. Urmson, *Berkeley* (Oxford: Oxford University Press, 1982), 28–31.

represented by the visual idea.) The visible line in the geometry book represents alternative visible lines (and no doubt a tangible line can equally represent other tangible lines). Its role in the demonstration, i.e. in the practice of geometry—not its role as the signification of the word "line"—is to represent any other visible line indifferently.

> And as that particular line becomes general, by being made a sign, so the name *line* which taken absolutely is particular, by being a sign is made general. And as the former owes its generality, not to its being the sign of an abstract or general line, but of all particular right lines that may possibly exist, so the latter must be thought to derive its generality from the same cause, namely, the various, particular lines which it indifferently denotes. (Introd., section 12)

These new-style general ideas represent as signs, not as copies; indeed, to represent as a sign just is to represent not as a copy. It is to be a representative without being a representation. The rest of us use words as geometers use diagrams—as conventions to convey information about things other than the signs themselves. The analogy has obvious limitations: the geometrical proof may still hold good when applied to the diagram used as a sign, whereas a verbal description of something does not hold good of the words used to make it. However, it is important for Berkeley's account of geometry, to see that the proof may *not* hold good when applied literally to the diagram and that this is why it is to be construed always as a sign:

> [A] line in the scheme, but an inch long, must be spoken of, as though it contained ten thousand parts, since it is regarded not in it self, but as it is universal; and it is universal only in its signification, whereby it represents innumerable lines greater than it self, in which may be distinguished ten thousand parts or more, though there may not be above an inch in it. After this manner the properties of the lines signified are (by a very usual figure) transferred to the sign, and thence through mistake thought to appertain to it considered in its own nature. (*Principles*, section 126)

One way to bring home the way in which Berkeley uses this analogy of the general idea—namely, to illumine the way in which general words also signify many particulars without signifying any intermediary—is to stress the point that he never actually cites any other general ideas in his own sense except those employed in the practice of geometry. He does offer another direct analogue—our ability to use figures as signs in arithmetic, without having to postulate the existence of abstract numbers (*Principles*, sections 119–22)—though in this case he suggests that language itself may be the more perspicuous model. Mathematics in its totality is the science par excellence of representative non-representations.[15]

VI

It is time to tie together some loose ends in Locke and Hume. First, Locke.

I have been concentrating on some cardinal features of Berkeley's philosophy and of his attack on Locke which have otherwise been overlooked or misconstrued. That these led him to a distorted picture of Locke's position will not seem like news to anyone familiar with Berkeley's lifelong caricature of Locke on the abstract general idea of triangle.[16] But enough has been said to put the latter episode also into perspective.

It is, indeed, perplexing why anyone of Berkeley's genius should be so sure that assembling "some parts of several different and inconsistent *Ideas*" was itself inconsistent; sure, to the point of repeating the mistake in three separate works over twenty-five years, and in draft materials for several years before. That he would rebel against the expression "all and none at once" is more understandable, though he made no great effort to understand the thinking behind it. This we can see by going back to Gassendi's formulation of the issues in terms of species and genus, and visualizing how classes are displayed in the Porphyrian schema.[17]

Where a general idea is formed by aggregation, it is complete or perfect proportionately to its inclusion of all the individuals in a species, or all the species in a genus. "If any idea of mankind embraces not only Europeans, Africans, and Asians, but also Americans, it will be more complete than if, in the habit of the ancients, it were to embrace only Europeans, Africans and Asians" (*Institutio Logica*, 1.8). This completeness is achieved by creating a larger aggregation out of groups whose differences still make them distinct. On the other hand, where a general idea is formed by abstraction, it is complete or perfect proportionately to its exclusion of those features which differentiate the groups or individuals that conform to it; so this completeness is achieved by eliminating differences—of size, age, color, etc.

---

[15] Cf. Berkeley's letters of 8 and 19 December 1709 to Samuel Molyneux (Luce, nos. 5–6).

[16] *Essay*, 4.7.9. Berkeley discusses this, obsessively, in Notebook A, entries 561, 687 ("the killing blow"); *New Theory of Vision*, section 125; *Principles*, ms. introd., fols. 12–13; printed introd., section 13; *Alciphron*, 7.5 (1st and 2nd eds.); *Defence of Free-thinking in Mathematics*, section 45.

[17] P. Gassendi, *Institutio Logica*, ed. H. Jones (see n. 3 above).

The result is that every class considered extensionally is all, and intension-
ally is none, of its members. Gassendi grants that man that is neither large,
small nor middling, etc., cannot be imagined, but, like any philosopher of
the period who distinguished sense from intellect, he saw no insuperable
difficulty in conceiving what could not be imagined. It is an irony, first
noticed by Monboddo, that the philosopher for whom sense was more
subordinate to intellect than for anyone else (namely, Berkeley) was the
one who found it hardest to dispense with sense. The distinction between
the activity of spiritual substances and the passivity of all else was so
fundamental for Berkeley, that there could be no bridging the gap between
notions and ideas.

Locke's abstract general ideas involve a partial integration into a single
account of the two kinds of generality distinguished by Gassendi.
Berkeleyan scruples aside, there is no reason why they cannot be inte-
grated—why we cannot both collect and look for the common thread in
the collection, indeed why the one process does not actually help the other.
The element of abstraction remains the dominant one in Locke's account,
but he tries to square this with the need for an alternative procedure for
higher-level simple ideas at 3.4.16; and there are a number of passages where
the motive to form general ideas is "comprehensiveness."

> Therefore to shorten its way to Knowledge, and make each Perception
> the more comprehensive; the first Thing it [the Mind] does, as the
> Foundation of the easier enlarging its Knowledge, either by Contempla-
> tion of the things themselves, that it would know; or conference with
> others about them, is to bind them into Bundles, and rank them so into
> sorts, that what Knowledge it gets of any of them, it may thereby with
> assurance extend to all of that sort; and so advance by larger steps in that,
> which is its great Business, Knowledge. This, as I have elsewhere shewed,
> is the Reason, why we collect Things under comprehensive *Ideas*, with
> Names annexed to them into *Genera* and *Species*. (2.32.6)

Locke's depiction of the triangle which is neither one thing nor another
is the most obvious of the Gassendist elements in his account.[18] But we do
not know its genealogy any more than we know whether there is a direct
line of descent from Gassendi's definitions of "idea" and "proposition" to
Locke's (*Inst.*, 1.1, 2 pref.; *Essay*, 1.1.8, 4.5.6). We are still underinformed
about the seventeenth-century logic book tradition. Locke was, however,

---

[18]   Gassendi also says that we cannot have a name for every particular (1.4; cf. *Essay*,
3.1.3, 3.3.2), and that noticing the "agreement" of individuals in certain respects is the
first step to forming an abstract idea (1.4; cf. *Essay*, 3.3.7).

nothing if not eclectic; and his identification of abstract ideas with "Patterns" and "Archetypes," like the distinction between "Archetypes" and "Ectypes," is patently neoplatonist, albeit without the theological undertones. Not that he need have been reading Plotinus: Cudworth would do.

In a central feature of his account, Locke is closer to the Port-Royal tradition. For Gassendi, the abstract idea "represents" not the many individuals that fall under it, but the species or genus: the mind "adopts such an idea as the general or universal idea 'man', in as much as there is represented in it not this or that or another particular man, but 'man' in general or in common" (*Inst.*, 1.4). Here, and again in 1.8, what an idea represents is equated with its content. For Port-Royal, on the other hand, the different ideas that we can form by abstracting from a particular equilateral triangle on paper may represent "all equilateral triangles," or "all kinds of triangles," or "all rectilineal figures," or, in the last resort, "extension itself" (*Logic*, 1.5). And while Gassendi would accept Locke's view that ideas such as that of the triangle "carry difficulty with them," it is Arnauld and Nicole who foreshadow Locke's explicit language of "Fictions and Contrivances of the Mind," of "something imperfect, that cannot exist," and (from a different context) "separating from them the circumstances of Time, and Place, and any other *Ideas*, that may determine them to this or that particular Existence" (*Essay*, 3.3.6).

VII

In conclusion, I bring the story back to Hume, who, on the account presented so far, had no more sense of what Berkeley was doing than Berkeley had of Locke. In one important respect, this is an unfair picture. Both Berkeley and Hume used the principle of the particularity of representative ideas to show the source of the belief in the infinite divisibility of space and time, and at the same time the impossibility of its being true. It was not in relation to this that Hume acknowledged his specific debt to Berkeley, but what he did claim to get out of his acknowledged reading is not without interest.

In the *Treatise*, Hume appears to commend Berkeley for an associationist theory which is actually a fusion of lines of thought that Berkeley himself kept distinct. He goes on to a substantive discussion of the determinate character of particular ideas, which is undoubtedly reminiscent of Berkeley but would also be found in a careful reading of Locke, and he repeats the textbook example of the triangle which has already run through the tradition from Arnauld to Berkeley. Unlike Berkeley (but like Arnauld and

Locke), Hume is interested in this not simply as part of the special subject matter of geometry, but as typical of the subject matter to which general terms descriptive of the natural world are applied. This is an idea "in itself individual," but "general in its representation," and its coming to be general in its representation is connected with our ability to recall alternative individuals among those joined by custom with the particular word. Hume is not restricting the application to mathematical objects, since he extends his account to such terms as "government," "church," "negotiation" and "conquest" (*Treatise*, 23). His discussion in the *Treatise* is nevertheless strategically placed, for its mathematical relevance, in a transitional position between Parts 1 and 2 of Book 1.

The limits to our powers of abstraction set bounds to what we can conceive, and thus to the possibilities for human knowledge. In particular, we cannot envisage a world of primary qualities without secondary, and we cannot envisage the infinite division of space and time. But Hume was not here merely mimicking Berkeley. The mechanisms of fictive association which for Hume replaced the more suspect psychological apparatus in Locke's account of abstract ideas not only fill a void which was still left in Berkeley's account; but they allow Hume to show more convincingly than Berkeley's principles allowed Berkeley, how we nevertheless come to believe some things that we cannot conceive.[19] This is different from the traditional view that we can conceive some things that we cannot imagine. Berkeley's rather simple psychology led him to consider that what was inconceivable was necessarily impossible, but this was not the lesson Hume himself derived from Berkeley. For Hume, as the *Enquiry* footnote makes clear, the natural consequence of Berkeley's anti-abstractionism was not, in the first instance, the replacement of materialist by immaterialist dogma, but simple scepticism (*Enquiry*, 155, n.).

Berkeley would have been scandalized at this inference from his philosophy. In the end, Hume does share Berkeley's rejection of infinite divisibility, because like him he finds it internally incoherent—based on the eminently Berkeleyan principle that "ideas are adequate representations of objects" (*Treatise*, 29). That is something stronger than saying just that we cannot conceive it. But even that agreement would be of little consolation to Berkeley. For Berkeley had wanted to eliminate the metaphysical

---

[19]   If belief is, for Hume, a mode of conception, the claim just made may seem puzzling. His point is that there are certain things of which we have no impressions, or no adequate impressions, and cannot therefore literally form ideas. What we do is form, as it were, proxy ideas, and project these on to the world in a way that creates the illusion and conviction of an objective experience. Some of these habits are corrigible, some not.

paradoxes of divisibility as a way of clearing away one more ground of impiety (*Principles*, section 133). This was hardly Hume's motive. In the literature on natural religion, the paradoxes of divisibility were trotted out with wearisome regularity, by all but Berkeley, to demonstrate the infirmity of human reason in order to safeguard the more paradoxical mysteries of the faith. Hume's psychological analysis of our thinking on space and time is an attempt (whether successful or not) to demystify one of the central mysteries in traditional metaphysics and thereby remove one of the favorite screens behind which natural religion had traditionally sheltered. It may be doubtful whether his discussion of abstraction was intended to have the prominence it has been accorded by subsequent historians of semantics; but even on a modest view of its significance, it must have ramifications for some of the most contentious issues of his day.[20]

---

[20] My thanks to Fred Michael, David Owen and David Raynor for comments on a first draft of this essay.

Reason, Revelation, and Experience in the Hymns of Addison and Watts

Arthur W. Wainwright

Hymns are not the place to look for a discussion of philosophical and theological problems. Their themes are praise, repentance, and prayer. They express and arouse emotions, and although they give utterance to theological statements, they are not the ideal vehicle for a examination of the pros and cons of intellectual disputes. Some of them, however, reflect their authors' attitudes to controversial issues. Luther's hymns reinforce his views on justification. Charles Wesley's reiterate Arminian doctrines in opposition to Calvinism. And several eighteenth-century hymns echo their writers' views on two issues that were to the forefront in the area where philosophy and theology overlap. One of these issues is the relationship between reason and revelation. The other is the nature and validity of religious experience.

The Deists' claim that reason was sufficient to provide a knowledge of God's existence and of the moral law was at the heart of much theological and philosophical discussion in the early eighteenth century. The basic truths of Christianity, Deists affirmed, could be discerned by reason apart from revelation. At the other end of the spectrum were visionaries who announced that they received special communications from God. Philosophers and theologians alike dismissed these visionary claims as enthusiasm.

Eighteenth-century England was abundant with hymn writers, and some of them showed an awareness of these issues. Attention will be paid to two of them, Joseph Addison (1672–1719) and Isaac Watts (1674–1748). Both of them were alert to the currents of thought in the intellectual world, and statements in their hymns reveal something of their views on these matters.

Addison is famous chiefly as an essayist, and in his own day he also won a reputation as a statesman and a dramatist. In the twentieth century it is likely that more people sing his hymns than read his essays. "When All Thy Mercies, O My God," and "The Spacious Firmament on High" remain in the repertoire. To students of history and literature it may seem ironical that this is the most widely known part of his literary output. But it may not have surprised Addison or displeased him.

In his writings Addison set out to be a popularizer of philosophy. "I shall be ambitious to have it said of me," he wrote, "that I have brought Philosophy out of the closets and libraries, schools and colleges, to dwell in clubs and assemblies, at tea-tables and in coffee-houses."[1] In fact, he was also a popularizer of theology. Many of his essays touch on theological themes, and to some of them he appended a hymn of his own composition. His output of hymns was small, especially when it is compared with the hundreds written by Watts and the thousands written by Charles Wesley. Addison wrote very few, but they had an enduring quality.

Addison was not a great original thinker. It was as a popularizer that he made his mark. The very medium that he used, the short essay in a popular journal, meant that his work did not have the thoroughness and detail of more rigorous treatises. But the essays that address ethical and theological issues and the hymns that he included in some of them give an insight into his views.

His opinions on reason and revelation are what might be expected from a Latitudinarian of that period. Reason, he contended, is primarily concerned with morality, and faith is concerned with revelation. The demarcation between the two is not rigid. Reason as well as revelation leads to conclusions about the nature of God.[2] It proves that there is a first cause who existed from all eternity (*Spectator*, 6 September 1714). "The Supreme Being," Addison wrote, "has made the best arguments for his own existence, in the formation of the heavens and the earth" (ibid., 23 August 1712).

The discovery of God through the natural universe is the theme of one of Addison's hymns, a paraphrase of the first four verses of Psalm 19. The psalm is a declaration of faith, not a philosophical argument. But Addison treated it as a proof of God's existence. In his stately English he elaborated on the psalm's opening words: "The heavens declare the glory of God: and the firmament showeth his handiwork."

> The spacious firmament on high,
> With all the blue ethereal sky,
> And spangled heavens, a shining frame,
> Their great original proclaim.

---

[1] *The Spectator*, 12 March 1711.

[2] J. Addison's *Evidences of the Christian Religion* (London: J. Tonson, 1730), a work written towards the end of his life and published posthumously, argues that miracles, the fulfilment of prophecy, and the reception of Christianity in the first three centuries are evidence in favor of the Christian religion. But this work appears to lack a final revision, and in any case his hymns and essays turn to other arguments to establish the truth of Christianity.

He did not introduce the idea of "reason" into the paraphrase until he reached the words, "There is neither speech nor language: but their voices are heard among them. Their sound is gone into all lands: and their words into the ends of the world."

> What though in solemn silence all
> Move round this dark terrestrial ball;
> What though no real voice or sound
> Amidst their radiant orbs be found:
> In reason's ear they all rejoice,
> And utter forth a glorious voice,
> For ever singing as they shine:
> The hand that made us is divine! (ibid.)

The words, "In reason's ear they all rejoice," inject reason with a strong dose of imagination. But in spite of that poetical fancy, Addison treated the psalm as a reasoned argument as well as a hymn of praise.

Addison openly admitted that he mixed his rational and imaginative faculties. It was not just calm intellectual reflection that led him to the idea of an Almighty Being. It was also his experience of the force of nature. He instanced his reaction to a storm at sea, probably during a voyage on the Mediterranean in 1700.[3] "Such an object naturally raises in my thoughts the idea of an Almighty Being, and convinces me of his existence as much as a metaphysical demonstration. The imagination prompts the understanding, and by the greatness of the sensible object, produces in it the idea of a Being who is neither circumscribed by time nor space." The sight of the rise and calming of the storm was evidence for Addison of the goodness and mercy of God, as can be seen from his hymn.

> Confusion dwelt in every face,
> And fear in every heart;
> When waves on waves, and gulf in gulfs,
> O'ercame the pilot's art.
>
> Yet then from all my griefs, O Lord,
> Thy mercy set me free,
> Whilst in the confidence of prayer
> My soul took hold on thee (*Spectator*, 14 September 1712).

Although reflection on his experience in the storm persuaded Addison of the mercy and goodness of God, it did not depict those attributes in such

---

[3]   P. Smithers, *The Life of Joseph Addison* (Oxford: Clarendon Press, 1954), 57.

a way as to offer him comfort when he contemplated his prospects of life after death. He had no difficulty in believing that he would survive death. Reason convinced him that souls are immortal. The soul's immateriality, its love of life, horror of death, and hope of immortality all supported, even if they did not prove, the doctrine of its immortality. So did the "Nature of the Supreme Being" and, in particular, God's "justice, goodness, wisdom, and veracity." But what impressed Addison the most was "the progress of the soul to its perfection, without a possibility of arriving at it." He thought it inconceivable that an infinitely good, wise, and powerful Creator would allow such a soul to perish soon after the beginning of its progress (ibid., 7 July 1711)

Having accepted the doctrine of the soul's immortality, his concern was about his destiny in that afterlife. At this point he was in sore need of assistance from revelation. When the soul is finally separated from the body and apprehends the Supreme Being, "a man must be lost in carelessness and stupidity who is not alarmed at such a thought." The prospect of a final examination before the eternal throne filled Addison with consternation. "I must confess, that I think there is no scheme of religion besides that of Christianity, which can possibly support the most virtuous person under this thought. . . . Our holy religion suggests to us the only means whereby our guilt may be taken away, and our imperfect obedience accepted" (ibid., 18 October 1712). While reason convinces us of the wisdom and power of God, faith gives us "more amiable ideas of the Supreme Being" (ibid., 16 August 1712). "If we would see him in all the wonders of his mercy, we must have recourse to revelation, which presents him to us, not only as infinitely great and glorious, but as infinitely good and just in his dispensations towards men"(ibid., 8 November 1712). In a hymn that seems to be based on his own experience of sickness, Addison appealed not to the manifestation of God in nature but to biblical revelation.

> For never shall my soul despair
>   Her pardon to procure,
> Who knows thine only Son has died
>   To make her pardon sure (ibid., 18 October 1712).

In speculating about the nature of life after death Addison cited Locke's theory that secondary qualities of color, taste, smell, and sound are "only ideas in the mind, and not qualities that have any existence in matter." He regarded this as a "great modern discovery, which is at present universally acknowledged by all the inquirers into natural philosophy." He likened human experience at death to finding oneself "on a barren heath, or in a solitary desert." At first there is no more experience of "beautiful castles,

woods, and meadows . . . the warbling of birds, and the purling of streams."
But Addison hoped that we might continue to perceive the secondary
qualities in that future existence. "It is possible the soul will not be deprived
of them, but perhaps find them excited by some other occasional cause, as
they are at present by the different impressions of the subtle matter or the
organ of sight (ibid., 24 June 1712)."

This hope may well underlie the final stanza of Addison's paraphrase
of the twenty-third psalm, published just over a month after the above
observations. Whatever the psalmist meant by the final words, "And I will
dwell in the house of the Lord for ever," Christian interpreters have
understood "for ever" to mean a life that extends beyond death; and that is
how Addison understood it. At the moment of death, he explained, when
the soul "is entering on another state of existence to converse with scenes,
and objects, and companions that are altogether new," it finds support by
casting its care "upon him who first gave her being, who has conducted her
through one stage of it, and will be always with her to guide and comfort
her in her progress through eternity." Since he had these thoughts in mind,
the final stanza of his hymn seems to imply that we can have sensations of
color and sound in that future life.

> Though in a bare and rugged way,
> Through devious lonely wilds I stray,
> Thy bounty shall my pains beguile;
> The barren wilderness shall smile
> With sudden greens and herbage crowned,
> And streams shall murmur all around (ibid., 26 July 1712)

Addison argued that ordinary human experience provides the ground
for the reasoning which leads to an idea of the Supreme Being. For this
insight he acknowledged his debt to Locke's assertion that "our complex
idea of God and separate spirits are made up of the simple ideas we receive
from reflection," and that these ideas are obtained from "what we experiment in ourselves."[4]

In one important respect Addison went much further than Locke. He
asserted that we could have direct experience of God. "The devout man
does not only believe, but feels that there is a Deity. He has actual sensations
of him; his experience concurs with his reason; he sees him more and more

---

[4]   J. Locke, *An Essay Concerning Human Understanding*, ed. P. H. Nidditch (Oxford:
Clarendon Press, 1975), 2.23.33. (References are to book, chapter, and section of this
work.) See J. Addison, *Spectator*, 8 November 1712.

in all his intercourses with him, and even in this life almost loses his faith in conviction" (*Spectator*, 23 August 1712).

At first glance this looks like the claim to special revelation that was regarded as enthusiasm. Enthusiasts, said Locke, are those "whose conceit of themselves has raised them into an Opinion of greater familiarity with God, and a nearer admittance to his Favour than is afforded to others" (*Essay* 4.19.5). Addison did not want to expose himself to the stigma of enthusiasm, which he criticized as a "kind of excess in devotion." "When the mind finds herself too much inflamed with her devotions, she is too much inclined to think they are not of her own kindling, but blown up by something Divine within her." Even in devotion, "we should be particularly careful to keep our reasons as cool as possible." Yet devotion is an activity to be pursued. Some animals may have "something like a faint glimmering of reason." But devotion is a uniquely human activity. When it is controlled by reason, it avoids the excesses of enthusiasm on the one hand and of superstition on the other (*Spectator*, 20 October 1711).

Although Addison spoke of the direct experience of God, other remarks of his give the impression that the experience is not as direct as he claimed it to be. "Our outward senses, he wrote, "are too gross to apprehend him; we may, however, taste and see how gracious he is, by his influence upon our minds, by those virtuous thoughts which he awakens in us, by those secret comforts and refreshments which he conveys into our souls, and by those ravishing joys and inward satisfactions, which are perpetually springing up and diffusing themselves among all the thoughts of good men (ibid., 23 July 1714)."

Addison seems to have identified the experience with the emotions that people feel when they reflect on the wonders of nature and on God's bounty to them in their own lives. It is an experience that occurs in devotion. "Faith and devotion naturally grow in the mind of every reasonable man, who sees the impressions of Divine power and wisdom in every object on which he casts his eye."

One of the sources of religious experience is the natural world. The countryside, Addison advised, is more conducive than the town to religious meditation. "In courts and cities we are entertained with the works of men; in the country with those of God. One is the province of art, the other of nature (ibid., 23 August 1712)."

Devotion also arises from contemplating how God has preserved us individually. A favourite word of Addison's was gratitude. He used it to describe personal recognition of God's bounty to individuals. Gratitude is not only a virtue. It is also an exercise of the mind that produces pleasure. "It exalts the soul into rapture, when it is employed on this great object of gratitude; on this beneficent Being, who has given us everything we already possess, and from whom we expect everything we hope for." Addison's poem on gratitude is one of his best known and exhibits a disciplined fervor.

> When all thy mercies, O my God,
>   My rising soul surveys;
> Transported with the view, I'm lost
>   In wonder love, and praise;
>
> O how shall words with equal warmth
>   The gratitude declare,
> That glows within my ravished heart!
>   But thou canst read it there.

The hymn recounts Addison's gratitude for divine protection from infancy through "the slippery paths of youth," and through "hidden dangers, toils, and deaths." Addison's religious experience arose from the adoration of God as creator, based on experiences of the natural world, the wonders and beauties of the creation. It also came from reflection on his own personal life. And while he attributed many of his private blessings to natural events, he also looked for solace in that aspect of God's mercy that is known only through revelation.

> When worn with sickness, oft hast thou
>   With health renewed my face,
> And when in sins and sorrows sunk,
>   Revived my soul with grace (ibid., 9 August 1712).

"Transported," "ravished," and "raptured" are the words he uses to describe his religious experiences. But they were experiences that followed rational reflection on the world of nature and on his personal fortunes. The glories of the natural world awaken in us "secret sensations of pleasure." "The cheerfulness of heart which springs up in us from the survey of nature's works is an admirable preparation for gratitude" (ibid., 31 May 1712). But it is as a result of gratitude that the experience of rapture occurs (ibid., 9 August 1712). Describing the devout individual, Addison observed, "In his deepest solitude and retirement, he knows that he is in company with the greatest of Beings; and perceives within himself such real sensations of his presence as are more delightful than anything that can be met with in the conversation of his creatures." God, he said, is "lodged in our very essence" (ibid., 23 July 1714).

Is this to be reckoned as enthusiasm? From Locke's point of view it is not. "If this internal Light," Locke wrote, "or any Proposition which under that Title we take for inspired, be conformable to the Principles of Reason or to the Word of GOD, which is attested by Revelation, *Reason* warrants it, and we may safely receive it for true, and be guided by it in our Beliefs and Actions" (*Essay* 4.19.15). One of the marks of an enthusiast is to claim to receive direct communication from God of new truths. Addison never made that claim. He believed himself to experience God in emotions of awe at the storm and of joy as he surveyed the blessings of his life. But he did not claim to receive new truths through these experiences.

The second writer to be considered is Isaac Watts. His background was very different from Addison's. He was brought up a Calvinist but was friendly towards other traditions, though he drew the line at Deism. When he wrote most of his hymns, he was orthodox in his beliefs, but towards the end of his life he displayed sympathy towards Arian and Unitarian viewpoints. He was educated at Thomas Rowe's dissenting academy in London, and became the minister of an independent congregation. His *Hymns and Spiritual Songs* were published in 1707, and his *Psalms of David* in 1719. The first book appeared before Addison's contributions to the *Spectator* and the second after his death. Addison was probably aware of many of Watts's hymns, and Watts was a reader of the *Spectator*, which published a letter that he wrote, including a paraphrase of Psalm 114 (19 August 1712). Watts was concerned, like Addison, to establish the relationship between reason and revelation and to avoid the charge of enthusiasm when he spoke of religious experience. But he laid more stress than did Addison on the subordination of reason to revelation and devoted a greater proportion of space to revealed doctrines like the atonement.

His reluctance to attach too much importance to reason is shown by his remarks about Locke. In the second edition of his *Horae Lyricae* (1709) he included verses about Locke, some of them written before the philosopher's death and some after the publication of his posthumous *Paraphrase and Notes on the Epistles of St. Paul*. When he learned that Locke was devoting his energies to the study of the scriptures, he had nothing but praise for him, and in 1704, when he discovered that Locke was seriously ill, he compared him with Elijah:

> Reason at length submits to wear
> The wings of faith; and lo, they rear
> Her chariot high, and nobly bear
> Her prophet to the skies.[5]

---

[5]   I. Watts, *The Works of the Rev. Isaac Watts, D.D.*, 7 vols. (Leeds: Printed by Edward Baker, 1800), 7:253.

But his opinion of Locke changed when he read the *Paraphrase*. Although the *Paraphrase* gave greater prominence to revelation than did any of Locke's previous writings, Watts complained that Locke's homage to reason prevented him from understanding the doctrines of the Trinity and the atonement.

> Reason could scarce sustain to see
> Th' almighty One, th' eternal Three,
> Or bear the infant deity;
> Scarce could her pride descend to own
> Her Maker stooping from his throne,
> And drest in glories so unknown.
> A ransom'd world, a bleeding God,
> And heaven appeas'd with flowing blood,
> Were themes too painful to be understood (ibid. 7:261).

In one of his hymns he probably had Locke, among others, in mind when he wrote:

> But all this glory lies conceal'd
> From men of prudence and of wit;
> The prince of darkness blinds their eyes,
> And their own pride resists the light.[6]

Watts regarded both reason and revelation as means by which truth could be ascertained. Neither of them told everything about God, but both of them provided evidence of God's existence. In his early *Horae Lyricae* (1706) Watts wrote,

> Nature and grace with all their pow'rs
> Confess the infinite Unknown (Watts, *Works*, 7:224).

But in his *Hymns* he put reason firmly in its place.

> Our reason stretches all its wings,
> And climbs above the skies;
> But still how far beneath thy feet
> Our grov'ling reason lies![7]

Addison envisaged the subordination of reason to revelation, but he never pictured it as grovelling.

---

[6] Ibid. 7:126 *Hymns and Spiritual Songs* (London: John Lawrence, 1707), Book 1, Hymn 11.

[7] Ibid. 7:123 (*Hymns* 2.87).

Watts's *Psalms*, published twelve years after the *Hymns*, are less severe in their treatment of reason. But they still give it a lower place than revelation. It is instructive to compare his paraphrase of Psalm 19 with Addison's. Addison says nothing of the superiority of revelation to reason. It is the central theme of Watts's hymn.

> The heav'ns declare thy glory, Lord;
> In ev'ry star thy wisdom shines;
> But when our eyes behold thy word,
> We read thy name in fairer lines.
>
> The rolling sun, the changing light,
> And nights and days thy pow'r confess;
> But the blest volume thou hast writ,
> Reveals thy justice and thy grace.[8]

Watts's prose writings, most of which were published after his hymns and psalms, confirm this position. His philosophical ability has been severely criticized, but he often discussed the relationships between reason and revelation. Among his works which deal with the subject are his *Logic: or, the Right Use of Reason in the Enquiry after Truth* (1724), *The Strength and Weakness of the Human Reason* (1731), and *The Ruin and Recovery of Mankind: or, An attempt to Vindicate the Scriptural Account of These Great Events upon the Plain Principles of Reason* (1740). In *The Rational Foundation of a Christian Church* (1747) he affirmed that reason provides information about morality, to which revelation does not greatly add. In "evangelical" matters it is otherwise. The doctrines of justification, resurrection, the Trinity, and the second advent are discoverable only through revelation (Watts, *Works*, 3:196–97).

Even in the area of morality, most of which is in theory discoverable by reason, our flawed human nature prevents us from using our reason effectively. Before the Fall Adam was a completely rational being, but even in that condition he was ready to submit to revelation. "If his maker were pleased to reveal any sublimer truth to him which his reason could not comprehend, then reason itself submitted to that revelation, believed the word of a speaking God, and resigned the throne to faith" (ibid. 1:110).

These speculations about Adam's pre-fallen state went well beyond the evidence of the Book of Genesis, but they gave strength to Watts's contention that reason was tainted by the Fall.

---

[8]   Watts, *Works* 7:44 (Psalm 19).

Bless'd with the joys of innocence,
Adam our father stood,
Till he debas'd his soul to sense,
And eat the unlawful food.

Now we are born a sensual race,
To sinful joys inclin'd;
Reason has lost its native place,
And flesh inslaves the mind.[9]

Religious experience was a central theme for Watts. He was as ready as Addison to speak of the raptures and pleasures of the Christian life. But he had no more desire than Addison had to be branded as an enthusiast. He was suspicious of the early Methodists and distanced himself from George Whitefield.[10] Enthusiasts, he wrote, "believe that reason is of no use in things of religion" (Watts, *Works*, 3:724). He feared that displays of emotion might have little substance. "The Christian life is no fantastic and visionary matter, that consists in warm imaginations, and pretends to inward light and rapture; it is a real change of heart and practice, from sin to holiness, and turn of the soul from earth toward heaven" (ibid. 1:106). Moreover, Watts knew that claims to religious experience were liable to ridicule, and that as a result of this ridicule many Christians resolved "to believe that nothing of experimental religion can be justified to strict reason." At the same time Watts insisted that a life of holiness and a feeling of happiness, a sense of sins forgiven and a persuasion of the special love of God are a direct witness given by the Spirit (ibid. 1:11).

He agreed with Locke that a genuine revelation needed evidence to confirm it, and cited, as Locke did, the miraculous power of Moses (ibid. 6:133). But he believed that the age of supernatural miracles was past. He therefore sought elsewhere for corroboration of the genuineness of a reve-lation. Watts mentioned three other kinds of evidence. The first was the fulfilment of prophecy. The second was the power of the gospel to change people's lives. The third was the inward witness. "Wheresoever persons have found this effect in their own hearts, wrought by a belief of the gospel of Christ, they have a witness in themselves of the truth of it, and abundant reason to believe it divine" (ibid. 6:134).

The inward witness consisted of a sense of sins forgiven and of a special love of God for the individual. Watts obviously claimed this experience for himself.

---

9   Ibid., 7:181 (*Hymns*, 2.128).

10   A. P. Davis, *Isaac Watts: His Life and Works* (New York: The Dryden Press, 1943), 45–49.

Jesus, thy witness speaks within;
The mercy which thy words reveal,
Refines the heart from sense and sin,
And stamps its own celestial seal (ibid. 1:37).

Yet Watts made a distinction between men and women who receive an inward assurance of forgiveness and the prophets and apostles who through "inspiration" receive new revelations of divine truth. "In the case of inspiration, the prophet not only exercises divine faith, in believing what God reveals, but he is under a superior heavenly impression, light, and evidence, whereby he is assured that God reveals it." The claim to inspiration, Watts said, needs external attestation by such means as miracles, and it only belongs to "a few favourites of heaven" (ibid. 6:91).

When Watts spoke of the inward witness of the Spirit, he was not claiming to receive a special revelation. He was claiming an experience which he believed to be available for every believer, and he was claiming to sense the divine presence within him. His viewpoint was like Addison's and the tradition was later developed by the Wesleys. Critics may dispute whether these feelings are actually God-given. It is possible to give a purely secular account of the removal of a sense of guilt or of the feelings of awe and wonder in the presence of natural beauty. But once a belief in God and the inner working of the Spirit is accepted, it is not a giant step to regard the feelings that Watts and Addison mention as experiences of God.

Watts's hymns have long been a part of the tradition of worship in English-speaking Protestantism. They were sung with great frequency in the eighteenth and nineteenth centuries. His *Psalms and Hymns* sold 60,000 copies in 1865 (Davis, *Watts*, 212–13). And even in the twentieth century many of the leading hymnals have included a substantial selection of his work.

Addison's hymns did not have as great an impact as did Watts's. But they have continued to be used from the time they were written until the present. Moreover, the *Spectator* essays, for which Addison wrote his hymns, were read widely throughout the eighteenth and nineteenth centuries; and the hymns have reached an even greater cross-section of the public than the essays have done.

Most of the people who have sung or read these hymns have known little about the intellectual atmosphere in which the writers lived. Probably few of them have recognized how the words reflected the writer's views on controversial issues of their time. But the hymns took shape under the influence of the theological and philosophical discussions of the early eighteenth century. Addison and Watts did not exclude reason. They were always concerned to be reasoned in their arguments, and they believed that reason proved the existence of God and established moral truths. But they both regarded revelation as essential to their salvation. Moreover, they gave sustained expression to religious emotion. The trend was already beginning towards a stress on individual religious experience that was characteristic of eighteenth-century revivalism. It did not claim to receive new truth by special revelation, but it laid great emphasis on a sense of assurance of God's love and mercy. And it regarded the emotions that accompanied this assurance as sensations of the divine presence.

Although Addison received some gibes because of his religious interests, it was difficult to accuse him of enthusiasm. He was the chronicler of Sir Roger de Coverley and an urbane commentator on the manners of polite society. He did not convey the impression of being a religious fanatic. Watts was more suspect. Religious activities were consistently at the center of his life. He was a well-known preacher and hymn writer. Because of the directness and simplicity of his language his allusions to religious experience were less restrained than Addison's. Yet both Watts and Addison were concerned to show that there could be religious experience without enthusiasm. Their position depended on understanding their feelings of awe, wonder, relief, and joy in the light of their faith.

Edmund Law and His Circle at Cambridge: Some Philosophical Activity of the 1730s.

John Stephens

One of John Yolton's many achievements has been to draw attention to the way in which minor figures play an important part in the history of philosophy as they prepare the ground and define the assumptions of those greater than they. Often these people also turn out to be of more significance than was first thought: certainly consideration of their work enables us to attempt to follow what was going on in a way that might have made sense to the original participants. This essay is an attempt to draw a sketch map of what was happening in Cambridge in the early 1730s. In 1731 Edmund Law, a young fellow of Christ's translated into English *De Origine Mali* by William King, sometime Archbishop of Dublin. This represented the first published fruit of a mass of philosophical activity in Cambridge in the preceding decade. The object of this essay is to disinter the participants and show something of their relevance to one another. Law himself is known, at least to eighteenth century specialists, as is John Gay. This cannot be said with any assurance of others such as John Clarke, Joseph Clarke, John Chapman, Thomas Rutherforth and Thomas Johnson, to say nothing of Phillips Gretton and Thomas Knowles. These forgotten figures will be briefly introduced in the course of this paper.

In 1781 Edmund Law rewrote the introduction to his translation first published exactly fifty years before.[1] He was then in his seventy-eighth year and was nearing the end of his career as a successful eighteenth century pluralist. He died six years later in 1787. Born in 1703, he had been educated at Cartmell and Kendall schools and as a sizar at St. John's College,

---

[1] William King's *De Origine Mali* was published in London and Dublin in 1702 though written in 1697. Edmund Law's translation was published in Cambridge in 1731. This was a quarto edition. A second edition which included additional material supplied by King's family appeared in two volumes (Cambridge, 1732). This and all subsequent editions appeared in octavo. These were Cambridge 1739, Cambridge 1758 and London 1781. References to the text are given to the 2nd edition of 1732 and, for Law's later introduction, briefly to the 5th edition of 1782.

Cambridge, graduating in 1724. Elected a fellow of Christ's, he remained there until 1737 when he occupied various Cumberland livings, becoming Archdeacon of Carlisle in 1743. However, his Cambridge connections did not cease: he proceeded D.D. in 1743, rather controversially since he held the doctrine of the sleep of the soul between death and resurrection. In 1756 he returned to Cambridge as Master of Peterhouse, in 1760 university librarian, and Knightsbridge Professor of Moral Philosophy in 1764. His career culminated in his appointment to the see of Carlisle in 1768. For a while he held this, again rather controversially, together with the university librarianship; the only time that office has been occupied by a bishop.[2] In the fifty years that had elapsed since Law had first written much had happened in Cambridge. It is true that as far as natural science was concerned Newton had already firmly entered the syllabus[3] but in many respects what was then taught represented a continuation of the seventeenth century scholastic curriculum.[4] In the period that Law was resident the curriculum was still in flux and much depended on the interests of the moderators charged with the conduct of each year's disputations. This appears to have been especially true in the 1730s although even then the developments which culminated in the establishment of the mathematical tripos as the principal examination for the B.A. degree in 1747 were already clear. Before this there was a brief flowering of philosophical inquiry in which Law played a crucial role.

In that 1781 fifth edition of his translation of King's work Law tells us something of himself, the origins of his translation, and his life at Cambridge at that time. In his first philosophical studies, he states, it was his "principal endeavour to get a competent knowledge of the several systems then in vogue, as well as of the general powers, and properties of human nature, and the rules by which they were to be directed; taking Mr. *Locke* as one of my chief guides in such enquiries" (Fifth edition xvi). It was as part of this process that in about 1723 he discovered King's work, itself originally

---

[2] J. Peile, *Biographical Register of Christ's College 1565–1905* (Cambridge: Cambridge University Press, 1913), 2: 200–201. D.J. McKitterick, *Cambridge University Library. A History: the Eighteenth and Nineteenth Centuries* (Cambridge: Cambridge University Press, 1986), 283ff. J. and J.A. Venn *Alumni Cantabrigienses* (Cambridge: Cambridge University Press, 1922): unless otherwise stated this is the source of all biographgical details given in this article.

[3] J. Gascoigne, *Cambridge in the Age of the Enlightenment* (Cambridge: Cambridge University Press, 1989), 142ff.

[4] W. T. Costello, *The Scholastic Curriculum in Early Seventeenth Century Cambridge*. (Cambridge, Mass: Harvard University Press, 1958)

published in 1702. Modesty, he states, made him produce the work in the form that he did, that is to say that the translation of the text is accompanied by extensive, often digressive, footnotes. This form of translation was not unprecedented and Law may well have had in mind Samuel Clarke's Latin translation of Rohault's physics. Law's notes clarify many of King's arguments in the context of his own extreme interpretation of Locke's empiricism in turn directed at Clarke's a priori arguments.

Law goes on to say that then at Cambridge there were some "remarked abuses in the training up of our youth" such as persisting in bringing them up in Aristotelian Logic rather than "laying some solid foundation in Natural Philosophy with its modern improvements, or *Natural Law* (as the whole Doctrine of *Morals* is now termed) which should be of constant use to these young disciples. . . ." (Fifth edition xviii). Law did not approve of the dominance of mathematics at Cambridge in the latter half of the century pointing out that these "favourite [i.e. Mathematical] speculations did not at first so far engross all the thoughts of our young Students as not to admit some points of a moral and metaphysical kind to accompany them; which last held their ground for about twenty years, and together with Mr Locke's Essay, Dr. Clarke went hand in hand thro' our public schools and lectures, tho' they were built on principles opposite to one another. . . ." However Clarke's insistence on "certain innate *Instincts*, or *absolute Fitnesses*" were completely at odds with Locke's empiricism "till at lenghth certain flaws being discovered in the Doctor's celebrated argument *a priori* . . . his doctrine fell into disrepute and was generally given up . . . " (Ibid, xix).

The attraction of King's work for Law was that it managed to combine an empiricist epistemology with at least the outlines of an empiricist ethical theory. King's book was published in 1702 though it was written five years earlier in 1697. King had had time to absorb Locke's *Essay*, although there were parts of it that he was not happy about, notably Locke's rejection of the doctrine of innate ideas and also the ambiguous ontological status of some of Locke's ideas.[5] These King had outlined in a letter to Locke sent via Molyneux which would have been available to Law.[6] By 1731 the context had changed and the doctrine of innate ideas could be easily, and

---

[5]   J. W. Yolton, *John Locke and the Way of Ideas* Oxford: Clarendon Press, 1956, 49ff. Yolton errs in supposing that King changed his mind on innate ideas. It was only in the second edition that Law had access to King's papers and the additions made from that source do not indicate a change of view.

[6]   William King to William Molyneux included in Molyneux to Locke 26/27 October 1697 in *John Locke The Correspondence . . .* ed. E.S. de Beer (Oxford: 1981) 4. No. 2339. This had been printed in Locke's *Some Familiar Letters* (London: A&J Churchill, 1708).

certainly was by Law, looked on as exploded. In his notes on King's first chapter, one of the most extensively annotated, Law also reprints, in the first edition, King's own notes with the exception of that on innate ideas, which he regards as unnecessary. Otherwise Law's intention is to underline King's ideas in a very specific way, most notably in insisting that many of our most important ideas such as space and time are abstract.

Law argues, following Locke, that abstract ideas exist "no where but in the Mind, neither have they any other foundation , nor can they be a proof of anything, beside the power which the mind has to form them." Abstract ideas are not a case of "making the idea of the Individual stand for the whole Species" as King and Peter Browne suggest since that would entail "that *Universals*, such as *Animal* or *Matter* have a real Existence in the same precise manner in which we consider them; whereas under such precision they are confessedly the creatures of our own Minds and exist nowhere else." (Second edition, (1732) 8). This is possibly to misunderstand King and Browne, neither of whom seem to have said any such thing.

King states that we must "attend to our own Thoughts and Sensations, which have no relation to external Things or to Quantity; and when our Minds are thus employed, there will appear to be the more necessity for the existence of Space than of Matter." King connects belief in the self-existence of Space with a peculiarity of our conception of ourselves: "For a finite Mind requires a Cause *from* which it may receive Existence no less than a Body does a Place in which it may exist: and from hence in reality: it is that we attribute *Self-existence* to Space because whenever we think of ourselves, we imagine ourselves to consist of both *Body* and *Soul*. While therefore we are conscious of our Existence, we form a Belief in Space also as necessarily existing, since it is connected with the Conception of *Body* i.e. of ourselves." (Second edition, 38–39). Certain experiences (hearing, smelling), can, says Law, have no connection with space. The mind when it thinks of its own operations can think of nothing but itself and its cause. The fact that in concept space cannot be partially annihilated is why we suppose it to be self-existent.

For King conceptions of external things are true in the sense that they "represent things as God would have them known to us." He recognises that this does not necessarily mean that we perceive things, even mediately, as they are. Of space he says that even if the whole world were annihilated, the "Idea of Space" would remain as of a thing yet existing. King wonders whether "this Inability of our Understanding to separate the Nature of *Space* from Existence, proceeds from the *same Nature* of Space or rather from the *Imperfections* of our Reason." For King this is still (just) a question. For Law it is a vital matter and accounts for both Joseph Clarke and Law himself writing on the nature of space. This debate on space in Cambridge in the 1730s was an important one. If space is an abstract idea and no more, it follows that the mind's conception of any reality outside itself necessarily includes ideas that are fictitious. It follows from hence that the mind is incapable of making certain deductions on the strength of ideas alone, thus dispensing with any *a priori* certainty. Those who took the other view argued that since space is something (i.e. not an abstract idea), it must be explicable, for example as a mode of some unknown substance.

King finally argues about the first cause. Reason tells us that an active principle exists even though we are not certain as to its exact nature. Although "by our outward Senses, and the Notions they convey to us, we cannot go beyond *Space, Matter, Motion, sensible Qualities*, and this *Active Principle* which we are speaking of we can conceive *within ourselves a Self-conscious* and *thinking principle* within us" which is entirely abstracted from any notion of internal and external. By analogy we can ascribe similar qualities to the first cause. This since it is infinite . . . in its Essence and Power . . . must be so likewise in *Intelligence*, viz. *omnipotent, and omniscient.*" (Second edition, 56–57) Being infinite in knowledge and power this cause works for an end. Since God is perfect in himself and since all things subsist by his Providence "and stand in need of him, but he of none" it follows that he made those things for no advantage of his own. What is wanting even to a perfect God was the exercise of his Attributes *without*, [i.e.] "the communication of his Power and Goodness." It was this that he attempted in the Creation. Any external existence can add nothing to God's nature and it is not necessary for God that he should have created the world. It was made for the "exercise of the Divine power and the Communication of his Goodness." (Second edition, 58–59). To say that the world was made for the glory of God is metaphorical: man may think so, God does not. King's argument is that God wishes to bring happiness "and more good arises to our whole species from the donation of . . . a self moving power together with all its forseen abuses, than could have been produced without it" (Fifth edition, xix).

However it is at this point that King's interests diverge from Law's and those of Law's circle. King's work is exactly what he says it is—an enquiry into the existence of moral evil. He is not attempting to construct a complete system of ethics. Law implicitly recognizes this in his preface in stating that the inquiry into the origin of evil "leads us into the most exalted Speculations concerning the Existence and Attributes of God, and the Original of Things." In other words, it is merely a stepping stone. Given that man is an imperfect creature, King examines the nature of his imperfection in the form of an examination of man's intention, good or bad. It is only in the section "On Moral Evil" that Law again annotates extensively and it is clear that his aim is to insist on man's free will; subsequently these notes expanded and by the third edition (1739) they had extended to include not only Anthony Collins but, for example Samuel Strutt, author of *Philosophical Enquiry into the Spring of Human Actions* (1732). The purchase of the argument in these works was to insist that some or all of our actions are determined, and hence bear no element of moral responsibility.[7] If God has created the world to spread happiness and that man has the freedom to pursue that end it must be possible to deduce the manner in whicn he intends that end to be attained. Law must have realized King's book and his annotations alone did not do this, which is why the translation is preceded by a "Preliminary Dissertation concerning the Fundamental Principle of Virtue or Morality" which attempts to marry a posteriori epistemology with a posteriori ethics. What is clear is that Law's translation was the first attempt at this synthesis, fragmentary and imperfect as it may be. The author of this piece—John Gay—was one of the first of Law's circle to try to take matters further.

They were, for the most part, young graduates newly elected to fellowships. These were B.A.s and M.A.s pursuing their studies for higher degrees with the eventual hope of ordination and a college living or other preferment. Although there were many people with similar interests at Cambridge at this time, their presence was transitory, and it was inevitable that their activity in a specifically Cambridge context was short lived. Law's translation is its first major published manifestation, and a number of works by Law's associates followed, almost all of which bear the imprint of the Cambridge publisher Thurlbourne. Apart from the evidence of these publications little seems to be known of Law at the time. One of the few with any sort of knowledge of him was William Paley, but he knew Law much later, and his memoir of him is, in any case, tantalizingly brief.[8] The acquaintances that Paley cites are Daniel Waterland, the Master of Magdalene, John Jortin and John Taylor. These latter were young men at that time and still had substantial reputations in the late eighteenth century, formed in classical scholarship and miscellaneous letters rather than philosophy. The acquain-

---

[7]   Strutt seems to have been influential at Cambridge at the time. Tinkler Duckett who was expelled from the University in 1738 looked on Strutt's *Philosophical Enquiry* as the infallible guide to his reaching the "ne plus ultra" of atheism. J. Venn, *Biographical History of Gonville and Caius College* (Cambridge: Cambridge University Press, 1898) 2: 28. British Library Add Manuscripts, 5822: f.90b et. seq.

[8]   W. Paley, *A Short Memoir of the Life of Edmund Law* (London: Davis, Taylor and Wilks, 1800) 2.

tances of Law that were in any sense philosphers had almost all long since died without trace. Paley was writing in the last decade of the eighteenth century, and it would have been natural only to mention those names still likely to be known.

However, Paley was right to identify Daniel Waterland as a crucial figure. He was much senior to Law—he was born in 1683—and had been Master of Magdalene since 1712 where he remained until his death in 1740. His reputation was that of a formidable defender of Christian orthodoxy, most specifically of the divinity of Christ. He was a man of immense learning and ability, a philosopher, but not in the sense that one now understands the term, but well able to undertake abstract thought when he thought it necessary. The arguments in his other books are based on immense citation of biblical and patristic sources. However, the thrust of Law's notes in his translation cannot but have appealed to him. The second edition of Law's translation (1732) is dedicated to Waterland, and Law in the dedication takes the opportunity of mentioning "the many private obligations which in a particular manner demand an acknowledgment" (Second edition vi). Waterland would have been pleased, since Law's insistence on the argument a posteriori could be shown to demonstrate the need for revelation, thus undermining the deist view that revelation was no more than a republication of the laws of nature.

This was a line taken by one of Waterland's most interesting protégés,[9] Thomas Johnson, who graduated in 1724–5, the year after Law, and became a fellow of Magdalene the same year. Johnson was a classical scholar who had collaborated with Law and others on an edition of Étienne's *Thesaurus* published in 1734–5. However he also had a serious interest in philosophy, particularly moral philosophy, and wrote a number of works on that subject. He produced *An Essay on Moral Obligation* attacking the deists Thomas Chubb and Thomas Morgan, a sermon *The Insufficiency of the Laws of Nature* (both in 1731), as well as *A Summary of Natural Religion* published in 1736. All these were printed for or by William Thurlbourne. Johnson seems to have been resident in Cambridge at least until 1734 when he produced *Quaestiones Philosophicae* (later editions 1735; 1741), a guide to the questions asked in the schools based on his experience as moderator in 1731–2. He became a Chaplain at Whitehall at some point before his early death in 1737. The second protégé was Joseph Clarke, educated at Westminster and who graduated in 1726–7 from Magdalene, where he was a pupil of Johnson:

---

[9]   Cf. Eamonn Duffy in P. Cunnich et. al., *A History of Magdalene College 1425–1988* (Cambridge: Magdalene College, 1994), 165. "Over the fellows, as over the undergraduates he exercised a firm though usually friendly discipline."

he became a fellow of Magdalene in 1732 and, like Johnson, died early in 1749. He wrote two pamphlets, published in 1733 and 1734, on the nature of space, defending the views expressed in Law's notes.[10]

A third member of this group was John Gay, the author of the "Prefatory Discourse" to Law's translation of King. He is much the most mysterious. He was born in 1699 and graduated from Sidney Sussex in 1721–2, that is to say a year before Law, and was a fellow of the college from 1724–1732, when he left for two Bedfordhire livings. He died only a little later than the others, in 1745, leaving a wife and five children in poverty.[11] Law, according to Paley, spoke of him with great respect—"In the Bible and in the writings of Mr Locke, no man . . . was so well versed." His versatility was shown in his college, where he occupied every college office other than the mastership in the space of five years. His authorship of the *Discourse* appears to have been an open secret in Cambridge—David Hartley, for example, was aware of it at the time, but it was only explicitly acknowledged by Law in the fourth edition (Cambridge, 1758) of the translation. In the last edition printed in Gay's lifetime, the third (Cambridge 1739), Law is only able to state "that the author of this dissertation is well known but I cannot have leave to mention him."

These four are the prime movers in what happened at Cambridge in the period we are concerned with. Others from a slightly later generation carried on the tradition; Thomas Knowles who published a pamphlet, *The Existence and Attributes of God Not Demonstrable a Priori* (Cambridge, 1746), and John Chapman who wrote an attack on Thomas Morgan, *Eusebius* (2 vols. Cambridge, 1739–1741). Chapman was of a later generation graduating B.A. from King's in 1727 whilst Knowles was later still graduating from Pembroke in 1744. More important though, at least in terms of his influence, was Thomas Rutherforth, who, graduating in 1729–1730, was a fellow of St. John's from 1733 to 1752, moderator in the schools in 1736 and Regius Professor of Divinity from 1756 until his death in 1771.

Cambridge in the early part of the eighteenth century was in as much political turmoil as the rest of the country. The triumph of Newtonianism within the university was a specifically Whig one, and Cambridge's loyalty to the Hanoverian dynasty was sealed by George I's gift of the great library

---

10   J. Clarke, *Dr. Clarke's Notion of Space Examined* (Cambridge: Cornelius Crownfield, 1733); *A Farther Examination of Dr. Clarke's Notions of Space* (Cambridge: Cornelius Crownfield, 1734).

11   Gascoigne, *Cambridge in the Age of the Enlightenment,* 128. He appears to have held no College Office after 1730. Cf. *Notes and Queries* 1st ser., 4: 389. The Rev — Gay. [signes] 'Fellow of Sidney Sussex College.' Nevertheless Gay's son entered the College in 1752.

of John Moore, Bishop of Ely, which was bought for the university by George I. A contemporary jibe about Oxford lacking loyalty and Cambridge learn-ing (hence the need of the gift of the library) may be justified by the fact that the only copies of the first and (until recently) the second, editions of Locke's *Essay* in Cambridge University Library came from that source. But by the time that Johnson published his *Quaestiones* Locke had entered the syllabus and Johnson even directs his pupils to such works as Henry Lee's *Antscepticism* (1700) and John Sergeant's *Solid Philosophy Asserted* (1697), both of them amongst the ablest replies to the *Essay*.

The bulk of the material referred to by Johnson relates to natural phi-losophy, but the sections on what in contemporary parlance we would call philosophy are fascinating. It certainly suggests that Johnson's expectations of his pupils were substantial and his own erudition and diligence staggering. He was, for example, reading Berkeley's *Alciphron* very shortly after publi-cation. Nevertheless, a large number of the sources that Johnson cites are scholastic Latin texts such as Aquinas and Albertus Magnus. The texts for logic are the standard seventeenth century ones—such as Aldrich, Burgers-dijk and Sanderson—with the addition of Isaac Watts's *Logick*. Locke's *Essay* is of course cited along with works by Balguy, Andrew Baxter, Berkeley, Peter Browne, Colliber, Collins, Edward Bentham, Fiddes, Norris, Perronet, and Wollaston. None of those had any current connection with Cam-bridge, although some had been educated there. Foreign authors cited in-clude Bayle, Crousaz, Le Clerc, Malebranche and Wolff. Samuel Clarke is of course prominent not least for his correspondence with Leibniz. As one would expect, the works of Law and his circle feature prominently. One source from Cambridge's past that is frequently cited for its arguments on space and time is Ralph Cudworth's *True Intellectual System of the Universe* (1678).

In 1736 Johnson published *A Summary of Natural Religion* which sets out his agenda in more general terms:

> And . . . with regard to the Being and Attributes of God, I am content with the Old Method of proceeding *a posteriori*, or from Effect to Cause, as I find I can lay no other hold of these famous mediums (*Space* and *Absolute Necessity*) which have been invented of late to build up a Demonstration *a priori*, than merely a *Entia Rationis*, or abstract Ideas, with out any objective reality. ([v]–[vi]

Of Law he states that he has:

> thrown a great deal of Light on several very important and nice Points which fall within the compass of our Enquiry: it were to be wish'd that he had given us a set Treatise on the Subject, rather than interspersed his

Notions here and there occasionally, or thrown them into a Corner where scarce any body will think of looking for them. Had he done so my labours might well have been spared as the World would have been furnished with a much better Treatise on the Subject before us, than I can pretend to give them. [iv]

This is significant, since Law had published an *Enquiry into the Ideas of Space, Time Immensity and Eternity* (Cambridge 1734) which much expanded the notes that he had published in 1731. Waterland had contributed a learned appendix to this, expounding arguments against the a priori argument from Albertus Magnus onwards: a virtuoso performance and perhaps Waterland's only purely philosophical work. Hence, by a "set Treatise" Johnson means something that brings together a posteriori reasoning in both metaphysics and morals. Evidently that is why he felt it necessary to write his own book two years later, and in this short period he was the only person to be overtly concerned with ethics. The bulk of the debate in Cambridge had concentrated on the more abstract questions of space and time on which the demolition of the validity of the a priori argument was seen to depend. In Cambridge itself Samuel Clarke had only one defender, John Clarke, a fellow of Corpus who produced *A Defence of Dr. Samuel Clarke's Demonstration of the Being and Attributes of God* (London 1731) followed by second (1733?) and third (1733) defenses: all but the last are anonymous. Clarke was Samuel's nephew and the son of John Clarke, Dean of Salisbury. He, in turn, was attacked by Joseph Clarke—apparently no relation—in *Dr. Clarke's Notion of Space Examined* (Cambridge 1733) followed by *A Farther Examination* published in 1734. Another player in the game was Phillips Gretton who had published *A Review of the Argument a Priori* in 1726 and whose act for his doctorate of divinity caused some commotion in 1732. This included a Latin sermon in which he attributed the works written by John Clarke of Corpus to his father: this is what caused the third of his defenses to be issued under his own name. Also of the pro Clarke faction was John Jackson,[12] sniping from his position as master of Wigston's Hospital in Leicester in which position he had succeeded Samuel Clarke, but he cannot be considered part of the Cambridge debate.

Rutherforth's *Essay on Virtue* (Cambridge 1744) is the last large scale work of the circle. He had graduated the year before Law had published his translation and by the publication of his book, probably based on lectures, he was able to take a lot for granted which had not been possible ten years before. His systematic treatment meant that he reverted to references to the

---

12   J. W. Yolton, *Perceptual Acquaintance* (Oxford: Basil Blackwell, 1984), 81–82.

seventeenth century natural law theorists such as Pufendorf and Grotius (whom he edited), and did not feel it necessary to refer to the writings of the early 1730s, a brief approving reference to Gay's *Treatise* excepted.[13] The later oblivion of most of the writers of the 1730s can probably be dated from this point. They all had in common a broadly utilitarian ethic and all rejected any form of a priori argument. Gay's *Dissertation* is still a standard text of the period but the others have been strangely neglected. This is not totally surprising, since, if one assumes utilitarianism to be a nineteenth century invention, its historians did not think it necessary to look too far beyond the year 1800. They looked back to David Hartley who graduated from St. John's in 1725–26 and was a Fellow until 1730 and whose *Observations on Man* was published in 1749. This was a popular text in the eighteenth century and often reprinted. The main set author at Cambridge was William Paley, senior wrangler in 1763 and a friend and contemporary of Law's son John, later Bishop of Elphin. Paley's *Principles of Moral Philosophy* (1786) was dedicated to Law. With this work, of which Richard Price asserted, "Never before have I met with a theory of morals which has appeared to me more exceptionable," the circle closes.[14]

Law's translation of King's work is on the whole regarded as the most convenient means of reading King's original text. Few have bothered to look at the notes and their significance. But the preliminary data presented here—not even scratching the surface, just looking at it—suggest that what was going on in Cambridge at this time was of unusual significance. The detailed debates on space and time are complex and of real philosophical interest. Although this aspect fell by the wayside, the demolition of the a priori arguments on space and time also went alongside the laying of the foundations for an ethical theory which was the precursor of the utilitarianism of the nineteenth century as it was expressed by late eighteenth-century writers such as Abraham Tucker and Jeremy Bentham. How all these were interrelated is difficult and complex: what is offered here is no more than a preliminary and doubtless inadequate prospectus.

---

[13]   T. Rutherforth, An Essay on the Nature and Obligations of Virtue (Cambridge: J. Bentham for William Thurlbourne, 1744), 250.

[14]   R. Price, A *Review of the Principal Questions of Morals* . . . ed. D.D. Raphael (Oxford: Clarendon Press, 1974), 283.

HUME, DESCARTES, AND THE MATERIALITY OF THE SOUL*

John P. Wright

Nearly two hundred and sixty years ago, in the summer of 1737, David Hume left La Fleche after a stay of two years to return to England to publish the first two books of his *Treatise of Human Nature*.[1] On his way back to Paris, at Tours, he wrote a letter to his friend Michael Ramsey, advising him to read four books which would aid in the understanding of the "metaphysical Parts of [his] Reasoning."[2] Of the four books which Hume cites, the most surprising is Descartes's *Meditations*. After mentioning Malebranche's *De la recherche de la vérité*, Berkeley's *Principles of Human Knowledge*, and the "metaphysical Articles of Baile's Dictionary such as those of Zeno and Spinoza," Hume adds that "Des-Cartes Meditations woud also be useful but (I) don't know if you will find it easily among your Acquaintances." Much serious scholarship has gone into describing the connections between Hume and the other three authors, far less on the connections between Hume and Descartes. Yet, especially in determining the basic principles of Hume's own philosophy of the soul or mind, the relation of his ideas to those of the seventeenth-century French thinker are particularly important. It is that aspect of the connection between the two philosophers which I will focus on in this paper.

It is difficult to believe that Hume's choice of La Fleche as the locale to write his masterwork was unrelated to the fact that the greatest of French philosophers had been educated at the Jesuit college (clearly the town's main attraction) over 120 years earlier. In his biography of Hume, E.C. Mossner writes that La Fleche "was still in 1735 a center of Cartesianism."

---

[1]   In *My Own Life* Hume wrote: "During my Retreat in France, first at Reims, but chiefly at Lafleche in Anjou, I composed my *Treatise of human Nature*. After passing three Years very agreeably in that Countrey, I came over to London in 1737" *The Letters of David Hume*, 2 vols., ed. J.Y.T. Greig [Oxford: Clarendon Press, 1932] Vol. 1, 2.

[2]   Tadeusz Kozanecki, "Dawida Hume'a Nieznane Listy W Zbiorach Muzeum Czartoryskich (Polska)," *Archiwum Historii Filozofii I Mysli Spolecznej* 9 (1963): 127–39 and Richard H. Popkin, "So Hume did read Berkeley," *Journal of Philosophy* 61 (1964): 773–78.

While I can find no evidence for this claim,[3] what seems to be true is that the hostility to Cartesianism by the Jesuits had waned by Hume's day and that the tenets of Cartesianism were commonly debated by them.[4] Hume's own philosophy engages the basic tenets of Cartesian philosophy at the deepest level, and La Fleche must at least have provided the symbolic ground where he believed he could do battle with the great French thinker.

The most obvious connection between Hume's *Treatise* and Descartes's *Meditations* lies in the fundamental project of the two books. In the introduction to the *Treatise* Hume wrote that his aim is to "propose a compleat system of the sciences, built on a foundation almost entirely new" (xvi). This metaphor had been central to Descartes's *Meditations*, where he announced that his purpose was "to demolish everything completely and start again right from the foundations" in order "to establish anything at all in the sciences which was stable and likely to last."[5] Like Descartes, Hume was interested in providing foundations for "Mathematics, Natural Philosophy and Natural Religion" as well as sciences whose connection with human nature is more obvious (*Treatise*, xv). Yet, it is clear that the foundations which the two authors sought were very different. Descartes founded the other sciences on principles which are certain and indubitable. The foundational science for Hume was a science of "human nature," a science whose principles had be gleaned from experience and "a cautious observation of human life" (ibid., xix). The basic principles of this science have, at best, a high degree of probability.

Hume and the Cartesian Principle of Metaphysical Reasoning

What then could Hume have expected Michael Ramsey to learn from an examination of the metaphysical reasoning of Descartes's *Meditations*? The principle of reasoning employed in the *Meditations* is that the analysis of our

---

3   E.C. Mossner, *The Life of David Hume*, 2d ed. (Oxford: Clarendon Press, 1980), 99. Mossner also claims that Descartes is implicitly mentioned in the *Treatise* when Hume refers to "the Cartesians" (104). This is misleading because both of Hume's references to the Cartesians in the *Treatise* are to the occasionalist views of Malebranche. See D. Hume, *A Treatise of Human Nature*, ed. L.A. Selby-Bigge, 2d ed., rev. by P.H. Nidditch (Oxford: Clarendon, 1978), 159, 249.

4   See G. Sortais, *Le cartésianisme chez les Jésuits français au xviie et au xviiie siècle* (Paris: Gabriel Beauchesne, 1929).

5   R. Descartes, *Meditations on First Philosophy*, in *The Philosophical Writings of Descartes*, 2 vols., trans. and ed. J. Cottingham et al. (Cambridge: Cambridge University Press, 1984), Vol. 2:12. Henceforth referred to as *Meditations* + page number.

mental contents or ideas is the basis for determining the truth about the structure of reality. Thus, at the beginning of Meditation 3 Descartes states his general rule that "whatever I perceive very clearly and distinctly is true" (*Meditations*, 24). According to Descartes, "we cannot have any knowledge of things except by the ideas we conceive of them," and "whatever conflicts with these ideas is absolutely impossible and involves a contradiction."[6] In his *Meditations* he went on to describe what he considered to be clear and distinct ideas of God, matter, and the soul. Descartes's analysis of these metaphysical concepts was designed to clear the ground for the foundation of his own mechanical conception of nature. However, by the time Hume was writing, Malebranche and Berkeley claimed to show that a correct interpretation of Cartesian idea analysis leads back to a totally theocentric conception of reality. In my *Sceptical Realism of David Hume*[7] I argue that Hume regarded the conclusions of Malebranche and Berkeley as involving a *reductio ad absurdum* of the Cartesian way of ideas. Hume held that a genuine analysis of our clear and distinct ideas, those based on our sense impressions, led to the paradoxical ontological conclusions of these philosophers—the conclusions that there are no real causes in the physical world and that there are no objects which exist unperceived. However, these are conclusions which Hume himself considered to be absurd and directly opposed to the fundamental beliefs of contemporary experimental science, as well as common sense. Thus Hume sought to provide an entirely different foundation for these beliefs in *human nature*—one which required recognition of the indispensable role of the natural and irrational processes of the imagination in gaining a purchase on reality.

However, there is one area in which Hume himself held that the Cartesian principle of metaphysical reasoning is valid, namely the soul itself. That is not to say that Hume himself held, like Descartes, that one could establish the simplicity and immateriality of the soul on the basis of an analysis of ideas. Indeed, Hume argued that a correct analysis of our ideas led to quite opposite conclusions. Nevertheless, Hume's faith in idea analysis in the limited realm of the soul led him into paradoxes from which he found it impossible to extricate himself. In the rest of this paper, I shall argue that it is Hume's acceptance of the Cartesian principle of metaphysical reasoning in this limited realm which led him to two of the most paradoxical conclusions of the *Treatise*—conclusions which he later left out of his

6   Letter to Gibieuf, 19 January 1642 in *Descartes: Philosophical Letters*, trans. and ed. by A. Kenny (Oxford: Clarendon Press, 1970), 124.

7   J. P. Wright, *The Sceptical Realism of David Hume* (Minneapolis: Minnesota University Press, 1983).

Enquiry concerning Human Understanding. I discuss an important, though often neglected section of Book 1 of Hume's *Treatise* entitled "Of the Immateriality of the Soul."[8] This is a section which is particularly important in understanding the relation of Hume's metaphysical reasoning to that of Descartes. I shall argue that Hume has the philosophical tools to dispense with the Cartesian principle as a foundation for our ontological beliefs about the soul itself, and so leaves the field open for an ontological materialism.

In the *Meditations* Descartes claims to establish the distinction between soul and body on the ground that we can form a complete and distinct idea of the one without the other. Indeed, in this discussion we find one of the clearest applications of his rule of metaphysical reasoning. In his sixth *Meditation* Descartes writes that,

> On the one hand I have a clear and distinct idea of myself, in so far as I am a thinking non-extended thing; and on the other hand I have a clear idea of body, in so far as this is simply an extended non-thinking thing. And accordingly, it is certain that I [that is, my soul by which I am what I am] am really distinct from my body, and can exist without it. (*Meditations*, 54)

By establishing the distinction between the mind and body in this way Descartes thought he was establishing "the first and most important prerequisite for the knowledge of the immortality of the soul." In the Synopsis to the *Meditations* he goes on to argue that the soul must be considered as a simple substance which is indivisible and hence "immortal by its very nature."[9]

Hume's strategy in "Of the Immateriality of the Soul" is to point out the conceptual difficulties with both materialism and immaterialism before turning to his own sceptical solution to the problem. In the course of his criticism of immaterialism Hume arrives at the positive conclusion that

---

8   *Treatise*, 1.4.5: pp. 232–51; Recent interest in this section is shown in two articles which discuss it in the context of the Clarke-Collins debate—Jane McIntyre's "Hume: Second Newton of the Moral Sciences," *Hume Studies* 20 (1): 3–18 and Paul Russell's "Hume's *Treatise* and the Clarke-Collins Controversy", *Hume Studies*, 21 (1): 95–115. See also Lorne Falkenstein's "Hume and Reid on the Simplicity of the Soul," *Hume Studies* 21 (1): 26–46. My own overall interpretation of the section is close to that of Paul Russell.

9   R. Descartes, *Philosophical Writings of Descartes*, Vol. 2: 9–10. In *The Achilles of Rationalist Arguments* (The Hague: Martinus Nijhoff, 1974), Ben Mijuskovic has argued that Descartes's use of this argument came as a kind of afterthought after his claim to prove the immortality of the soul was challenged by various critics. This is a complex issue. But Descartes's failure to produce any proof of immortality in the soul of the *Meditations* does suggest that his main purpose in writing this work was not to establish this theological claim.

each of our perceptions is a distinct existence and can exist independently from everything else in the universe. In criticising materialism Hume concludes that most of our perceptions exist nowhere and cannot be conceived to be conjoined with matter. Indeed, he points out that reason "shows us the impossibility of such an union" (*Treatise*, 238) While neither of these claims are Cartesian, they are, I would argue, based on the kind of metaphysical reasoning which is endorsed in Descartes's *Meditations*. Nevertheless, Hume argues that whatever conceptual difficulties exist in determining the relation of matter in motion to our perceptions, we have every evidence through experience that the former really does cause the latter. Indeed, when he clearly states his own view in his essay "Of the Immortality of the Soul"[10], an essay which may well have been excised from Book 1, Part 4 of the *Treatise* for prudential reasons,[11] he claims that "the existence" of the soul "must be dependent on" that of the body since "the organs of the one are all of them the organs of the other" (596).

Hume's Arguments against a Simple Immaterial Soul

Hume begins Book 1, Part 4, Section 5 of the *Treatise* by pointing out that we can have no conception of either a material or immaterial substance in which our various perceptions are supposed to inhere. In the section "Of the Ancient Philosophy" he had argued that the belief that there is an underlying substance which is both simple and identical though a series of changes arises from a fiction of the imagination, not a genuine idea (*Treatise*, 220–21). Here, in "Of the Immateriality of the Soul", he argues specifically that we can have no idea of a soul substance, since there can be no impression to represent it. According to the proponents of a simple soul substance, an impression has none of the "peculiar properties or characteristics of a substance" (ibid., 233). But, Hume argues, all representation requires resemblance, and since no impression is simple and unchanging, it follows that no impression or idea can represent the soul. Hume concludes that the question whether all our perceptions inhere in a simple and unchanging soul is absolutely unintelligible.

However, Hume clearly does not want to rest his case on this simple assertion that we *lack* an idea of a simple unchanging substance. In fact,

---

10   D. Hume, *Essays: Moral, Political, and Literary*, ed. E. F. Miller, rev. ed. (Indianapolis: Liberty Classics, 1987), 590–98.

11   This interesting conjecture has been made by J. Gaskin, *Hume's Philosophy of Religion*, 2d ed. (London: Macmillan Press, 1988), 182.

close to half of "Of the Immateriality of the Soul" involves a consideration of the question whether our thoughts of external objects can be contained in a simple and indivisible soul. Hume wrote that though he has condemned the question "as utterly unintelligible, yet [he] cannot forebear proposing some farther reflections concerning it" (ibid., 240). I believe that the argument which he puts forward on the next seven pages throws a great deal of light on his own philosophical views, especially as they relate to Descartes's principle that we can determine ontological truth through an analysis of our ideas.

In these pages Hume adapts arguments which Pierre Bayle[12] had used to show the absurdity of the Spinozist conception of God, to show the absurdity of the theologians' conception of a simple soul. Just as Bayle had argued that the claim that the material world inheres in a simple, unchanging substance called God is self-contradictory, so Hume argues for the self-contradictory character of the view that our perceptions inhere in a simple, unchanging substance called the soul. In showing that the same argument must apply in both cases, Hume appeals to what he appears to regard as a corollary of the Cartesian maxim of metaphysics—namely the principle that *what we ascribe to external reality on the basis of an analysis of our mental contents must be true of those mental contents themselves (i.e. our impressions and ideas)*. Instead of arguing, as Descartes had, that whatever is true of our mental contents is certainly true of the objects which they represent, Hume points out that the certainty works the other way round. He writes that

> any conclusion we form concerning the connexion and repugnance of impressions, will not be known certainly to be applicable to objects; but that on the other hand, whatever conclusions of this kind we form concerning objects, will most certainly be applicable to impressions. (*Treatise*, 241)

In his argument against the immaterialists Hume notes that the conclusions they arrive at concerning the "connexion or repugnancy" of external objects must apply to the impressions and ideas through which those objects are supposed to be known.

---

12   That is, in the article entitled "Spinoza" in Bayle's *Dictionary*, referred to by Hume in his letter from Tours. For Bayle's own arguments see Pierre Bayle, *The Historical and Critical Dictionary of Mr. Peter Bayle*, 2d ed., 5 vols., trans. & ed. P. Des Maizeaux (London: J.J. Knapton et al., 1734–8), Vol. 5: 208–11, Note N. See also, N. K. Smith's *The Philosophy of David Hume* (London: Macmillan, 1966), 506–16.

Hume goes on to employ this principle in showing that the theologians' criticisms of Spinozism can be turned on themselves. Hume writes that there are "two different systems of beings presented, to which I suppose myself under a necessity of assigning some substance, or ground of inhesion" (ibid., 242). The first is the "universe of objects or of body: The sun, moon and stars; the earth, seas, plants, animals, men, ships, houses. . . . " The second is

> the universe of thought, or my impressions and ideas. There I observe another sun, moon and stars; an earth, and seas, cover'd and inhabited by plants and animals; towns, mountains, rivers; and in short every thing I can discover or conceive in the first system. (ibid., 242)

Hume notes that while everyone treats Spinoza's hypothesis that external bodies inhere in a simple, unchanging substance with "detestation and scorn," they treat the hypothesis that perceptions are contained in a simple, unchanging soul "with applause and veneration" (ibid., 243). But since any claim concerning impossibility in the first system is derived from our analysis of our impressions, it follows that the epithets which apply to the first hypothesis must also apply to the second. Thus the view that all our perceptions inhere in a simple unchanging soul, like the view of Spinoza, is a "hideous hypothesis" (ibid., 241) and a "dangerous and irrecoverable atheism" (ibid., 244).

John Yolton has written of this discussion of "two different systems of beings" as a "satirical characterization",[13] but this appears to me to misrepresent Hume's arguments against immaterialism. Yolton thinks that Hume is parodying the theory of perception of Malebranche which treats ideas as entities which are distinct from bodies. But, if there is a parody here it is a parody of the rejection of Spinoza's system by pious theologians who, at the same time, wish to maintain the absolute simplicity of the soul. This parody *presupposes* that there are indeed two systems of beings and that any conclusions we arrive at concerning external objects must apply to our internal objects.

Hume takes note of three arguments which Bayle had given against Spinoza's view that extended substances are merely modifications of the deity (*Treatise*, 243–44). In the first place, Bayle had argued that since a substance is not distinct from an attribute, on Spinoza's view God must be identical with the extended universe. But this implies that what is

---

13   J. Yolton, *Thinking Matter: Materialism in Eighteenth-Century Britain* (Minneapolis: Minnesota University Press, 1983), 49–63, esp. 56. Cf. J. Yolton, *Perceptual Acquaintance from Descartes to Reid* (Minneapolis: University of Minnesota Press, 1984) 147–64.

indivisible expand itself and become divisible or that what is divisible contract and become indivisible. Bayle argued that both possibilities are absurd.[14] But, according to Hume, since our knowledge of absurdity can only be through our perceptions, and we cannot conceive of the difference between an external object and a perception, it follows that the same argument applies to our extended perceptions and the simple essence of the soul. Our perceptions of extended objects cannot be mere modifications of an indivisible soul.

Secondly, Bayle argued that we do in fact consider the parts of matter to consist of distinct substances, not modifications as Spinoza claimed. We consider each part of matter to be a substance in the sense that it can exist by itself and apart from anything else.[15] According to Hume, it follows that the impressions which represent those parts of matter are also distinct and separable. Thus he asserts that if we define a substance as "*something, that can exist by itself,* 'tis evident every perception is a substance and every distinct part of a perception is a distinct substance" (*Treatise*, 244).

In the third argument, Bayle pointed out that Spinoza's view implies that one and the same thing can have two contradictory predicates at one and the same time.[16] God is, at one and the same time, both the square table in the corner and the round table beside it. But this is absurd since one and the same thing cannot be both round and square at the same time. Similarly, Hume asked how the impressions of the round and square table can coexist at once, in a simple soul substance. If perceptions were mere modifications it would follow that the soul itself would have contradictory predicates at the same time.

It is important to realize that these reflections, which Hume bases on his corollary of the Cartesian maxim of metaphysics, led him to more than a purely negative conclusion about the soul. His reasoning led him to assert

---

[14]   Hume's description of Bayle's first argument is very loose. Bayle writes that Spinoza "owns, as all other Philosophers do, that the attribute of a substance does not really differ from that substance. . . . He cannot say that extension in general is distinct from the substance of God: for should he say so, it would follow that this substance is in itself unextended: and therefore it could never have acquired the three dimensions but by creating them. . . . But Spinoza did not believe that something can be created out of nothing. Again, it is manifest, that a substance, unextended by it's nature, can never become the subject of the three dimensions; for how could they be placed upon a mathematical point?" (*Historical and Critical Dictionary*, Vol. 5: 208b.)

[15]   Again, Hume's characterization of the argument is loose. But this fits Bayle's discussion in the third paragraph of Note N of the article on Spinoza (*Dictionary*, 5: 209a).

[16]   See the fourth and fifth paragraphs of Note N of the article on Spinoza (*Dictionary*, Vol. 5: 209 a & b).

positively that perceptions themselves really are distinct and separate from each other. Hume writes that

> As we conclude from the distinction and separability of their ideas, that external objects have a separate existence from each other; so when we make these ideas themselves our objects, we must draw the same conclusion concerning *them*, according to the precedent reasoning. (*Treatise*, 245)

It is Hume's own interpretation of the Cartesian maxim which leads him to make "ideas themselves our objects." According to Hume, our perceptions do not merely represent objects which are independent and separate one from the other; in order for us to think that they do, the perceptions must themselves *be* independent and separate from one another. According to his argument, even if it should turn out that the external objects were not distinct and separable, this would still be true of the perceptions from which we drew the conclusions that they were.

Personal Identity & the Mental Transparency Principle

In this argument, Hume treats our perceptions themselves as distinct entities. It is this "ontologizing" of perceptions which led Hume to the problem he encountered when he sought to explain our belief in the unity of ourselves in the next section of the *Treatise*, "Of Personal Identity" (1.4.6). In the Appendix to his book he explains that problem as follows:

> There are two principles, which I cannot render consistent; nor is it in my power to renounce either of them, viz. that all our distinct perceptions are distinct existences, and that the mind never perceives any real connexion among distinct existences. (636)

Hume's problem is that, having concluded from the fact that I perceive things distinctly that the perceptions themselves are distinct, he then cannot explain how we come to believe that they are united in one simple consciousness. He had argued in the section entitled "Of Personal Identity" that one perception causes another and when we reflect on them in memory, we read this real causal relation as one of identity (see 261). But the problem he confronts in the Appendix to the *Treatise* is that the causal relation would then have to be perceivable. In the case of external objects, it is still possible for one object to cause another and for their *perceptions* to be distinct. In fact, Hume argues that this is always so. "We only *feel* a connexion or determination of the thought" when they become associated in the mind through experience (635). On the other hand, in the case of our perceptions themselves a real causal connection—which precludes distinctness[17]—would have to be perceived. Since in the case of the mind, what appears to be distinct must really be distinct, it follows that there can be no real causal connection between perceptions. Thus, in his Appendix Hume came to realize that his earlier proposed explanation of "the principles, that unite our successive perceptions in our thought or consciousness" failed (*Treatise*, 636).

Hume also runs into the problem he does in explaining our belief in personal identity because he retains the Cartesian principle that the mind is transparent to itself and that, in the case of an attentive mind, what is the case also appears to be the case.[18] In discussing the source of our belief in an external world in another section of the *Treatise*, he writes that "every thing that enters the mind, being in *reality* a perception, 'tis impossible any thing shou'd to *feeling* appear different." His point is that we cannot be mistaken about our impressions themselves. It is not "conceivable that our senses shou'd be more capable of deceiving us in the situation and relations, than in the nature of our impressions." (190). Hume employs this principle to argue that we cannot derive a belief in the externality of our impressions from any rational examination of those impressions. Similarly, if our impressions are really causally connected then they must appear that way when we reflect on them. In the case of the mind itself, appearances cannot differ from reality.

The Arguments against Materialism

Hume balances his discussion of the impossibility of an immaterial soul with an account of the difficulties of materialism. He argues that certain perceptions can have no spatial conjunction with matter. An important step in Descartes's argument that the mind can be conceived entirely separately from the body involves showing that there are a set of purely intellectual ideas which, unlike those of extension, cannot be imagined.[19] These include

---

17   See my *Sceptical Realism*, pp. 135ff.

18   In his second Meditation Descartes writes: " . . . I am now seeing light, hearing a noise, feeling heat. But I am asleep , so all this is false. I certainly *seem* to see, to hear and to be warmed. This cannot be false" (*Philosophical Writings of Descartes*, Vol. 2: 19).

19   This is a central theme of the second Meditation and the sixth Meditation. In the latter Descartes writes that he "can clearly and distinctly understand [him-]self as a whole" without the faculties of imagination and sensory perception (*Meditations*, p. 54).

the idea of God and our idea of ourselves as thinking substances. While Hume denied the existence of such clear and distinct ideas, he did hold that all ideas except those of sight and touch "are simple, and exist no where, (and) are incapable of any conjunction in place with matter or body, which is extended and divisible" (*Treatise*, 236). Thus, "a moral reflection cannot be plac'd on the right or on the left hand of a passion, nor can a smell or sound be either of a circular or a square figure." Such a perception has nothing in common with matter and hence, according to Hume, cannot be spatially conjoined with it.

Hume goes on to explain how, through a principle of the imagination, we naturally come to suppose that certain simple objects, such as tastes and smells, combine with the extended objects which cause them. For example,

> We suppose, that the taste exists within the circumference of the body, but in such a manner, that it fill the whole without extension, and exists entire in every part without separation (ibid., 238).

He stresses that this supposition is entirely absurd from the point of view of reason and that we cannot conceive how an unextended object can be combined with an extended one. His solution is to admit that tastes and smells "exist without any place" (ibid., 239). Thus these impressions, as well as all those simple impressions he discusses, while they might be causally connected to an extended brain, need not be located at any place in that brain.

It is important to see that, in showing the difficulties with materialism as well as immaterialism, Hume ends up adopting the point of view of reason rather than the natural suppositions of the understanding. I believe that this results from his commitment to his own version of the Cartesian principle of ontological reasoning. He thinks that what we determine about the connections or repugnances of perceptions applies to those perceptions themselves, even though it might not apply to their objects. Indeed, Hume notes in this section that "by an irregular kind of reasoning from experience" we can "discover a connexion or repugnance betwixt objects, which extends not to impressions" (*Treatise*, 242). Such suppositions are formed by the imagination and allow us to ascribe relations to *objects* which differ from those which we would attain through an examination of their *impressions*. The most important relations of this kind are those which lead us to believe that the objects continue to exist while unperceived and that they are necessarily connected. But, Hume's own theory of ideas leads him to assert that impressions are fully understood in themselves and that all connections and repugnances which we discover through analysis of these impressions really do apply to them. It is no co-incidence that the two most paradoxical features of Hume's own philosophy in the *Treatise*—the claims that the mind consists of wholly distinct perceptions and that some of those perceptions exist nowhere—both result from his adoption of the Cartesian principle of metaphysics in relation to the contents of the mind. It is also important to note, as I mentioned earlier, that both of these paradoxes were entirely dropped from Hume's rewriting of Book 1 of the *Treatise* in his *Enquiry concerning Human Understanding*.

Favouring Materialism: Causality and the Unintelligible Real Connection of the Soul and the Body

Given his remarks against materialism it is rather surprising to find that Hume thinks that the conclusion of last main topic he discusses in 1.4.5 of the *Treatise* "evidently gives the advantage to the materialists above their opponents" (250). This is the question "concerning the *cause* of our perceptions" (ibid., 246).

Hume begins his discussion by considering and dispensing with an argument which is based on the Cartesian maxim of metaphysics. It is supposed to establish that matter in motion cannot be the cause of thought because we never can conceive how the first can produce the second:

> 'Tis absurd to imagine, that motion in a circle, for instance, shou'd be nothing but merely motion in a circle: while motion in another direction, as in an ellipse, shou'd also be a passion or a moral reflexion: That the shocking of two globular particles shou'd become a sensation of pain, and that the meeting of two triangular ones shou'd afford a pleasure (ibid., 246).

Hume says that "few have been able to withstand the seeming evidence of this argument" (ibid., 247). He may have had in mind the discussion in Bayle's *Dictionary* article on Dicearchus:

> no Body that I know of ever dared hitherto to say that he clearly conceived, that, in order to make a substance pass from the privation of all thought to actual thinking, it was sufficient to put it into Motion, so that this change of Situation was, for instance, a sense of Joy, an Affirmation, and idea of moral Virtue, &c.[20]

Bayle includes Locke among those who found this argument persuasive. He points out that in spite of his great efforts which Locke made to understand how matter might be able to think he was forced to admit that this is incomprehensible. Bayle writes:

---

[20]   See Dicearchus, Note K, *Dictionary*, Vol. 2: 661 b.

> Among other Arguments he makes use of this, *That it cannot be conceived*
> *how matter can think*. Mr. Locke confesses the Truth of this Principle, and
> contents himself with denying the Consequence; for he pretends that God
> can do things which are incomprehensible to human Understanding. . . . [21]

As John Yolton has shown,[22] Locke's discussion in Book 4 of the *Essay*
concerning Human Understanding was key in debates about the soul's materiality in the eighteenth century.

Hume goes further than Locke, for he does not require any supernatural
being to make matter think. Unlike Locke, he does not accept the Cartesian
type of reasoning from the incomprehensibility of a thing to the conclusion
that thing cannot come about in a natural way. Hume claims that those
who argue against the possibility of a causal relation "from the mere
consideration of the ideas" argue too hastily (*Treatise*, 247). For we never
perceive any connection between cause and effect, even in the case of purely
physical events. All causation is merely determined through our experience
of constant conjunction and "all objects, which are not contrary, are
susceptible of a constant conjunction."

According to Hume, we do in fact experience the constant conjunction
of matter and motion with thought:

> 'Tis not only possible we may have such an experience, but 'tis certain we
> have it; since everyone may perceive, that the different dispositions of his
> body change his thoughts and sentiments (ibid., 248).

Hume goes on to reject the view of the occasionalists "that nothing can be
the cause of another, but where the mind can perceive the connexion in its
idea of the objects" (ibid., 248). Rather, according to Hume, we should
accept constant conjunction as evidence of a genuine though unperceived
connection between cause and effect.[23] He then concludes that this argument favors the materialists, who he had earlier defined as those "who
conjoin *all* thought with extension" (ibid., 250, 239, my italics).

In his essay "Of the Immortality of the Soul", Hume took this causal
argument one step further. He presented what he called "physical arguments" designed to show not merely that the soul is affected by changes in
the body, but rather that *the very existence of the soul depends on that of the*

---

[21]   Dicearchus, Note M, *Dictionary*, Vol. 2: 662 a.

[22]   See *Thinking Matter*.

[23]   I have discussed this argument in "Hume's Criticism of Malebranche's Theory of
Causation: a Lesson in the Historiography of Philosophy", ed. S. Brown, *Malebranche*
and His Critics (Assen/Maastrict: Van Gorcum, 1991), 116–130.

body. He pointed out that sleep, which involves "a very small effect on the body, is attended with a temporary extinction; at least, a great confusion in the soul" and that the weakness of the body in infancy and old age are conjoined with a similar weakness in the mind.[24] Further, he pointed out that since the "analogy of nature" shows us that a very slight change in the environment of any living being destroys that being, there is every reason to think that the soul must be destroyed with the body. It is tempting to conclude that Hume fully embraces materialism when he concludes with the claim that I mentioned earlier, that the organs of thought are also organs of the body. Is Hume not very close to the claim made later in the century by Cabanis that the brain secretes thought like the liver secretes bile?

At the end of "Of the Immateriality of the Soul" Hume had denied that his arguments detract from the belief in the immortality of the soul, since this belief rests on "moral arguments and on those derived from the analogy of nature" (*Treatise*, 250). But this claim was probably disingenuous. For, in his essay "Of the Immortality of the Soul" he rejects both of these sorts of arguments and merely notes the belief in immortality must be based on revelation.

Conclusion

Thus Hume concluded from experience that our soul is material and mortal. He therefore opposed two of the explicit conclusions of Descartes's *Meditations*.

However, having reached these conclusions from experience, Hume is still faced with major problems which arise from his own adoption of the Cartesian principle of metaphysical reasoning within the realm of the mind itself. As we have seen from our discussion of Hume's arguments against materialism in the *Treatise*, this principle led him to deny that most of our perceptions can be spatially conjoined with matter. Moreover, in the Appendix to the *Treatise*, Hume was forced to admit that he was unable explain the unity we ascribe to the soul. His reason is that we are not able to perceive the necessary causal connection between perceptions which his explanation postulates. Thus, by retaining the Cartesian principle, he was led into an incoherent theory of the soul itself and of its connection with matter.

This was clearly not the point at which he expected to arrive when he began writing the section "Of the Immateriality of the Soul". He wrote that

---

24   *Essays: Moral, Political, and Literary*, 596.

the intellectual world, tho' involv'd in infinite obscurities, is not perplex'd
with any such contradictions, as those we have discover'd in the natural.
What is known concerning it agrees with itself. . . (ibid., 232).

However, as we have seen, he is forced to admit that there are contradictions
in his own account of the soul. The conclusions to which Hume is led by
experience and imagination are directly opposed to those which he reaches
through the Cartesian principle of the analysis of ideas.

There is, I believe, a solution to Hume's problem. He needs to recognize
that the mind itself is not better known than the body, and that it is through
the natural principles of the imagination rather than reason that we learn
about the basic structure, not only of the external world, but also of the soul
itself. While we cannot understand how our unextended impressions are
connected with extended matter, it does not follow that they are really
distinct from it. We can affirm the existence of an unknown connection,
based on our experience of their constant conjunction. For it may well be
that these perceptions are not in themselves such as they appear to us. Thus,
in reality, my anger may be identical to the neural motions with which it is
constantly conjoined, just as, on Hume's own explicit account, the color of
a globe of black marble is identical with its shape (ibid., 25). There is only
a "distinction of reason" between them. I am not suggesting that Hume
thought that we could ever make the necessary causal connection intelligible. His scepticism concerning causality precludes that. Nevertheless, his
account of distinctions of reason shows us how, in spite of the lack of perspicu-
ity of our own ideas, we can understand—in a general way—how matter in
motion might be identical with our unextended perceptions. Hume has the
apparatus in his philosophical system to effect, at least on the ontological level,
what our own contemporary philosophy calls "eliminative materialism."

This suggestion is very much in keeping with the methodological
principle for the study of human nature which Hume lays out in the
Introduction to the *Treatise*. Here he rejects introspection as a method for
discovering those principles of the mind which underlie our behaviour:

> Reflection and premeditation would so disturb the operation of my natural
> principles, as must render it impossible to form any just conclusion from
> the phænomenon. We must therefore glean our experiments in this
> science from a cautious observation of human life, and take them as they
> appear in the common course of the world, by men's behaviour in
> company, in affairs, and in their pleasures. (ibid., xix)

Hume suggests that the scientist of human nature should rely on a cautious
induction from observation of human behavior and so explain "all effects

from the simplest and fewest causes" (ibid., xvii). While he refuses to dogmatically put forth a theory which states the "ultimate original qualities of human nature," he makes clear his own belief that the most "specious and plausible" hypothesis is in terms of mechanical events in the brain:

> As the mind is endow'd with a power of exciting any idea it pleases; whenever it dispatches the spirits into that region of the brain, in which the idea is plac'd; these spirits always excite the idea, when they run precisely into the proper traces, and rummage that cell, which belongs to the idea (ibid., 60–61).

He goes on to suggest that ideas are associated by resemblance because they are located in contiguous portions of the brain. This and other passages[25] show that he believed that the ultimate principles underlying human psychology involve the mechanism of the brain, a mechanism which is not immediately discoverable by introspection.

In the light of these reflections it is clear why Hume did not believe, as others have, that his failure to explain the unity of the self was a definitive objection to his philosophy. It is true that each of our perceptions can appear distinct from one another on reflection. At the same time, there is good reason to believe that the unity which we feel when we remember the past events of our lives is a real unity imposed by the genuine causal connection of our perceptions. The fact that the necessary connection fails to appear to us when we reflect on our past perceptions does not prove its non-existence. Memory and the *feeling* of unity which it contributes may well be caused by physical events in the brain (for Hume this would have been movements of animal spirits) which stimulate trains of ideas in certain regular sequences.

Endnote

*An earlier version of this paper was read in La Fleche on 1 July 1992 at the Nineteenth Hume Society Conference. The argument relates back to discussions I had with John Yolton in the mid-1970s—discussions which had a profound influence on my own understanding of Hume's epistemology and metaphysics. I am indebted to both John Yolton and David Raynor for written criticisms of the earlier version of this paper.

---

25   In my *Sceptical Realism* (esp. 68–71 and 211 ff.) I argued that this model underlies some of the central psychological principles of Hume's *Treatise*.

Foucault's Critique of the Enlightenment

Shadia B. Drury

The current philosophical atmosphere is so charged with anti-Enlighten-ment sentiments that John W. Yolton's Enlightenment studies can no longer be regarded as a matter of antiquarian interests. Postmodernism has vilified the Enlightenment by attributing to its ideas all the ills of our time. Postmodernists, like Michel Foucault, depict the modern world in terms of the tyranny of a cold and heartless rationalism. In this paper I will show that a despotic, chilly and arid portrait of reason is a necessary pre-requisite for the postmodern romanticization of madness, unreason, fury and frenzy. In light of these developments, Yolton's work redresses the balance in two important ways. First, his meticulous historical method sets the record straight. Second, his philosophical incisiveness teaches us the extent to which the Enlightenment was not a homogeneous intellectual phenomenon, but a time filled with exciting philosophical debates—many of which are perennial philosophical concerns. The centrality of the En-lightenment in contemporary postmodern thought makes his contribution invaluable.

In this essay, I will focus on Michel Foucault's demonization of Enlight-enment rationalism and show how the defamation of reason is part of his subtle celebration of the violent, dark, and demonic. My thesis is not that Foucault suffered from some personal perversions and obsessions. My view is that Foucault is part of a way of looking at the modern world as a conspiracy to supress everything which does not conform to a cold and arid rationalism. This leads to the mistaken belief that whatever is forbidden or condemned is worthy of being liberated, exalted and extolled; it gives the impression that whatever is hidden, suppressed or driven under-ground has a reality which is more fundamental, more real, more vital than what is conventional, accepted and approved. This way of thinking contains a profound dualism coupled with a dark romanticism that give postmod-ernism its appeal. One need not have any proclivity for the demonic or any other mental disorders to be seduced by this way of thinking.[1] The best antidote to these enchantments is developing one's capacity for critical reasoning—and for that, I owe a profound debt to my greatest teacher, John W. Yolton.

Critique of Enlightenment

According to Foucault, the Enlightenment, or the "classical age," as he likes to call it, has established a "new regime of power" which amounts to a tyranny of reason unlike anything ever known to man. The Enlightenment "project" sets out to resolve the perennial conflict between freedom and authority in the trickiest manner. Foucault takes Kant as paradigmatic, but we can recognize the ideas as belonging equally to Rousseau and Hegel.[2] On the Enlightenment view, the reconciliation of freedom and authority is possible if each submits to the demands of reason. If the individual desires only what is good and rational, and the state demands only what is good and rational, then the conflict between them dissolves. In obeying the state, one obeys only oneself and is as free as one was before becoming a subject. In this way, a harmony of power and freedom is achieved.

According to Foucault, the Enlightenment project makes sense only if we accept the following assumptions. First, that reason is neutral and

---

[1]   This paper was written prior to the appearance of James Miller's *The Passion of Michel Foucault* (New York: Simon & Schuster, 1993). Miller's biographical narrative is gripping and there is much in his accounts of Foucault's life which is not surprising to me and which lends support to my thesis. But there is an important difference between my approach and Miller's. Unlike Miller, I make no claims about the relationship between Foucault's life and his work. Unlike Miller, I do not think that Foucault's ideas are intimately connected to his own peculiarities, fascinations and obsessions. I believe that Foucault's way of thinking is much more widespread and has its source in Alexandre Kojève's "end of history" thesis which regards modernity as the global triumph of reason. I develop this thesis in my *Alexandre Kojève: The Roots of Postmodern Politics* (New York: St. Martin's Press, 1994). Miller does not mention Kojève; however, he documents the intellectual debt of Foucault to Jean Hyppolite who was the successful academic version of Kojève and who introduced Foucault to the same set of existential Marxist ideas which Kojève expressed more boldly and dramatically.

What I find disturbing about Miller's book is that it is a bold exposé of Foucault's life, but it is philosophically uncritical about the Foucauldian assumption that the darkest sentiments in the heart of man are somehow a clue to knowledge of reality. Miller is disturbed by what he uncovers precisely because he suspects it is not intellectually cogent and therefore does not make the effort to subject it to critical reasoning.

[2]   M. Foucault, "What is Enlightenment," in *The Foucault Reader*, ed. P. Rabinow (New York: Pantheon Books, 1984), 32–50.

good—that it is neither an instrument of domination nor a product of power. Second, that freedom from domination by irrational and arbitrary forces, internal or external, is a genuine possibility for the individual. And third, that a regime free of arbitrary domination or mastery of man by man is attainable—which is to say that a regime which embodies truth, justice and freedom is within reach.

Foucault rejects these assumptions. He denies that reason yields any knowledge or truth independent of power. He balks at the idea that reason is not coercive. He regards all appeals to rationality as manifestations of the coercive machinery of domination. He laughs at the idea that there can be a regime of truth and justice (and history laughs with him). He believes that every truth is someone's truth, and every justice is someone's justice.[3] He demolishes any hope of liberation or freedom from domination by maintaining that the human *subject* is itself constituted by power. He therefore eschews all reference to "ideology," not just because the term "always stands in virtual opposition to something else which is supposed to count as truth," but also because the term presupposes a *subject* unduped by ideology, and this is not possible (ibid., 118).

Foucault aims to convince us not only that the Enlightenment project is impossible but also that it is a hoax by which we have been duped into submission to a regime of unbridled tyranny. In fact, Enlightenment rationalism, and the scientific spirit it has engendered, has proven to be the most effective mechanism of domination of all time. Posing as freedom, Enlightenment rationalism has succeeded in legitimizing a new and more terrible form of power than any we have ever known before. Foucault calls this new form of power *disciplinary* power, and contrasts it with the old form which power has generally assumed—*sovereign power*.

Sovereign Power and Disciplinary Power

Foucault regards the modern world as a legacy of Enlightenment rationalism. Since the dawn of that "classical age," a type of power, hitherto unknown, has been steadily gaining strength and usurping more and more of the traditional domain of *sovereign power*. We cannot understand the insidious nature of modern forms of domination without understanding the nature of the new *disciplinary power*—how it differs from sovereign power,

---

[3]   See for example, "On Popular Justice: A Discussion with Maoists," in *Power/Knowledge, Selected Interviews and Other Writings, 1972–1977*, ed. C. Gordon, (New York: Pantheon Books, 1980), 1–36.

and how it has managed to usurp the domain of the latter and rule supreme, and with our blessings.

Sovereign power is an overt and conspicuous form of power which Foucault describes dramatically in *Discipline and Punish*. Sovereign power is pompous and grand. In the days of old, it had no qualms about displaying itself—its superiority, its prowess, and its grandeur. The public execution was one of these occasions for display.[4] Foucault describes how the "spectacle of the scaffold" was an exercise in "terror" meant to make everyone aware of the "unrestrained presence of the sovereign" (ibid., 49). By showing that the sovereign did not shrink from atrocities, the public execution intended to strike fear into the hearts of the subjects. According to Foucault, public executions did not serve the function of reestablishing justice, but of "reactivating power." The imbalance of powers between the sovereign and the accused highlights the power of the sovereign. The crime was to be understood as a crime against the sovereign—a personal affront to the King or Queen—and hence, an assault on the established order itself. The punishment was therefore not intended simply to expiate the crime, but to reinforce the power of the sovereign, and the vigor of the established order. And, just to display its total freedom, power may choose *not* to punish; instead, it may suspend both the law and vengeance with a *pardon* delivered dramatically at the eleventh hour. These pardons were often received with cries of "God save the King!" In this way, sovereign power sought renewal in the very act of displaying itself as a superpower.

Despite all the atrocities of this old form of power, Foucault claims that it was limited in nature. First, it acted only on the *body* of the subject. Foucault makes his point by providing eye witness reports of Damiens, the regicide, being drawn and quartered in 1757. Foucault goes to great lengths to describe how his flesh was torn away, boiling oil and resin poured over his body, his limbs ripped apart by horses, etc.. The point of dwelling on the details of this ordeal is to illustrate the physical nature of the punishment. Foucault aims to show us that, for all its horror, sovereign power was limited to the body of the accused; it was not equipped to act on the mind or alter the passions and desires of the subject.

Second, sovereign power understood itself as power, and as such, was dependent on the consent or support of its subjects. The public execution gave people the opportunity to give their support to the sovereign power or to withhold that support. They could withhold their support by voicing their discontent; they could revolt when they saw a man of the people

---

[4]   M. Foucault, *Discipline and Punish*, trans. A. Sheridan, (New York: Random House, 1977, 1979), 48.

punished severely for a crime, when someone better born would have suffered a much lighter sentence (ibid., 61). In this way, the people still had power; for sovereign power still depended on their support. Moreover, the people were in a position to determine what would pass for truth. For example, they could transform a criminal into a hero and a crime into a great deed. They could delay the executioner, pretend a pardon was on the way, and eventually compel the sovereign to grant a pardon. In this way, they could turn the guilty into the innocent. And so, they remained makers of truth and therefore the proprietors of power, and not just its victims. Foucault does not mean to belittle sovereign power. He means only to show that, for all its spectacular atrocities, it was still limited in nature.

Sovereign power used the coercive force of law as its instrument. It therefore created an order which was characterized by external conformity to law. It also generated a "discourse of right" to lend it support and validity. This discourse articulated the legitimate domain of sovereignty. One only has to think of the language of Hobbes or Locke. As we shall see, the discourse of right served not only to justify sovereign power, but ultimately to limit it even further.

Although it has not disappeared, sovereign power has lost its monopoly of power in modern society. Side by side with sovereign power, a new form of power has emerged—Foucault calls it disciplinary power. Unlike sovereign power, disciplinary power is not pompous or grand, overt or conspicuous, terrible or terrifying. The new power is silent, unobtrusive, covert, and clandestine. It may *look* less awesome, but appearances are deceptive. It may *seem* less terrible, but it is more vigilant. For it is "possessed of highly specific procedural techniques, completely novel instruments, quite different apparatuses" (*Power/Knowledge*, 104). The success of the new power lies in the fact that its locus of operation is not centralized. Unlike sovereign power, the new power is widely dispersed and operates on many different fronts. Its "polymorphous techniques of subjugation" are located in a great variety of "micro-powers" (ibid., 96). And this has enabled disciplinary power not merely to usurp the domain of sovereign power, but to stake out new territories.

According to Foucault, the strategies and tactics of disciplinary power are constantly being refined. Instead of acting only on the body of the subject, as sovereign power does, disciplinary power acts also on the mind. Instead of relying on coercive force, it resorts to new mechanisms of domination, like psychology.

Instead of a "society of law," disciplinary power has generated a "society of normalization." Just as law was the instrument of sovereign power, so the *norm* is the instrument of disciplinary power. Foucault seems to think that the *norm* is a far more powerful instrument because it can operate in domains inaccessible to law.

Foucault's histories, which he prefers to call genealogies, are intended to reveal how the new power has managed to extend its arid rationality to areas of human life that were completely beyond the scope of sovereign power. Unlike a history, a genealogy does not take continuity and gradual change for granted; a genealogy seeks out *discontinuities* and uncovers strange new beginnings and eruptions.[5] Foucault's genealogies are meant to show us how the age of Enlightenment is a watershed, a break with everything that went before.

What is so dreadful about disciplinary power is the fact that it regards every aspect of life—social, cultural, economic and biological as its rightful domain of control and surveillance.[6] This extensive control over the populace and the territory requires a detailed knowledge of citizens, their productivity, their incomes, their employment, their skills, their marriages, their divorces, their birth rates, their diseases, their delinquencies, their accidents, their gerontology and their deaths. The new "savoir" lends itself to a totalitarian regime and its police (ibid., 21). Foucault is right to warn us that this totalizing power is growing at an alarming rate before our very eyes. We are in the grip of the enlightenment ideology, and Foucault means to shake us out of our rationalistic slumber. The question is: How does Foucault hope to break the spell of disciplinary power? His detractors say that he cannot, because on his own admission, truth is always a function of power. Even language and discourse are products of power. To use the words of T.S. Eliot, we are formulated, sprawling on a pin; we are pinned and wriggling on the wall.

Power and Truth

Foucault does indeed emphasize the dependence of truth on power—so much so that he does not think that the notion of truth can be understood apart from its relation to power.[7] However, his understanding of the relation between power and truth is not as simpleminded as it is often portrayed. Foucault is largely responsible for the bastardization of his work—since his style is notoriously evasive and inconclusive. Nevertheless, Foucault is not

---

5   See Foucault, "Nietzsche Genealogy, History," in *The Foucault Reader*, 76–100.

6   Foucault, "Governmentality," *Ideology and Consciousness*, nos. 6–9 (Autumn 1979–Winter 1981/82): 10.

7   *Power/Knowledge*, 93, 105, 106, 107; *Discipline and Punish*, 27.

just a new Thrasymachus, telling us that those in power make truth, or that might is right or that justice is the interest of the stronger, or that those in power determine what is right and wrong by fiat. His position is more sophisticated. I would describe it as follows. Power generates truth or a "discourse of truth." Truth in turn lends support to the power which has generated it. It gives it legitimacy, just as the "discourse of right" legitimized sovereign power by providing reasons for obedience. But truth is not, not even for Foucault, a *mere* product of power. Truth is much more than a slave to power. For a "discourse of truth," once it comes into being, has a vitality of its own which enables it to become *alienated* from the power which gave it birth. Once it becomes alienated from power, this new discourse can launch an attack on the existing order. Confronted with the new discourse, power retreats and devises new "strategies" compatible with the new "discourse of truth." Finally, a new power or a new form of power may emerge—a form of power legitimized by the new discourse. In this way, power creates truth, *and* truth in turn creates power.

When a discourse acquires a power of its own, that "power of truth" is capable of launching an assault on the very power which generated it. This is what happened in the case of the "discourse" generated by sovereign power (*Power/Knowledge*, 93–94, 105). Like every form of power, sovereign power generated a "discourse of truth" to lend it support and give it legitimacy. The "discourse of right" is the special "discourse of truth" generated by sovereign power. The "discourse of right" has been the dominant discourse of political philosophy from Hobbes to the present. This discourse is preoccupied with questions of legitimacy, jurisdiction, obligation, powers, rights and laws (ibid., 92, 94). Its object is to legitimize sovereign power by providing reasons for obedience or inventing theories of obligation.

The "discourse of right" which was originally created by sovereign power, has not continued to be its slave. It has managed to acquire a power of its own, and in so doing, has launched an assault against sovereign power. But sovereign power did not simply collapse when it was persecuted by its own discourse of right. It withdrew—but, only to regroup its energies and reemerge in a new form compatible with the new discourse of right. The "discourse of right" managed to set limits to sovereign power; it forced it to submit to the laws it imposed on it subjects. In this way, absolute monarchy gave way to constitutional monarchy. The discourse of right was therefore responsible for generating a new and more limited form of sovereign power.

Like sovereign power, disciplinary power has generated its own "discourse of truth" and its own "apparatuses of knowledge." Instead of a "discourse of right" based on law, it has generated a "discourse of normalization," based on the idea of a *norm*. This discourse is the secret of the success of the new power. For the discourse of normalization is the discourse of science. In other words, science is the handmaid of disciplinary power. This new form of power has imposed its scientific discourse on almost every aspect of human life—madness, punishment, and sexuality, to name a few. Disciplinary power has medicalized these aspects of human life, and turned them into objects of science. Disciplinary power extends its ambitions to every sphere of life; it aims to control every gesture, every thought and every desire.

Despite the success of disciplinary power in controlling our lives, sovereign power has not been totally eclipsed, not so much because of its inherent vitality, but because disciplinary power has found it useful. In particular, the "discourse of right" engendered by sovereign power is a convenient instrument which serves to "conceal" the domination inherent in the polymorphous techniques and mechanisms of disciplinary society (ibid., 105). The explanation is that the discourse of right, having tamed the sovereign, has become democratized. As a result, it reinforces the *illusion* of liberty, while eliminating any obstacles that might thwart the development of disciplinary society. This is why Foucault thinks that appealing to sovereign power and resorting to its discourse of right as a means of defeating disciplinary power is a "blind alley" (ibid., 108).

If disciplinary power is to be defeated, a new "discourse of truth" has to be invented that is neither a "discourse of right" nor a "discourse of normalization." But Foucault has no pretensions about the new discourse; he does not pretend that it will be the true discourse of freedom—that is, a discourse free from power. It will no doubt engender a new power, since it will inevitably spring from a newly emerging form of power.

There is a note of hopelessness in Foucault's work. We can disentangle ourselves from one form of power only to become ensnared in another. The hopelessness stems not so much from the difficulty of defeating disciplinary power, but from the impossibility of establishing a domain of *truth* and *freedom*.

For all its despondency, Foucault's work is nevertheless permeated with the exhilaration of unmasking. The excitement of reading Foucault is not unlike the thrill of following a noble and handsome prince slay a formidable dragon, even though there is no beautiful princess to liberate and marry at the end.

Despite his apparent rejection of the project of liberation, Foucault poses as a liberator. Foucault presents his work as a task, nay an urgent mission, a mission of liberating us from the hateful prejudices of disciplinary power. Nothing short of our salvation seems to be at stake. Foucault aims to teach us that the cost of normalization is our humanity—we are destitute of spirit, divested of madness, and robbed of desire. In the perennial struggle between reason and passion, reason has gained a victory which is total, and has established a totalitarian regime, where madness has been banished, nay "cured" and where every rebel against the regime is disempowered or silenced.

Those who believe that Foucault's position is contradictory or self-defeating, or that he exempts his own thought from the verdict he imposes on all others, are mistaken.[8] There is nothing logically inconsistent in wanting to be free of the current forces of domination while admitting that new forces are likely to replace the old ones. The process of liberation is exiliharating, even if it lasts only for a moment. And, if we understand the dialectic of power and knowledge as I have explained it above, then we can avoid the charge that all claims to knowledge are just manifestations of the will to power, which can never liberate. Moreover, Foucault is honest enough to admit that his own thought is rooted in certain preferences which he cannot and does not account for, but takes for granted—namely, that freedom is good and desirable, whereas being enslaved and dominated is not.

Foucault's celebration of freedom would not be troublesome if it did not go hand in hand with a demonization of reason.

The Demonization of Reason and the Cult of Madness

We can best understand the nature of postmodernism if we think of it as a retelling of an old story about the perennial battle between reason and passion. In the classic version of the tale, reason is noble, nay, divine.

---

[8]   Most of the commentators on Foucault believe that his position is contradictory or incoherent. I do not think that this is the case. To accuse Foucault of self-contradiction is to silence him. K. Minogue, "Can Radicalism Survive Michel Foucault?" *Critical Review*, 3, no. 1 (Winter 1989): 138–154; Jurgen Habermas, "Taking Aim at The Heart of the Present," in *Foucault: A Critical Reader*, ed. D. C. Hoy (New York: Basil Blackwell, 1986); M. Walzer, "The Politics of Michel Foucault," also in *Foucault: A Critical Reader*; C. Taylor, "Foucault on Freedom and Truth," also in *Foucault: A Critical Reader*; see also C. Taylor and W. Connolly, "Michel Foucault: An Exchange," *Political Theory*, 13, no. 3 (August 1985): 365–85; see also T. Keenan, "The Paradox of Knowledge and Power: Reading Foucault on a Bias," *Political Theory*, 15, no. 1 (February 1987): 5–37; and P. Bove,"Forward: The Foucault Phenomena: the Problematics of Style," in G. Deleuze, *Foucault*, (Minneapolis: University of Minnesota Press, 1986); and P. Pasquino, "Michel Foucault: the Will to Knowledge," *Economy and Society*, 15, no. 1 (February 1986): 97–122; C. Gordon, "Question, Ethos, Event: Foucault on Kant," *Economy and Society*, 15, no. 1 (February, 1986): 71–87.

Reason is the golden chord that tugs gently at our conscience. Some believe that reason does battle with those dark and unruly passions which Plato portrays as the multiform beast within. But this is not so, for reason is sweet, feminine and lovely. She is not in the business of doing battle, let alone with the multiform beast. If she triumphs, she does so simply on the strength of her power of persuasion. And even then, she does not shout, and it is a miracle she is ever heard or heeded. In any case, if we are not to wait for miracles, we may pray that some powerful passions will love reason, and ardently defend her. It is to that end that Plato, the classic teller of the tale, invented that third part of the soul, the spirited part. Postmodernism does little more than turn Plato's story on its head.

In the postmodern version of the tale, the history of the West is the story of the triumph of reason. Reason has gotten the upper hand, and has tyrannized over man; in the name of truth and justice she has enslaved him to her every demand. She has accomplished this total subordination of man because she is as bullish as she is beguiling. Reason has been particularly merciless where her enemies, the passions, are concerned.[9] By banishing the passions, she has exorcised everything glorious, resplendent, splendiferous and sublime from the modern world. Modernity is the legacy of reason—predictable, tiresome, mundane and monotonous.

The most fundamental characteristic of postmodernism is its demonization of reason which goes hand in hand with a fashionable *Kulturpessimismus*. Postmodernism paints an arid picture of reason—cold, heartless, uncompromising, technical, and grim. It portrays the modern technological world as the ineluctable outcome of the absolute and uncompromising triumph of reason. It concocts Bosch-like images to describe the world in which we live—modernity has given birth to these vile "last men" (Nietzsche); its excessive rationalism has returned man to "animality"

---

[9]   Albrecht Dürer, one of Foucault's favorite artists, provides a pictorial illustration of the postmodern version of the tale. In his etching of "Hercules at the crossroads between Virtue and Vice," Virtue is portrayed as vicious. Her face filled with hatred and vengeance, she lashes out against Vice and would have demolished her with a big stick, were it not for the intervention of Hercules. In contrast to the hateful virtue, vice is the picture of innocence. She is quietly cavorting with a satyr in the woods, not disturbing anyone, when she is suddenly besieged by Virtue. Vice is puzzled. What is the matter with Virtue? Why is she so harsh, vengeful and tyrannical? Virtue is in the business of poking her nose into other people's affairs and depriving them of their supposedly innocent pleasures. The painting is intended to show how easily virtue turns into its opposite. It is intended to show how zealous and meddling the virtuous are inclined to be. However, the painting could also be understood more radically. Virtue and Vice may be regarded as corresponding to Reason and Passion.

(Kojève); deaf to the calls of Being, modernity is the "night of the world" (Heidegger); trapped in an "iron cage," modern life is reduced to "mechanized petrifaction" (Weber). And all this is the consequence of the deadly devotion to reason.[10]

It is my contention that the postmodern demonization of reason, subtly, but unmistakably, celebrates madness, unreason, and their excesses. Postmodernism does not simply describe our predicament in the most dire terms. It has an activist side. It is not prescriptive in the strict sense of prescribing what we ought to do or what is right to do. It abandons the domain of right as a domain belonging to reason, and its established tyranny. Instead, it tells us subtly what we *must* do, what we are compelled to do, if we hope to stop wallowing in our "mechanized petrifaction." In order to escape the clutches of a world understood as a rational tyranny, postmodernism feels *compelled* to exalt the wild, bestial, mad, violent, dark, deranged, distraught and demented. The subtle message is that, if we wish to break out of the "iron cage," it behooves us to unleash our wildest passions, become unreasonable, unbridled, unruly, and unhinged. The romantic excesses of postmodernism are great sources of its appeal. However, this postmodern romanticism aims to liberate much more than warm passions and harmless instincts.

Foucault is a case in point. His demonization of reason bring him dangerously close to the celebration of madness and even crime. He regards madness as one of the "subjugated knowledges" which he aims to liberate. And, he is sympathetic to cold blooded murderers like Pierre Rivière because he mistakes them for rebels against the unbearable oppressions of rationalism.

Foucault's aversion to reason makes his love of freedom indiscriminate. It makes him unable to distinguish between liberty and license. He aims to liberate all of the "subjugated knowledges," regardless of their nature. His book, *Madness and Civilization*, illustrates his fascination, not just with the mysterious and sublime, but with the demonic. His admiration of the art of Hieronymus Bosch, Mathias Grünewald, Stephan Lochner and Albrecht Dürer is telling. The irrational and diabolical world they depict, is a world for which Foucault is nostalgic. Diabolical madness is an antidote to the

---

10   F. Nietzsche, *Thus Spoke Zarathustra*, trans. W. Kaufmann, (New York: Penguin, 1954), Zarathustra's Prologue, sec. 5; M. Heidegger, "Overcoming Metaphysics," and "Only a God Could Save Us," in *The Heidegger Controversy*, ed. R. Wolin (New York: Columbia University Press, 1991); M. Weber, *The Protestant Ethic and the Spirit of Capitalism*, trans. T. Parsons, (New York: Charles Scribner's Sons, 1958): 181–82; A. Kojève, *Introduction to the Reading of Hegel*, trans. J. H. Nichols, Jr. (New York: Basic Books, 1969), 160–61.

arid rationalism and "mechanized petrifaction" that he assumes is the legacy
of Enlightenment.

Foucault claims to be giving a neutral and impartial account of the
history of madness, punishment, medicine, and sexuality. He tells us again
and again that he is not recommending anything, but that he is merely
describing our predicament. He pretends to be neutral, but as is obvious to
any reader, his neutrality is a sham. In general, it is not easy to describe
without implicitly prescribing.[11] Foucault's histories in particular are always
histoires a thèse which he himself describes as "fictions."

In *Madness and Civilization* Foucault illustrates how madness was treated
before and after the onslaught of the "classical age" or age of Enlightenment.
His point in this book, as in *Discipline and Punish*, is to show that the
abominations of the days of old are negligible in comparison to the cold
horrors of our own world. According to Foucault, the Renaissance gave
madness its rightful place as a manifestation of that part of the human soul
which, after Freud, came to be called the unconscious. And, as representatives of that dark and mysterious part of the soul, the mad were
regarded with both fear and reverence. They represented another world—
mysterious, hidden, and inscrutable—a world whose total otherness is as
terrifying as it is beguiling. The mad represent a world which is enticing
enough to beckon all of us. One thing is clear: madness threatens the sanity
of our world, and is therefore a cause for disquiet. Renaissance society dealt
with madness by sending the mad off to sea—hence the popularity of the
"ship of fools" motif in art and literature. Perhaps they hoped the mad might
get lost at sea. Perhaps they thought the mad belonged to the sea because
it was as mad as they were. Perhaps they expected that the water might
purify them. Whatever the explanation, Foucault believes that the "pres-
tige" of navigation rubbed off on madness.

The paintings of Hieronymus Bosch, Mathias Grünewald and others
also served to dignify madness and give it legitimacy. According to Foucault,
these paintings depicted the great disquiet which loomed on the horizon of
European culture at the end of the Middle Ages. They represented the

---

[11] I am deeply indebted to J.G.Merquior, *Foucault* (Berkeley: University of California
Press, 1985), 57, 73, 77, for his excellent discussion of this point. Merquior characterizes
Foucault's position as anarchistic radicalism, which has dispensed with the old worn out
concepts of the left—truth, history, and utopianism. Merquior's book is a delight. He
tackles Foucault with the clearheadedness of an English mind unseduced by Foucault's
subliminal charm.

[12] M. Foucault, *Madness and Civilization*, trans. R. Howard (New York: Random House,
1965): 13.

"dizzying unreason of the world that began to dawn with the passing of the old order."[12] The order of God and his angels was shaken, and the Devil became more transparent. Foucault subtly applauds this madness as an appropriate response to the macabre of the world.[13]

The "classical age" is one of these grand historical "discontinuities." In the age of Enlightenment, reason tightens her grip. Madness disappears from view. The mad are nowhere to be seen—on or off ships. Instead, they are confined to hospitals and entrusted to physicians. There are no madmen anymore—only the mentally ill. Foucault paints the classical age as a monologue of reason about madness—a monologue called psychiatry. True to its character, the "classical age" banishes from the world everything mysterious and sublime—it outlaws both God and the Devil. Religious men, dismayed with the spiritual wasteland of secular society, regard Foucault as an ally. But those who embrace him, fail to understand that Foucault is on the side of all subjugated knowledges—he does not prefer God to the Devil. Foucault has no way of discriminating between the sublime and the demonic. His only criterion is "otherness." He is enthusiastic about anything which to him seems "other" than the dominant reality, "other" than reason.

Foucault's attraction to madness, even madness which ends in crime, is particularly evident in his approach to Pierre Rivière, a nineteenth century parricide, whose memoirs were edited and published by Foucault, along with details of the trial.[14] This is a story of a young man who slaughtered his pregnant mother, his sister, and his brother, in cold blood—with an axe. The trial was of particular interest to Foucault because it came at a time when psychologists and psychiatrists were beginning to exert a significant influence on the law and the courts. The defense maintained that Pierre Rivière was mad, at least during the time he committed the crime, and as such, he could not be held responsible for his crimes. The jury condemned him to death, but his sentence was later commuted to life in prison. Rivière committed suicide in jail. What is particularly interesting about the case, is the fact that Rivière wrote a very long, detailed and articulate memoir in which he gave details of his life and the reasons for his crime. The memoir reveals that Rivière's crime was not a crime of passion, but a premeditated one. It also reveals that Rivière knew exactly what he was doing and that he was willing to accept his own death as the consequence of his crime. The memoir does not read like the incoherent ravings of a madman. Nevertheless, it contains a gruesome logic.

---

13   Foucault refers to Guyot Marchant's painting, "Danse Macabre."

14   M. Foucault, ed., *I, Pierre Rivière: a Case of Parricide in the 19th Century*, (Lincoln: University of Nebraska Press, 1975).

Rivière explains that his crime was intended to liberate his father from the countless humiliations and incessant torments to which his willful and capricious wife (Rivière's mother) had subjected him for years. Moreover, Rivière considered his mother to be the representative of a new world order in which Woman ruled supreme, and in which men were the helpless victims of endless grief, caprices, persecutions, and torments. So, in liberating his father from the tyranny of his mother (which was no doubt real), Rivière imagined that he was liberating the world from the tyranny of Woman.[15] He was willing to die in order to accomplish his self-appointed mission of world salvation.

Foucault objects to those psychiatrists who declared Rivière mad in their testimonies before the court. He argues convincingly that the manuscript left behind could not have been written by a mere imbecile. The memoir clearly reveals that Rivière knew what he was doing, and was willing to accept the consequences of his actions—his own death.

I agree with Foucault that Rivière was entitled to be treated as one who was worthy of being held responsible for his acts. I think that Foucault is right in thinking that the defense of madness belittles a man. But Foucault goes much further. On behalf of Rivière, Foucault protests that in declaring Rivière to be mad, the court has silenced an act of protest against the regime of reason. By declaring him mad, the court divested all his actions of their significance. By placing his actions outside the domain of sanity, the regime of reason makes Rivière's actions null and void. In this way, the regime emasculates, disempowers, and disarms all its critics. No doubt, Foucault regards this as the "cunning of reason" by which she manages to dissolve every act of protest against her despotic rule. The new order, the post-revolutionary order, may appear soft, feminine, and compassionate, but its despotic tyranny is more cunning than any that man has ever encountered before.

Foucault makes an effort to be impartial. But here, as elsewhere, his "neutrality" is a failure. Foucault's "impartial" account is hardly distinguishable from Rivière's version of the story. Foucault does not focus on the event as a *murder*, but as a *protest*—not an act of killing, but an act of dying and sacrificing. Foucault asserts that Rivière was deprived of the "glory" he sought by "risking his life." He implies that Rivière was deprived of something to which he was entitled.

---

[15]   This view closely resembles Alexandre Kojève's claim that the Feminine has triumphed in the modern world and the Masculine has been eclipsed. It also bears some resemblance to Nietzsche's claim that the Feminine morality (which has its source in Christianity) has triumphed.

By siding with Rivière's vision of the world, Foucault implies that risking one's life and killing others is a route to glory from which modernity deprives men like Rivière. There is no doubt that there are circumstances under which risking one's life is glorious. But "risking one's life" by killing one's mother in cold blood is not one of them—not even if a "memoir" identifies the mother with the new and wildly tyrannical regime of WOMAN. Such identification is a "madness" of sorts, even if it is not the madness of one who cannot be responsible for his deeds. In siding with Rivière's vision of the world, in trying to "liberate" his "subjugated knowledge," Foucault reveals his own madness.

Conclusion

First, it behooves us not to follow Foucault and the postmodernists in thinking that our predicament is totally unique, or that disciplinary power is more insidious in its capacity to act on the mind than any power has ever been before. For there has never been a power worthy of the name that has not acted on the mind; every power that can boast a modest success, has been internalized by its subjects. Even sovereign power was not confined to acting on the body, whatever Foucault may say. If it focused on the body, that was precisely because it believed that in coercing the body, it would ultimately train the mind. Law may be considered, as it was by Plato and Aristotle, to be an instrument of moral training. What people may initially do only out of fear, they may come to do habitually in the absence of coercion. They may even come to like it. Foucault is wrong to think that the process of internalizing social norms is a recent invention of the Enlightenment.

Second, Foucault assumes (without argument) that the "inner voice" is always the voice of power which has been internalized. Like Freud, Foucault thinks that the inner voice is the product of convention.[16] However, it may be that conscience has a natural as well as a conventional dimension. In other words, it may be more plausible to think that the very presence of this inner voice makes it possible for power to socialize us as it does. The tragedy (as Aquinas and others have recognized) is that power can silence conscience or usurp its place in one's heart. The quest to liberate

---

[16]   In most of his genealogies, Foucault assumes that the inner voice is necessarily repressive. In his later writings Foucault discovered what he called the "positivity" of power. He abandoned Freud and Marx's suspicions. But this "discovery" seems to make nonsense out of much of what he has written.

ourselves from *every* inner voice is not a project of liberation, but of dehumanization. The question is not how to liberate ourselves from the inner voice, but how to decide which of the voices, and to which of the powers (doing their utmost to lure and seduce us) we should succumb.

Third, the appeal of postmodernism stems from its ability to express, however inarticulately, the sense of helplessness, disenchantment and *ennui* that modern men and women no doubt experience. It sensitizes us to the fact that man's triumph over nature has not yielded the promised liberation. Paradoxically, the more mankind triumphs over nature, the more individuals find themselves helpless in the face of impersonal forces beyond their control. Postmodernism gives vent to our frustration with modern technological existence. But we would do well to remember that we are not the first or the last generation to be disenchanted with our existence. Disenchantment is man's lot. So, if we are to show our mettle, we must prevent our disenchantment from driving us to the lure of madness.

Finally, the Foucauldian picture of the world as a tyranny of reason contrived by Enlightenment philosophers can only be refuted by empirical evidence to the contrary—observation of our violent and furious world and knowledge of the Enlightenment philosophers and their spirit. And in light of these developments, Yolton's contribution to Enlightenment studies is critical in ferreting out the claims about the relationship of the modern world to the Enlightenment. What we need is history which can be distinguished from fiction.

Curriculum Vitae of
John W. Yolton: August 1995

Vital Statistics

Born 10 November 1921, in Birmingham, Alabama
Married September 1945 to Jean Mary (née Sebastian)
Children: 2 daughters, born in 1948 and 1953

Education

B.A. with honors in philosophy, University of Cincinnati, June 1945
M.A. in philosophy, University of Cincinnati, June 1946. Thesis: "British Empiricism and our Knowledge of the External World," supervised by Prof. Julius R. Weinberg
Graduate student and teaching assistant, University of California at Berkeley, 1946-49
University Fellow in philosophy, University of California at Berkeley, 1949-50
Fulbright Grantee at Balliol College, 1950-52
D.Phil. (Oxon.) from Oxford University, October 1952. Thesis: "John Locke and the Way of Ideas; a Study of the impact of Locke's Epistemology and Metaphysics upon His Contemporaries," supervised by Prof. Gilbert Ryle; examined by Prof. R.I. Aaron and A.D. Woozley
LL.D.(Hon.) York University, June 1974
D.Litt. (Hon.) McMaster University, May 1976

Appointments

Visiting lecturer in philosophy, Johns Hopkins University, 1952-53
Lecturer in philosophy, University of Baltimore, fall term 1952

Assistant professor and Jonathan Dickinson Bicentennial Preceptor, Philosophy Department, Princeton University, 1953-56 (Study leave 1955-56)

Assistant professor of philosophy, Princeton University 1956-57

Associate professor of philosophy, Kenyon College, Gambier, Ohio, 1957-60

American Council of Learned Societies Fellow, 1960-61

Professor of philosophy, University of Maryland, College Park, 1961-63

Professor of philosophy, York University, Toronto, 1963-July 1978; chairman, Department of Philosophy,1963-January 1973; acting dean, Faculty of Graduate Studies, 1967-68; acting president, January 1973-June 1974 (absent on leave, Canada Council Grant, 1968-69; sabbatical leave, 1974-75)

Dean of Rutgers College, Rutgers University, New Brunswick, N.J., August 1978-July 1985

Acting chairman, Department of Philosophy, Rutgers University, September 1987-June 30 1988

Professor of philosophy, Rutgers University, August 1978 - July 1992

John Locke Professor of the History of Philosophy, Rutgers University, July 1989-92.

Professor emeritus, Rutgers University, July 1992

Director of the seminar, "Space and Time, Matter and Mind," September-December 1981, at the Folger Shakespeare Library, Washington, D.C. in the Folger Institute of Renaissance and Eighteenth-Century Studies

National Endowment for the Humanities Fellowship, 1988-89.

Activities

Member of editorial board and consultant to
American Philosophical Quarterly, 1964-83
History of Philosophy Quarterly, 1984-90
Studies in the History and Philosophy of Science
Journal of the History of Philosophy
Philosophy of the Social Sciences
Journal of the History of Ideas
Studi Internazionali di Filosofia
Eighteenth Century Studies, 1982-85
British Journal for the History of Philosophy, 1992-
Associate editor, 1985-86; editor, 1986-88, *Studies in Eighteenth-Century Culture* (Publication of the American Society of Eighteenth-Century Studies)

General editor, *Blackwell Companion to the Enlightenment*, 1992.
General editor, *The Library of the History of Ideas*. A 13 volume set of essays reprinted by the University of Rochester Press from the *Journal of the History of Ideas*, 1990-95.
Member of the editorial committee for the Clarendon Edition of the *Works of John Locke*, 1972-92 (general editor, 1983-92)
Member of the board of editors, *Journal of the History of Ideas*, 1986- ; member of the board of directors, 1990 (Vice President, 1991-).
Member of the Advisory Editorial Board for the Bertrand Russell Archives at McMaster University, 1973-1986
Member of the Board of Governors of York University, faculty constituency, July 1972-January 1973
Member of the research committee, Council of Ontario Universities, 1964-1968 (under its earlier name: Committee of Presidents of Universities of Ontario); of its Ontario Committee on Graduate Studies, 1967-68; of its appraisals committee (for assessing new graduate programs in Ontario) 1966-August 1971; of its advisory committee on academic planning (for advanced degree programs) September 1971-June 1974
Member of the President's Commission on Goals and Objectives for the Future of York University, September 1975-June 1978
President, Canadian Philosophical Association, July 1973-June 1974
Member, New Jersey Committee for the Humanities, July 1979 - July 1985 (Treasurer, 1981-1985)
Member, International Council on the Future of the University (founded by the late Charles Frankel) April 1976-June 1982
Vice-president, 1981-82, and president, 1982-83, of the Northeast American Society for 18th Century Studies

Prizes

The F.C.S. Schiller Essay Prize, at the University of California at Berkeley, 1948. Topic: "F.C.S. Schiller and British Empiricism"
A.S. Eddington Essay contest, sponsored by the Institut International des Sciences Théoriques, Brussels (offered 1951). Awarded first prize in February 1956 by the Association Internationale de Collaboration Scientifique. Topic: "The Philosophy of Science of A.S. Eddington"
Leonard Nelson Essay Contest, sponsored by the Leonard Nelson Foundation. Awarded first prize, Janruary 1959. Topic: "Concept Analysis"

Books

John Locke and the Way of Ideas. London: Oxford University Press, 1956. Oxford Classical and Philosophical Monographs. Bristol: Thoemmes Press: Reprint out of series, 1968, and 1993.

The Philosophy of A. S. Eddington. The Hague: M. Nijhoff, 1960.

(Editor) Locke's Essay concerning Human Understanding. London: Dent, 1961. 2 vols. (Everyman's Library 332, 984)

———2d revised edition, ibid., 1965

———3d revised edition, ibid., 1971

———Abridgment (in one vol.), ibid., 1976; reprinted with additional apparatus, 1993.

Thinking and Perceiving: a Study in the Philosophy of Mind. LaSalle, Ill.: Open Court Publishing Co., 1962

(Editor) Locke's Essay concerning Human Understanding. Abridged and edited with an introduction. Toronto: Dent's of Canada, 1965 (Dent's University Paperbacks, no.1)

(Editor) Theory of Knowledge. New York: Macmillan, 1965. (Sources in Philosophy)

Metaphysical Analysis. Toronto: University of Toronto Press; London: Allen and Unwin, 1967

(Editor) John Locke: Problems and Perspectives. Cambridge: Cambridge University Press, 1969.

Locke and the Compass of Human Understanding. Cambridge: Cambridge University Press, 1970.

Locke and Education. New York: Random House, 1971.

(Editor) The Locke Reader. New York: Cambridge University Press, 1977.

Thinking Matter: Materialism in Eighteenth-Century Britain. Minneapolis: University of Minnesota Press and Oxford: Basil Blackwell, 1984.

Perceptual Acquaintance from Descartes to Reid. Minneapolis: University of Minnesota Press and Oxford: Basil Blackwell, 1984.

John Locke: A Reference Guide. Boston: G.K. Hall Co., 1985 (jointly with J.S. Yolton).

(Editor, with L.E. Brown) Studies in Eighteenth-Century Culture, 17 (1987) and 18 (1988). Colleagues Press.

John Locke: An Introduction. Oxford and New York: B.H. Blackwell, 1985. Translated into Italian by Bruno Morcavallo, Universale Paperbacks, Bologna: Il Mulino, 1990.

(Editor, with J.S. Yolton) Some Thoughts Concerning Education, by John Locke. Edited with an introduction, notes and critical apparatus. Clarendon Edition of the Works of John Locke. Oxford: Clarendon Press, 1989.

Locke and French Materialism. Oxford: Clarendon Press, 1991.

(Editor) *Philosophy, Religion and Science in the 17th and 18th Centuries.* Rochester, NY: University of Rochester Press, 1990.

(General Editor) *The Blackwell Companion to the Enlightenment.* Oxford: Blackwell Reference, 1992. (Author of approximately 35 entries).

A Locke Dictionary. Oxford: Blackwell, 1993. A Portuguese translation, 1996.

Perception and Reality: A History from Descartes to Kant. Ithaca, NY: Cornell University Press, 1996, (forthcoming).

Introductions to Reprints

William Carroll, A Dissertation upon the Tenth Chapter of the Fourth Book of Locke's Essay, 1706 (Reprinted by Thoemmes Antiquarian Books Ltd, 1990).

Isaac Watts, Philosophical Essays on Various Subjects, 1742 (Reprinted by Thoemmes Antiquarian Books Ltd, 1990).

Thomas Webb, The Intellectualism of Locke, 1857 (Reprinted by Thoemmes Antiquarian Books Ltd, 1990).

George Santayana, Character and Opinion in the United States, 1921 (Reprinted by Transaction Publishers, 1991).

Samuel Colliber, Free Thoughts concerning Souls, 1734 (Reprinted by Thoemmes Antiquarian Books Ltd, 1990.

Vincent Perronet, A Second Vindication of Mr. Locke, Wherein his Sentiments relating to Personal Identity are clear'd up from some Mistakes of The Rev. Dr. Butler, 1738 (Reprinted by Thoemmes Antiquarian Books Ltd, 1991).

Locke, John. Conduct of the Understanding, 1706 (Reprinted by Thoemmes Antiquarian Books, 1993).

Articles

"A Defence of Sense-Data. *Mind*," 57 (January 1948): 2-16.

"The Ontological Status of Sense-Data in Plato's Theory of Perception." *Review of Metaphysics*, 3 (September 1949): 21-59.

"F.C.S. Schiller's Pragmatism and British Empiricism." *Philosophy and Phenomenological Research*, 11 (September 1950): 40-57.

"Notes on Santayana's 'The Last Puritan.'" *The Philosophical Review*, 60 (April 1951): 234-42.

"The Metaphysic of 'En-Soi' and 'Pour-Soi.' " *Journal of Philosophy*, 48 (August 1951): 548-56.

"Locke's Unpublished Marginal Replies to John Sergeant." *Journal of the History of Ideas*, 12 (October 1951): 528-59.

"The Psyche as Social Determinant." *Journal of Philosophy*, 49 (March 27, 1952): 232-39. Reprinted in *Animal Faith and Spiritual Life*, edited by John Lachs (1967).

"Linguistic and Epistemological Dualism." *Mind*, 62 (January 1953): 20-43.

"The Dialectic of Loyalty Tests." *Philosophy and Phenomological Research*, 13 (March 1953): 337-51.

"The Dualism of Mind." *Journal of Philosophy*, 51 (March 18, 1954):173-80.

"History and Meta-History." *Philosophy and Phenomenological Research*, 15 (June 1955): 477-92.

"Criticism and Histrionic Understanding." *Ethics*, 65 (April 1955): 206-12.

"Locke and the Seventeenth-Century Logic of Ideas." *Journal of the History of Ideas*, 16 (October 1955): 431-53.

"Individuality, Leadership and Democracy." *Diogenes*, 12 (Winter 1955): 76-86.

"Bacon, Hobbes, and Other Philosophical Writers: A Bibliography." *The Cambridge Bibliography of English Literature*, vol. 5 Supplement, pp.1025-32. Revised and enlarged for *The New Cambridge Bibliography of English Literature* (Cambridge University Press, 1974) vol.1, cols. 2321-2342.

"Ascriptions, Descriptions, and Action Sentences." *Ethics*, 67 (July 1957): 307-10.

"Philosophical and Scientific Explanation." *Journal of Philosophy*, 55 (February 13,1958): 133-43.

"Locke on the Law of Nature." *The Philosophical Review*, 67 (October 1958): 477-98.

"Philosophical Realism and Psychological Data." *Philosophy and Phenomenological Research*, 18 (June 1959): 486-501.

"Explanation." *British Journal for the Philosophy of Science*, 10 (November 1959): 194-208.

"A Metaphysic of Experience." *Review of Metaphysics*, 12 (June 1959): 612-23.

"Sense-Data and Cartesian Doubt." *Philosophical Studies*, 11 (January 1960): 25-30.

"Broad's Views on the Nature and Existence of External Objects." In *The Philosophy of C.D. Broad*, edited by Paul A. Schilpp (New York: Tudor Publishing Co., 1960): pp. 511-36.

"Seeming and Being." *The Philosophical Quarterly*, 11, n. 43 (April 1961): 114-222.

"Professor Malcolm on St. Anselm, Belief, and Existence." *Philosophy*, 36 (October 1961): 367-70.

"Concept Analysis." *Kantstudien*, 52, pt. 4 (1960-61): 467-84.

"Act and Circumstance." *Journal of Philosophy*, 59, n. 13 (June 21, 1962): 337-50.

"The Form and Development of Experience." *Acta Psychologica* (Amsterdam: North-Holland Publishing Co.), 21, n. 4/5 (1963): 357-70.

"The Concept of Experience in Locke and Hume." *Journal of the History of Philosophy*, 1, n. 1 (October 1963): 53-71. The "Locke" part reprinted in *Locke & Berkeley: A Collection of Critical Essays*, edited by C.B. Martin and D.M. Armstrong, 1968)

"Agent Causality." *American Philosophical Quarterly*, 3 (1966): 14-26.

"My Hand Goes Out to You." *Philosophy*, 41, n. 156 (April 1966): 140-52.

"Sartre's Ontology" (jointly with Albert Shalom). *Dialogue*, 6, n. 3 (1967): 383-98.

"Gibson's Realism." *Synthèse*, 19 (1968-69): 400-407.

"Perceptual Consciousness." In *Knowledge and Necessity* (Royal Institute of Philosophy Lectures, vol. 3, 1969-70, edited by G. Vesey): pp.34-50.

"Locke on Knowledge of Body." In *Jowett Papers 1968-1969*; edited by B.Y. Khanbai, R.S. Katz, and R.A. Pineau (Oxford: B. Blackwell): pp.69-94.

"The Science of Nature." In *John Locke: Problems and Perspectives* (Edited by J. W. Yolton. Cambridge: University Press, 1969): pp.183-94.

"George Santayana's Literary Psychology." In *Proceedings of the 7th Inter-American Congress of Philosophy*, held in 1967; vol. 2, pp.369-73.

"Appearance and Reality." In *Dictionary of the History of Ideas* (Edited by Philip P. Wiener, 1972), vol. 1, pp.94-99.

"Philosophy of Science from Descartes to Kant." (Discussion review of *Metaphysics and the Philosophy of Science*, by Gerd Buchdahl). *History of Science*, 10 (1971): 102-13.

"John Locke and Essay Concerning Human Understanding;" [articles]. *Encyclopedia Americana*. 1971 edition.

"Méthode et métaphysique dans la philosophie de John Locke." *Revue philosophique de la France et de l'étranger* 163 (1971): 171-85.

"Action: Metaphysic and Modality." *American Philosophical Quarterly* 10 (April 1973): 71-85.

"Action Theory as the Foundation for the Sciences of Man." *Philosophy of the Social Sciences*, 3 (1973): 81-90.

"Ideas and Knowledge in Seventeenth-Century Philosophy." *Journal of the History of Philosophy*, 13 (April 1975): 145-66.

"Comments on Professor Schouls' Paper." *Canadian Journal of Philosophy*, 4 (June 1975): 611-15.

"On Being Present to the Mind: A Sketch for the History of an Idea."
    Dialogue (September 1975): 373-88.
"Textual vs. Conceptual Analysis in the History of Philosophy." *Journal of
    the History of Philosophy*, 13 (October 1975): 505-12.
"Critical Note: *John Locke*, by J.D. Mabbott (1973)." *Canadian Journal of
    Philosophy*, 6 (June 1976): 327-37.
"Pragmatism Revisited: an Examination of Professor Rescher's Conceptual
    Idealism." *Idealistic Studies*, 6 (September 1976): 218-38.
"Can a University Be an Institution of Higher Learning? Convocation
    address at McMaster University, May 27, 1976." *York* [University]
    Gazette, 7 no. 5 (12 October 1976): 34-36.
"G.H.von Wright's Account of Causing and Producing [review-discussion
    of his *Essays on Explanation and Understanding*]." *Philosophy of the Social
    Sciences*, 7 (1977): 397-404.
"As in a Looking-Glass: Perceptual Acquaintance in Eighteenth-Century
    Britain." *Journal of the History of Ideas*, 40 (June 1979): 207-34.
"How is Knowledge of the World Possible?" In *The Philosophy of Nicholas Rescher*,
    edited by E. Sosa (Dordrecht, Holland: D. Reidel, 1979), pp. 175-85.
"Hume's Abstract in the 'Bibliothèque Raisonnée'." *Journal of the History of
    Ideas*, 40 (Jan.-March 1979): 157-58.
"Hume's Ideas." *Hume Studies*, 6 (April 1980): 1-25.
"Locke and Malebranche: Two Concepts of Ideas." In *John Locke: Sympo-
    sium Wolfenbuttel 1979* (edited by R. Brandt. Berlin: W. de Gruyter,
    1981), pp. 208-34.
"Phenomenology and Pragmatism;" [review-discussion of Richard Rorty's
    Philosophy and the Mirror of Nature, 5]. *Philosophical Books*, 22 (April
    1981): 129-34.
"Perceptual Cognition with Descartes." *Studia Cartesiana*, 2 (1981): 63-83.
"Ideas." An Audio Tape Discussion with G. Vesey on the term 'idea' in
    seventeenth and eighteenth century thought. Open University (Mil-
    ton Keynes, England), November 1982. (Part of course offered on
    "Reason and Experience").
"Locke's Suggestion of Thinking Matter and Some 18th-Century Portuguese
    Reactions." *Journal of the History of Ideas*, XLV (April-June 1984):
    303-07. (with J.S. Yolton)
"Locke, John." *The Social Science Encyclopedia*, ed. by A & J Kuper. (London,
    Boston: Routledge and Kegan Paul), pp.472-73.
"Some Remarks on the Historiography of Philosophy." *Journal of the History
    of Philosophy* (October 1985): 571-78.
"Is There a History of Philosophy? Some Difficulties and Suggestions."
    Synthese, 67 (1986):1-21.

"Schoolmen, Logic and Philosophy." *The History of the University of Oxford*, vol. 5, edited by L.S. Sutherland and L.G. Mitchell, chapter 20, pp.565-91. (Clarendon Press, 1986)

"French Materialist Disciples of Locke." *The Journal of the History of Philosophy*, 25 (Jan 1987): 83-103.

"Representation and Realism: Some Reflections on the Way of Ideas." *Mind*, (July 1987): 318-30.

"Locke and Materialism: The French Connection." *Revue Internationale de Philosophie*, 42 no. 165 (1988): 229-53.

"John Locke," *The Age of William III and Mary II*, ed. by P.B. Maccubin and M. Hamilton-Phillips (College of William and Mary, 1989), 153-5.

"Mirrors and Veils, Thoughts and Things: The Epistemological Problematic." In *Reading Rorty*, ed. by Alan Malachowski, Oxford: B.H. Blackwell, 1990: 58-73.

"The Way of Ideas: A Retrospective." *Journal of Philosophy*, LXXXVII (1990), 510-16. Paper in the APA Symposium: John Locke after Three-hundred Years.

"The Term *Idea* in Seventeenth and Eighteenth-Century British Philosophy." Proceedings of the VI Colloquio Internazionale su Idea, held in Rome at the Lessico

"Intellettuale Europeo, Jan 1989." Rome: Edizioni dell'Ateneo, 1990, 237-63.

"Empiricism." *Handbook of Metaphysics and Ontology*. Munich: Philosophia, 1991.

Book Reviews

Pieper, Joseph: Leisure, the Basis of Culture. *The Philosopical Review* 52 (1953): 151-53.

O'Connor, D. J.: John Locke; **and** Klemmt, Alfred: John Locke, Theoretische Philosophie. *Journal of Philosophy* 50 (1953): 435-441.

O'Connor, D. J.: John Locke. *The Philosophical Review* 62 (1953): 459-60.

Gotlind, Erik: Russell's Theories of Causation; **and** Russell's Construction of the External World, by C.A. Fritz; **and** Bertrand Russell, O.M., by H.W. Leggett. *Philosophy and Phenomenological Research* 14 (1953): 110-12.

Hyppolite, Jean: Logique et existence, essai sur la logique de Hegel. *Philosophy and Phenomenological Research* 14 (1953): 274-75.

Lean, Martin: Sense-Perception and Matter. *The Philosophical Review* 63 (1954): 263-66.

Santayana, George: Dominations and Powers. *Mind* 63 (1954): 419-23.

John Locke: Essays on the Law of Nature, edited by W. von Leyden. *The Philosophical Review* 64 (1955): 487-91.

Parkinson, C.H.: Spinoza's Theory of Knowledge and Tulane Studies in Philosophy, vol. 3: a Symposium on Kant. *Canadian Forum* 35 (1955): 91.

Polin, Raymond: Politique et philosophie chez Thomas Hobbes. *Philosophy and Phenomenological Research* 15 (1955): 431-33.

Cranston, Maurice: John Locke, a Biography. *The Philosophical Review* 67 (1958): 554-57.

Natanson, Maurice: The Social Dynamics of G.H. Mead. *Journal of Philosophy* 56 (1959): 140-45.

Chisholm, Roderick M.: Perceiving, a Philosophical Study. *Philosophy of Science* 25 (October 1958): 302-05.

Basson, A.H.: David Hume. *Journal of Philosophy* 56 (1959): 545-50.

Tuveson, E.L.: The Imagination as a Means of Grace. *Journal of Aesthetics and Art Criticism* September 1961.

Cox, Richard H.: Locke on War and Peace. *The Philosophical Review* 71 (April 1962): 269-71.

Furlong, E.J.: Imagination. *Journal of Philosophy* 59 (June 7, 1962): 329-32.

Armstrong, D.M.: Perception and the Physical World. *Journal of Philosophy* 59 no.14 (July 5, 1962): 384-88.

"In the Soup": a review of Tree and Leaf, by J.R.R. Tolkien. *Kenyon Review* 27 (1965): 565-67.

Scheffler, Israel: Conditions of Knowledge. *Harvard Educational Review* 36 (1966): 71-74.

Jonas, Hans: The Phenomenon of Life. *Journal of Philosophy* 64 (1967): 254-58.

Garnett, A.C.: The Perceptual Process and Grossman, R.: The Structure of Mind. *Synthèse* 17 (1967): 223-29.

Straus, Erwin: The Primary World of the Senses. *Philosophy of Science* 34 (1967): 84-85.

John Locke: Two Tracts on Government, edited by Philip Abrams. *Journal of the History of Philosophy* 6 (1968): 291-94.

Lachs, John, editor: Animal Faith and Spiritual Life, by George Santayana. *Dialogue* 7 (1968): 129-31.

Ayers, M.R.: The Refutation of Determinism. *Mind* 78 no. 312 (1969): 616-22.

Von Leyden, W.: Seventeenth-Century Metaphysics and The Cambridge Platonists, edited by G.R. Cragg. *Mind* 79 no. 314 (1970): 364-66.

Weinberg, Julius: Ideas and Concepts. *Dialogue* 10 (1971): 349-53.

Woolhouse, R.S.: Locke's Philosophy of Science and Knowledge. *The Philosopical Quarterly* 22 no. 88 (1972): 269-71.

Santayana, George: Lotze's System of Logic. *Dialogue* 11 (1972): 293-95.

Glanvill, Joseph: The Vanity of Dogmatizing, the Three 'Versions' [facism. reprint edited by Stephen Medcalf]. *Journal of the History of Philosophy* 10 (1972): 359-60.

Taylor, Daniel: Explanation and Meaning. *Philosophy of the Social Sciences* 1 (1974): 345-50.

Matilal, B.K.: Epistemology, Logic and Grammar in Indian Philosophical Analysis. *Journal of Indian Philosophy* 2 (1974): 384-86.

Duchesneau, François: L'empirisme de Locke. *Journal of the History of Philosophy* 13 (1975): 410-13.

Mijuskovic, B.L.: The Achilles of Rationalist Arguments. *Philosophical Books* 16 (1975): 17-19.

Ree, Jonathan: Descartes. *Philosophical Books* 16 (1975): 22-25.

Hacking, Ian: The Emergence of Probability. *Philosophical Books* 17 (1976): 57-59.

Ferguson, J.P.: The Philosophy of Samuel Clarke. *Philosophical Books* 18 (1977): 19-20.

Mischel, Theodore: Understanding Other Persons. *Philosophy of the Social Sciences* 7 (March 1977): 104-09.

Radner, Daisie: Malebranche. *Philosophical Books* 21 (1980): 15-17.

Bedford, R.D.: Defence of Truth. *Philosophical Books* 22 (1981): 87-89.

De Beer, E.S., editor: The Correspondence of the John Locke. *Eighteenth-Century, a Current Bibliography* new ser. 3 (1977): 239-40.

Franklin, Julian H.: John Locke and the Theory of Sovereignty. *Political Science* 9 (May 1981): 266-68.

Loeb, Louis E.: From Descartes to Hume. *Philosophical Books* 23 (July 1982): 155-57.

Condillac, E.B. de: La logique, translated with introd. by W.R. Albury **and** Hobbes, Thomas: Computatio sive Logica, translated with commentary by A.P. Martinich. *Philosophical Books* 23 (1982): 158.

Hobart, Michael E.: Science and Religion in the Thought of Nicolas Malebranche. *Philosophical Books* 24 (1983): 77-79.

Centore, F.F.: Persons: A Comparative Account of Six Possible Theories; and Mischel, Theodore: The Self: Psychological and Philosophical Issues. *Philosophy of the Social Sciences* 13 (1983): 519-24.

Grave, S.A.: Locke and Burnet. *Philosophical Books* 24 (1983): 144-47.

Wood, Neal: The Politics of Locke's Philosophy: A Social Study of "An Essay

Concerning Human Understanding". *Eighteenth-Century Studies* 18 (1985): 227-32.

Reed, Edward and Jones, Rebecca (eds.): Reasons for Realism. Selected Essays of James J. Gibson. *Philosophy of the Social Sciences* 14 (1984): 430.

Galgan, Gerald J.: The Logic of Modernity. *Philosophical Books* 25 (1984): 63-64.

Talmor, Sascha.: Glanvill: The Uses and Abuses of Scepticism. *Philosophical Books* 25 (1984): 103-05.

Nuchelmans, Gabriel. Judgment and Proposition: From Descartes to Kant. *Philosophical Books* 25 (1984): 200-02.

Shapiro, Barbara J.: Probability and Certainty in Seventeenth-Century England: A Study of the Relationships between Natural Science, Religion, History, Law, and

Literature. *Renaissance Quarterly* 37 (1984): 280-82.

Tarcov, Nathan: Locke's Education for Liberty. *Political Theory*, November 1985: 638-43.

Force, James: William Whiston, Honest Newtonian. *History and Philosophy of Logic*, 1986.

Alexander, Peter: Ideas and Qualities and Corpuscles: Locke and Boyle on the External World. *Eighteenth-Century Studies*, 20 (Winter 1986-87), 235-38.

Schøsler, Jørn: La Bibliothèque raisonnée (1728-1753). Les réactions d'un périodique français à la philosophie de Locke au XVIIIe siècle. *Modern Language Review*, 1987.

Watson, R.A. The Breakdown of Cartesian Metaphysics (New York: Humanities Press 1987), *Review of Metaphysics* 41 (1988): 641-3.

Morman, Paul J. Noel Aubert de Versé: A Study in the Concept of Toleration. *English Historical Review*, Fall 1989.

Barrell, Rex A. Anthony Ashley Cooper, Earl of Shaftesbury 1671-1713 and Le Réfuge français: Correspondence (Lampeter, 1989), *English Historical Review*, July 1993.

Ferreira, M. Jamie. Scepticism and Reasonable Doubt: the British Naturalist Tradition in Wilkins, Hume, Reid, and Newman (Oxford: Clarendon Press, 1986), *Studies in the Philosophy of the Scottish Enlightenment*, ed. by M.A. Stewart (Oxford University Press, 1990): 303-6

Craig, Edward. The Mind of God and the Works of Man (Oxford University Press, 1990), *Studies in the Philosophy of the Scotish Enlightenment*, ed. by M.S. Stewart (Oxford University Press, 1990), 306-11.

Lee, Sang Hyun: The Philosophy of Jonathan Edwards (Princeton University Press, 1988), *International Journal for Philosophy of Religion*, 1990.

Constantine George Caffentzis. Clipped Coins, Abused Words and Civil Government: John Locke's Philosophy of Money (Brooklyn, New York: Automedia, 1989), *Eighteenth-Century Studies*, 24 (fall 1990): 130-132.

Steven Nadler. Arnauld and the Cartesian Philosophy of Ideas (Manchester University Press, 1989), *Journal of Philosophy*, Jan 1990.

Reid, Thomas: Practical Ethics: Being Lectures and Papers on Natural Religion, Self-Government, Natural Jurisprudence, and the Law of Nations. Edited from the Manuscripts with an Introduction and a Commentary, by Knud Haakonssen. (Princeton University Press, 1990), *Albion*, 1991.

John W. Danford: David Hume and the Problem of Reason: Recovering the Human Sciences. (Yale University Press, 1990), *Albion*, 1991.

Haakonssen, Knud: Thomas Reid. Practical Ethics: Being Lectures and Papers on Natural Religion, Self-Government, Natural Jurisprudence, and the Law of Nations. (Princeton University Press, 1990), *Albion*, 1991.

Index

Tabula Gratulatoria

Subscribers

Jean-Marie Beyssade

Chester Chapin

William J. Connell

Henry L. Fulton

Mark Goldie

Knud Haakonssen

Donald R. Kelley

Kevin C. Loudon

Victor Nuovo

H. B. Paksoy

Nicholas Phillipson

J. S. A. Pocock

J. L. Rynning

Trinity University Library

James Turner

Charles G. S. Williams